The Supreme Court

The Supreme Court

Ninth Edition

Lawrence Baum
Ohio State University

CQ PRESS

A Division of Congressional Quarterly Inc.
Washington, D.C.

CQ Press
1255 22nd Street, NW, Suite 400
Washington, DC 20037

Phone: 202-729-1900; toll-free, 1-866-4CQ-PRESS (1-866-427-7737)

Web: www.cqpress.com

Cover design: Diane Buric

Cover photo: Photos.com

Photo credits: AP/ Wide World Photos: page 4 (Nick Ut), 17 (Bob Child), 59, 76 (Kevin Wolf), 97 (Dave Martin), 109 (Dana Verkouteren), 118, 163 (Faleh Kheiber), 192 (Charles V. Tines), 207 (Christina Dicken), 219 (Mike Derer). Congressional Quarterly: frontispiece (Ken Heinen). UPI/Landov: page 35 (Kevin Dietsch).

♾ The paper used in this publication exceeds the requirements of the American National Standard for Information Sciences—Permanence of Paper for Printed Library Materials, ANSI Z39.48-1992.

Printed and bound in the United States of America

10   09   08   07   06   1   2   3   4   5

Library of Congress Cataloging-in-Publication Data

Baum, Lawrence.
   The Supreme Court / Lawrence Baum.—9th ed.
      p. cm.
   Includes bibliographical references and index.
   ISBN-13: 978-1-933116-85-3 (alk. paper)
   ISBN-10: 1-933116-85-4 (alk. paper)
   1. United States. Supreme Court. 2. Constitutional law—United States. 3. Courts of last resort—United States. 4. Judicial review —United States.   I. Title.
   KF8742.B35 2007
   347.73'26—dc22   2006025340

To my mother,
Ruth Klein Baum

Contents

Tables, Figures, and Boxes

Tables

Figures

Boxes

Preface

On June 29, 2006, the last day of its annual term, the Supreme Court decided *Hamdan v. Rumsfeld*. In its decision, the Court ruled that the military commissions established to try prisoners detained at Guantánamo Bay were illegal.

The impact of *Hamdan* depends on the reactions of the president and Congress, so that impact will be uncertain for some time. Whatever the consequences of the Court's decision, it illustrated the role that the Supreme Court plays as a policymaker. As they had two years earlier, the justices collectively agreed to rule on issues growing out of the government's efforts to deal with terrorism. And both times, the Court ruled against policies adopted by the president and his administration.

The Supreme Court's involvement in this issue did not surprise most people, because the Court has a long history of participation in consequential and controversial issues. At least as far back as the *Dred Scott* decision of 1857, the Court has made rulings on race and racial discrimination. For more than thirty years, it has been at the center of the debates over national policy on abortion. And it addresses a variety of other matters that range from the powers of Congress to the use of the death penalty.

Despite the general recognition of its importance, the Supreme Court is not as well understood as it might be. On the whole, Americans know more about the president and Congress than they do about the Court. One reason is that the Court limits what one may find out about it. The justices do most of their work in private, and their public sessions can be seen only by the small number of people who attend them. Another reason is the Court's role as interpreter of law, a role that adds considerable complexity to its work. For these reasons, even people who care a good deal about government and politics often know little about how the Court functions or about the forces that shape its decisions and their impact.

My goal in this book is to provide a better understanding of the Supreme Court. The book is intended to serve as a short but comprehensive guide to the Court, both for readers who already know much about the Court and for those who have a more limited understanding of it. The book puts the Court in its historical context, but it gives primary attention to the Court of the current era. This edition incorporates recent developments in and around the Court. Most prominent are the new appointments to the Court in 2005 and 2006 that have shifted its ideological balance. There has been a burgeoning of scholarship on the Court in the past few years, and the new edition takes advantage of the information and insights in that work.

The first chapter introduces the Supreme Court. It discusses the Court's role in general terms, examines the Court's place in the judicial system, analyzes the Court as an institution, and presents a brief summary of its history.

Each of the other chapters deals with an important aspect of the Court. Chapter 2 focuses on the justices: their selection, their backgrounds and careers, and the circumstances under which they leave the Court. Chapter 3 discusses how cases reach the Court and how the Court selects the small portion of those cases that it will hear.

Chapter 4 looks at decision making in the cases that the Court accepts for full decisions. After outlining the Court's decision-making procedures, I turn to the chapter's primary concern: the factors that influence the Court's choices among alternative decisions and policies. Chapter 5 deals with the kinds of issues on which the Court concentrates, the policies it supports, and the extent of its activism in the making of public policy. I give special attention to changes in the Court's role as a policymaker and the sources of those changes. The final chapter examines the ways in which other government policymakers respond to the Court's decisions as well as the Court's impact on American society as a whole. The chapter concludes with an assessment of the Court's significance as a force in American life.

This new edition of the book reflects the very considerable help that many people gave me with earlier editions. In writing this edition, I benefited from the information provided by Susan Lawrence, Kevin Scott, the Office of the Solicitor General, and the Public Information Office of the Supreme Court. The book was strengthened by the suggestions for revision from Mark S. Hurwitz, Western Michigan University; Mark P. Petracca, University of California, Irvine; and Kirk A. Randazzo, University of Kentucky.

As always, the professionals at CQ Press did a great deal to make my life easier and, more important, to make the book better. Dwain Smith assisted in preparing for the new edition of the book. As editors, Joanne S. Ainsworth and Anne Stewart were enormously helpful, and Joanne did much to improve the presentation of material. Charisse Kiino coordinated the revision and provided her usual (and much-appreciated) encouragement.

Throughout the life of the book, my faculty colleagues and the graduate and undergraduate students at Ohio State University have been an abundant source of ideas. I appreciate their continuing help.

Chapter 1

The Court

In the summer of 2005, Supreme Court Justice Sandra Day O'Connor announced her retirement and then Chief Justice William Rehnquist died. As a result, President George W. Bush gained his first opportunities to choose new members of the Court. The president had good reasons to take his choices seriously. During his four years in office the Court had ruled on some of his policies, such as the detention of suspected terrorists. Many of the voters who put Bush into office were deeply opposed to *Roe v. Wade* and other Supreme Court decisions on social issues. And the Court's decision in *Bush v. Gore* ensured that Bush became president in 2000 by resolving the conflict over Florida's electoral votes in his favor. The president certainly understood the impact of the nine people who make Supreme Court decisions, and that understanding was reflected in the effort that he and his administration devoted to choosing replacements for O'Connor and Rehnquist.

President Bush is hardly the only person who recognizes the importance of the Supreme Court. The Court receives a good deal of attention from the public and even more attention from people in government. The justices are regularly praised and denounced for their decisions. People who talk about the Court often exaggerate its impact, ascribing to the justices more power than they actually hold. But that exaggeration is understandable in light of the Court's prominence and the impact that it does exert. It is impossible to understand American government and society without understanding the Supreme Court.

This book is an effort to help provide that understanding. Who serves on the Court, and how do they get there? What determines which cases and issues the Court decides? In resolving the cases before it, how does the Court choose between alternative decisions? In what policy areas is it active, and what kinds of policies does it make? Finally, what happens to the Court's decisions after they are handed down, and what impact do they have?

Each of these questions is the subject of a chapter in the book. As I focus on each question, I try to show not only what happens in and around the

Court but also why things work as they do. This first chapter is an introduction to the Court, providing background for the chapters that follow.

A Perspective on the Court

The Supreme Court's place in government is more ambiguous than the places of Congress and the president, so it is appropriate to begin by considering the Court's characteristics as an institution and its work as a policymaker.

The Court in Law and Politics

The Supreme Court is, first of all, a court—the highest court in the federal judicial system. Like other courts, it has jurisdiction to hear and decide certain kinds of cases. Like other courts, it can decide legal issues only in cases that are brought to it. And as a court, it makes decisions within a legal framework. Congress simply writes new law, but the Court interprets existing law. In this respect, the Court operates within a constraint from which legislators are free.

In another respect, the Supreme Court's identity as a court reduces the constraints on it. The widespread belief that courts should be insulated from the political process gives the Court a degree of actual insulation. The justices' lifetime appointments allow them some freedom from concerns about whether political leaders and voters approve of their decisions. Justices usually avoid open involvement in partisan activity, because such involvement is perceived as inappropriate. And because direct contact between lobbyists and justices is generally considered unacceptable, interest group activity in the Court is basically restricted to the formal channels of legal argument.

The Court's insulation from politics should not be exaggerated, however. People sometimes speak of courts as if they are, or at least ought to be, "nonpolitical." In a literal sense, this is impossible: as a part of government, courts are political institutions by definition. What people really mean when they refer to courts as nonpolitical is that courts are separate from the political process and that their decisions are affected only by legal considerations. This too is impossible—for courts in general and certainly for the Supreme Court.

The Court is political chiefly because it makes important decisions on major issues. People care about those decisions and want to influence them. As a result, appointments to the Court frequently involve political battles. Interest groups bring cases and present arguments to the Court in an effort to help shape its policies. Because members of Congress pay attention to the Court's decisions and hold powers over the Court, the justices may take Congress into account when they decide cases. Finally, the justices' political values affect the votes they cast and the opinions they write in the Court's decisions.

Thus, the Supreme Court should be viewed as a legal institution and a political institution. Both the political process and the legal system influence what it does. This ambiguous position makes the Court more complex in some ways than most political institutions; it also makes the Court an interesting case study in political behavior.

The Court as a Policymaker

This book examines the Supreme Court broadly, but it emphasizes the Court's role in making public policy—the authoritative rules by which people in government institutions seek to influence government itself and to shape society as a whole. Legislation to provide subsidies for wheat farmers, a judge's ruling in an auto accident case, and a Supreme Court decision that makes rules of police procedure are all examples of public policy. The Court may be viewed as part of a policymaking system that includes lower courts as well as the other branches of government.

As I have noted, the Supreme Court makes public policy by interpreting provisions of law. Issues of public policy come to the Court in the form of legal questions. In this respect the Court's policymaking differs fundamentally in form from that of Congress.

The Court does not face legal questions in the abstract. Rather, it addresses these questions in the process of settling specific controversies between parties (sometimes called litigants) that bring cases to it. In a sense, then, every decision by the Court has three aspects: it is a judgment about the specific dispute brought to it, an interpretation of the legal issues in that dispute, and a position on the policy questions that are raised by the legal issues.

These three aspects of the Court's rulings are illustrated by its decisions on police powers to search automobiles. In the past decade the Court has decided more than a dozen cases involving the circumstances under which car searches are acceptable and the permissible scope of those searches.[1] In each case, it ruled on the specific dispute, determining whether the evidence obtained from a search could be admitted in the trial of a particular defendant. If a state supreme court or federal court of appeals had ruled against the defendant, the Supreme Court could affirm that judgment and allow the defendant's conviction to become final. Alternatively, the Court could reverse the conviction and remand the case, sending it back to the lower court for further action in line with the Court's ruling.

The Court's decision in each case was also a judgment on the law of search and seizure. The Court determines how the Fourth and Fourteenth Amendments should be interpreted in relation to the specific situation in a

Police officers search cars arriving at the Academy Awards ceremony in 2003. The Supreme Court's rulings on the legality of specific automobile searches also establish general rules and policies for such searches.

case. Lower courts then are obliged to apply the Court's interpretation of the Constitution to any other case that involves the same kind of auto search.

Finally, the Court's decisions shape public policy on police powers to engage in searches for evidence. In recent years the Court generally has given broad interpretations to those powers, in turn giving law enforcement agencies more freedom to engage in searches. Because the legal limits on police searches are determined primarily by the courts, the Supreme Court's expansions of search powers are an important component of government policy in this field.

The Supreme Court's role in government policy on police searches is not unusual. Through its individual decisions and lines of decisions, the Court contributes a great deal to policy on a variety of important issues. The Court's assumption of this role has been facilitated by several circumstances. For one thing, as the French observer Alexis de Tocqueville noted more than a century ago, "Scarcely any political question arises in the United States that is not resolved, sooner or later, into a judicial question."[2] One reason that policy disputes tend to reach the courts is the existence of a written Constitution whose provisions offer a basis for challenging the legality of government actions. Because so many policy questions come to the courts, the Supreme Court has the opportunity to shape a wide range of policies. And during much of its history the Court has welcomed that opportunity, frequently ruling on major issues and shaping public policy on those issues.

At the same time, the Court's role in policymaking is limited by several conditions, of which two are especially important. First, the Court can do only so much with the relatively few decisions it makes in a year. The Court currently issues decisions with full opinions in an average of about eighty cases each year. In deciding such a small number of cases, the Court addresses only a select group of policy issues. Inevitably, there are whole fields of policy that it barely touches. Even in the areas in which the Court does act, it can deal with only a limited number of the issues that exist at a given time.

Second, the actions of other policymakers limit the impact of the Court's decisions. The Court is seldom the final government institution to deal with the policy issues it addresses. Its decisions are generally implemented by lower-court judges and administrators, who often have considerable discretion over how they put a ruling into effect. The effect of a decision concerning police searches for evidence depends largely on how police officers react to it. Congress and the president influence how the Court's decisions are carried out, and they can overcome its interpretations of federal statutes simply by amending those statutes. There may be a considerable difference between what the Court rules on an issue and the public policy that ultimately results from government actions on that issue.

For these reasons, those who see the Supreme Court as the dominant force in the U.S. government almost surely are wrong. But if not dominant, the Court is an important policymaker. Certainly, the extent of its power is extraordinary for a court.

The Court in the Judicial System

The Supreme Court is part of a court system, and its place in that system structures its role by determining what cases it can hear and the routes those cases take.

State and Federal Court Systems

The United States has a federal court system and a separate court system in each state. Federal courts can hear only those cases that Congress has put under their jurisdiction. Most of the jurisdiction of the federal courts falls into three categories.

First are the criminal and civil cases that arise under federal laws, including the Constitution. A prosecution for bank robbery, which is a violation of federal criminal law, is brought to federal court. So are civil cases based on federal patent and copyright laws.

Second are cases to which the U.S. government is a party. When the federal government sues an individual to recover what it claims to be owed from a student loan, or when an individual sues the federal government over disputed Social Security benefits, the case almost always goes to federal court.

Third are civil cases involving citizens of different states, if the amount in question is more than $75,000; if this condition is met, either party may bring the case to federal court. If a citizen of New Jersey sues a citizen of Texas for $100,000 as compensation for injuries resulting from an auto accident, the plaintiff (the New Jersey resident) might bring the case to federal court, or the defendant (the Texan) might have the case "removed" from state court to federal court. If neither does so, the case will be heard in state court—generally, in the state where the accident occurred.

These categories encompass only a small proportion of all court cases. The most common kinds of cases—criminal prosecutions, personal injury suits, divorces, actions to collect debts—typically are heard in state court. The trial courts of a single populous state such as Illinois or Florida hear far more cases than do the federal trial courts. However, federal cases are more likely than state cases to raise major issues of public policy.

State court systems vary considerably in their structure, but some general patterns exist (see Figure 1-1). Each state system has courts that are primarily trial courts, which hear cases initially as they enter the court system, and courts that are primarily appellate courts, which review lower-court decisions that are appealed to them. Most states have two sets of trial courts, one to handle major cases and the other to deal with minor cases. Major criminal cases usually concern what the law defines as felonies; major civil cases are those involving large sums of money. Most often, appeals from decisions of minor trial courts are heard by major trial courts.

Appellate courts are structured in two ways. Eleven states, generally those with the smallest populations, have a single appellate court—usually called the state supreme court. All appeals from major trial courts go to this supreme court. The other thirty-nine states have a set of intermediate appellate courts below the supreme court. These intermediate courts initially hear most appeals from major trial courts. State supreme courts are required to hear certain appeals brought directly from the trial courts or from the intermediate courts, but for the most part they have discretionary jurisdiction over challenges to the decisions of intermediate courts. Discretionary jurisdiction means simply that a court can choose to hear some cases and refuse to hear others; cases that a court is required to hear fall under its mandatory jurisdiction.

The structure of federal courts is shown in Figure 1-2. At the base of the federal court system are the federal district courts. The United States has ninety-four district courts; each state has between one and four, and there is a district court in the District of Columbia and in some of the territories,

FIGURE 1-1
Most Common State Court Structures

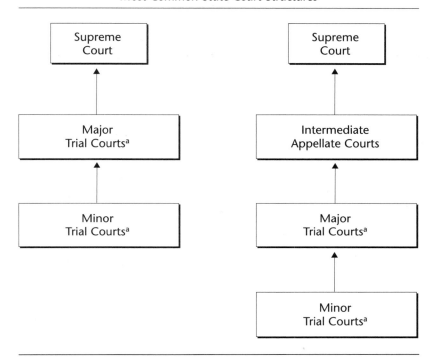

Note: Arrows indicate most common routes of appeals.

a. In many states, major trial courts or minor trial courts (or both) are composed of two or more different sets of courts. For instance, New York has several types of minor trial courts.

such as Guam. The district courts hear all federal cases at the trial level, with the exception of a few types of cases that are heard in specialized courts.

Above the district courts are the twelve courts of appeals, each of which hears appeals in one of the federal judicial circuits. The District of Columbia constitutes one circuit; each of the other eleven circuits covers three or more states. The Second Circuit, for example, includes Connecticut, New York, and Vermont. Appeals from the district courts in one circuit generally go to the court of appeals for that circuit, along with appeals from the Tax Court and from some administrative agencies. Patent cases and some claims against the federal government go from the district courts to the specialized Court of Appeals for the Federal Circuit, as do appeals from three specialized trial courts. The Court of Appeals for the Armed Forces hears cases from lower courts in the military system.

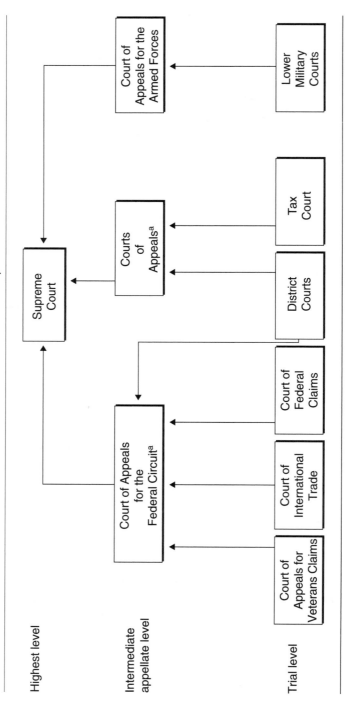

FIGURE 1-2
Basic Structure of the Federal Court System

Highest level

Intermediate appellate level

Trial level

Court of Appeals for the Armed Forces

Lower Military Courts

Supreme Court

Courts of Appeals[a]

Tax Court

District Courts

Court of Federal Claims

Court of Appeals for the Federal Circuit[a]

Court of International Trade

Court of Appeals for Veterans Claims

Note: Arrows indicate most common routes of appeals. Some specialized courts of minor importance are excluded.

a. These courts also hear appeals from administrative agencies.

TABLE 1-1
Summary of Supreme Court Jurisdiction

Types of jurisdiction	Categories of cases
Original	Disputes between states[a]
	Some types of cases brought by a state
	Disputes between a state and the federal government
	Cases involving foreign diplomatic personnel
Appellate[b]	All decisions of federal courts of appeals and specialized federal appellate courts
	All decisions of the highest state court with jurisdiction over a case, concerning issues of federal law
	Decisions of special three-judge federal district courts (mandatory)

a. It is unclear whether these cases are mandatory, and the Court treats them as discretionary.
b. Some minor categories are not listed.

The Supreme Court's Jurisdiction

The Supreme Court stands at the top of the federal judicial system. Its jurisdiction, summarized in Table 1-1, is of two types. First, the Constitution gives the Court jurisdiction over certain specified classes of cases as a trial court—what is called original jurisdiction. Those cases may be brought directly to the Court. The Court's original jurisdiction includes some cases to which a state is a party and cases involving ambassadors. Most cases within the Court's original jurisdiction can be heard alternatively by a district court. Lawsuits between two states can be heard only by the Supreme Court, and these lawsuits—often involving disputed state borders—account for most of the decisions based on the Court's original jurisdiction. A typical example is *Kansas v. Colorado* (2004), in which the two states disagreed about rights to water from the Arkansas River. The Court frequently refuses to hear cases under its original jurisdiction, even some lawsuits by one state against another. In part for this reason, full decisions in these cases are not plentiful—only about 180 such decisions in the Court's history.[3] When the Court does accept a case under its original jurisdiction, it usually appoints a "special master" to gather facts and propose a decision, which the Court tends to ratify.[4] Parties pay the fees charged by special masters, and the fees can add up. In a dispute between New Jersey and New York over how the border between the two states applied to Ellis Island, the total was more than $700,000.[5]

TABLE 1-2
Sources of Supreme Court Cases in Recent Periods (percent)

	Federal courts			
	Courts of appeals	District courts	Specialized courts	State courts
Cases brought to the Court[a]	76.4	0.0	1.6	22.0
Cases heard by the Court[b]	83.2	1.3	2.0	13.4

Source: Data on cases heard by the Court are from the U.S. Supreme Court Database, compiled by Harold Spaeth, Michigan State University.

Note: Original jurisdiction cases are not included. Nonfederal courts of the District of Columbia and of U.S. territories are treated as state courts. For cases heard by the Court, each oral argument is counted once unless it involves consolidated cases from two different categories of courts.

a. Cases in which the Court ruled on petitions for hearings, October 3, 2005 (1,719 cases).
b. Cases in which the Court heard oral argument, 2003 and 2004 terms (149 cases).

Second, the Court has appellate jurisdiction to hear cases brought by parties dissatisfied with certain lower-court decisions. In the federal system, such cases can come from the federal courts of appeals and from the two specialized appellate courts. Cases may also come directly from special three-judge district courts, which hear a few classes of cases. Most cases that reach the Court from the three-judge district courts concern voting and election issues.

Cases can come to the Supreme Court after decisions by the state supreme courts if they involve claims arising under federal law, including the Constitution. If a state supreme court chooses not to hear a case, the losing party can then go to the Supreme Court. For example, in 2003 the Court decided a case that had been heard only by a West Virginia trial court.[6] Table 1-2 shows that a substantial majority of the cases that come to the Court, and an even larger majority of the cases that it hears, originated in federal court rather than in state court.

The rule under which state cases come to the Supreme Court may be confusing, because cases arising under federal law ordinarily start in federal court. But cases brought to state courts on the basis of state law sometimes contain issues of federal law as well. This situation is common in criminal cases. A person accused of burglary under state law will be tried in a state court. During the state court proceedings, the defendant may argue that the police violated rights protected by the U.S. Constitution during a search. The case eventually can be brought to the Supreme Court on that issue. If it is, the Court will have the power to rule only on the federal issue, not on the issues of state law involved in the case. For example, the Court cannot rule on whether the defendant actually committed the burglary.

Nearly all cases brought to the Court are under its discretionary jurisdiction, so it can choose whether to hear them. They come to the Court primarily in the form of petitions for a writ of certiorari, a legal device by which the Court calls up a case for decision from a lower court. The Court must hear certain cases, called appeals. In a series of steps culminating in 1988, Congress converted the Court's jurisdiction from mostly mandatory to almost entirely discretionary. Today, appeals can be brought in only the few small classes of cases that come directly from three-judge district courts. The McCain-Feingold campaign funding law of 2002 provided this procedure for constitutional challenges to the law, so the appeals from the three-judge district court decision in the case went directly to the Supreme Court.[7]

The Supreme Court hears only a fraction of 1 percent of the cases brought to federal and state courts. As this figure suggests, courts other than the Supreme Court have ample opportunity to make policy on their own. Moreover, their decisions help to determine the ultimate impact of the Court's policies. Important though it is, the Supreme Court is not the only court that matters.

An Overview of the Court

The Court's Structure

The Supreme Court did not move into its own building until 1935. In its first decade, the Court met first in New York and then in Philadelphia. The Court moved to Washington, D.C., with the rest of the federal government at the beginning of the nineteenth century. For the next 130 years, it sat in the Capitol, a "tenant" of Congress.

The Court's accommodations in the Capitol were not entirely adequate. Among other things, the lack of office space meant that justices did most of their work at home. After an intensive lobbying effort by Chief Justice William Howard Taft, Congress appropriated money for the Supreme Court building in 1929. The five-story structure, completed in 1935, occupies a full square block across the street from the Capitol. Because the primary material in the impressive building is marble, it has been called a "marble palace." The aging of the Court's building and the need to house a staff that had grown considerably led to a major renovation project begun in 2003 and scheduled for completion in 2008.

The building houses all the facilities necessary for the Court's operation. Formal sessions are held in the courtroom on the first floor. Behind the courtroom is the conference room, where the justices meet to decide cases. Also near the courtroom are the chambers that contain offices for the associate justices and their staffs. Reflecting the chief justice's special status, the chief's chambers are attached to the conference room.

Personnel: The Justices

Under the Constitution, members of the Supreme Court must be nominated by the president and confirmed by a majority vote in the Senate. The Constitution establishes that they will hold office "during good behavior"—that is, for life unless they relinquish their posts voluntarily or are removed through impeachment proceedings. Beyond these basic rules, questions such as the number of justices, their qualifications, and their duties have been settled by federal statutes and by tradition.

People today are accustomed to a Court of nine members, but the number of justices was changed several times during the Court's first century. The Judiciary Act of 1789 provided for six justices. Subsequent statutes changed the number successively to five, six, seven, nine, ten, seven, and nine. The changes were made in part to accommodate the justices' duties in the lower federal courts, in part to serve partisan and policy goals of the president and Congress. The most recent change to nine members was made in 1869, and any further changes in size appear quite unlikely.

In 2006 each associate justice received a salary of $203,000, and the chief justice received $212,100. Substantial as these salaries are, they are considerably lower than leading lawyers receive at large private law firms. Justices are limited to about $23,000 in outside income from activities such as teaching, but there are no limits on income from books. Clarence Thomas reportedly will receive an advance payment totaling $1.5 million for the life story he is writing.[8] Some justices have considerable personal wealth: Stephen Breyer, Ruth Bader Ginsburg, John Roberts, David Souter, and John Paul Stevens all appear to be millionaires.[9]

The primary duty of the justices is to participate in the collective decisions of the Court: determining which cases to hear, deciding cases, and writing and contributing to opinions. Ordinarily, the Court's decisions are made by all nine members, but exceptions occur. At times the Court has only eight members because a justice has resigned, retired, or died, and a replacement has not been appointed. A justice's illness may leave the Court temporarily shorthanded. In the 2004 term William Rehnquist was absent from a dozen cases that the Court decided on the merits because of his severe health problems. After Samuel Alito succeeded Sandra Day O'Connor in 2006, Alito was unable to participate in several cases because oral argument had been held before he joined the Court. Or a justice may decide not to participate in a case because of a perceived conflict of interest. Under federal law, judges should withdraw from cases—"recuse" themselves—when a decision would affect their self-interest substantially or their impartiality "might reasonably be questioned."[10] The Court leaves this decision entirely to the individual justices.

Justices do not explain the reasons for their recusals, but the most common reason is a financial interest in a case, usually a result of their stock holdings. Other recusals result from personal ties between justices and the litigants or lawyers in a case. In 2003 Antonin Scalia recused himself from a case at the request of one of the parties because he had criticized the lower court's decision in a speech.[11] The next year Scalia was involved in a controversy over recusal that received considerable publicity. In that case two groups sought information about an energy task force over which Vice President Richard Cheney had presided. Scalia and Cheney were friends, and after the Court accepted this case the two were among the participants in a duck-hunting trip to Louisiana. One of Cheney's opponents in the case asked that Scalia recuse himself, but he declined to do so and issued a detailed memorandum explaining why he thought recusal was unnecessary.[12] Two years later, Scalia said, "I think the proudest thing I have done on the bench is not allowed myself to be chased off that case."[13]

When only eight justices participate in a decision, the Court may divide 4–4. This was the result in a 2002 environmental case from which Justice Anthony Kennedy withdrew because he was acquainted with one of the litigants.[14] A tie vote affirms the lower-court decision, the votes of individual justices are not announced, and no opinions are written. In rare instances, the Court fails to achieve a quorum of six members. This situation, like a tie vote, results in affirmance of the lower-court decision.

In addition to their participation in collective decisions, the justices make some decisions individually, as circuit justices. The United States has always been divided into federal judicial circuits. Originally, most appeals within a circuit were heard by ad hoc courts composed of a federal trial judge and two members of the Supreme Court assigned to that area as circuit justices. The circuit duties were arduous, particularly when long-distance travel was difficult. Some justices even suffered ill health from "circuit riding."[15] The justices' circuit-riding responsibilities were reduced in several steps and eliminated altogether when Congress created the courts of appeals in 1891.

The justices today retain some duties as circuit justices, with each justice assigned to one or more of the judicial circuits. As circuit justices they deal with applications for special action, such as a request to stay a lower-court decision (prevent it from taking effect) until the Court decides whether to hear the case. Ordinarily, such an application must go first to the circuit justice. That justice may rule on the application as an individual or refer the case to the whole Court. If the circuit justice rejects an application, it can then be made to a second justice. That justice ordinarily refers it to the whole Court.

One common subject of stay requests is the death penalty. The Court is confronted with numerous requests to stay executions or vacate (remove) stays of execution, many of which come near the scheduled execution time. In the past decade the Court has granted only a small proportion of requests for stays of execution, well under 10 percent in most years.[16] In the year from July 2004 to June 2005 the Court granted 2 of 55 motions to stay executions and 2 of the 3 motions to vacate stays.

Some stay requests involve important issues of policy or politics. Ohio was widely regarded as the key state in the 2004 presidential election. A few hours before the polls opened circuit justice John Paul Stevens was asked to vacate a lower-court stay and thereby reinstate limits on Republican challenges of prospective Ohio voters. Justice Stevens denied the request.[17]

For the most part, the nine justices are equal in formal power. The exception is the chief justice, who is the formal leader of the Court. The chief justice presides over the Court's public sessions and conferences and assigns the Court's opinion whenever the chief voted with the majority. The chief also supervises administration of the Court, with the assistance of committees of justices such as the Committee for the Budget and the Cafeteria Committee.[18]

The chief justice is the formal leader of the federal judicial system as well.[19] That role is symbolized by the official title, "Chief Justice of the United States." In this role the chief chairs the Judicial Conference and conveys to Congress the views of the conference on legislative issues. The chief justice appoints judges to administrative committees and some specialized courts. The chief also delivers an annual "state of the judiciary" message, directed primarily at Congress. In his first message, issued at the beginning of 2006, Chief Justice Roberts emphasized what he saw as inadequate budgets for the federal courts and inadequate salaries for their judges.[20]

Personnel: Law Clerks and Other Support Staff

A staff of about 450 people supports the justices. Most of the staff members carry out custodial and police functions under the supervision of the marshal of the Court. The police force has grown with concerns about security for the Court. These concerns were heightened by an incident in 2001: after anthrax bacteria were discovered in the Court's mailroom, the Court building was closed for a week, and oral arguments were held at a nearby federal court.

Several other offices help carry out the Court's work. The clerk of the Court is responsible for the clerical processing of all the cases that come to the Court. The reporter of decisions supervises preparation of the official record of the Court's decisions, the *United States Reports*. The librarian is in charge of the libraries in the Supreme Court building.

Of all the members of the support staff, the law clerks have the most direct effect on the Court's decisions.[21] Associate justices may employ four clerks each, the chief justice five. Clerks usually work with a justice for only one year. The typical clerk is a recent, high-ranked graduate of a prestigious law school. In the 2001–2005 terms, 43 percent came from Harvard and Yale. The great majority clerked in a federal court of appeals before coming to the Supreme Court, and some spent a short time in legal practice after their stints in a court of appeals.[22] There has been a growing tendency for the justices, especially the most conservative, to draw clerks from court of appeals judges who share the justices' ideological positions.[23]

Clerks typically spend much of their time on the petitions for hearings by the Court, reading the petitions and the lower-court records and summarizing them for the justices. Clerks also work on cases that have been accepted for decision. This work includes analysis of case materials and issues, discussions of issues with their justices, and drafting opinions. John Paul Stevens apparently was the only justice sitting in 2004 who wrote the first drafts of opinions rather than delegating them to law clerks.[24]

The extent of law clerks' influence over the Court's decisions is a matter of considerable interest and wide disagreement.[25] Observers who depict the clerks as quite powerful probably underestimate the justices' ability to maintain control over their decisions. Still, the jobs that justices give to their clerks ensure significant influence, influence that has grown over time. Writing drafts of opinions, for instance, allows clerks to shape the content of those opinions, whether or not they seek to do so. The same is true of the other work that clerks do.

After leaving the Court, most law clerks initially go into the private practice of law. With "signing bonuses" that can run as high as $200,000, these clerks often earn far more than the justices in their first year after Court service.[26] Many former clerks go on to distinguished careers. Indeed, Stephen Breyer, William Rehnquist, John Roberts, and John Paul Stevens were once law clerks in the Court. Roberts is a "second-generation" clerk-turned-justice, having clerked for Rehnquist in the Court's 1980 term and then succeeding him as chief justice.

The Court and the Outside World

Supreme Court justices differ in the extent and form of their public activity outside the Court.[27] David Souter seldom makes public appearances outside the Court. "In a perfect world," he told a colleague in 1990, "I would never give another speech, address, talk, lecture or whatever as long as I live."[28] In contrast, many of his colleagues are quite active. Their most common activity is speaking and lecturing at colleges, usually law schools. They often participate in judicial conferences and meetings of lawyers' groups. Sandra Day O'Connor was unusual for the number of her appearances before nonlawyers. In 2004, for instance, she appeared at the annual festival of the Mid-America Windmill Museum in Indiana. A year earlier she reported that she had spoken in every state.[29]

Some of the justices engage in off-the-Court writing. Chief Justice Rehnquist wrote four books about law and courts. Justice O'Connor published a book about her childhood on a ranch and one of essays on the Court's history and other topics. Some justices write law review articles, often based on their talks at law schools.

The justices' outside activities can have implications for policy or politics. Their speeches and lectures often convey a sense of their views on public issues. Justice Kennedy, for instance, has discussed issues such as sentencing policy. Justice Scalia frequently discusses his judicial philosophy and his views on issues such as the role of religion in public life, and he sometimes criticizes Court decisions in which he dissented. Scalia enjoys taking provocative positions, and one reporter said that of the justices, he "is the most likely to offer the jurisprudential equivalent of smashing a guitar onstage."[30] Largely as a response to Scalia, Justice Breyer gave a set of lectures at Harvard University in 2004 to lay out his quite different judicial philosophy. He later published the lectures as a book, and he made several public appearances to present the arguments in the book.[31]

Justices sometimes become involved in the political process more directly. In past eras some justices consulted with presidents. Abe Fortas, a long-time adviser to Lyndon Johnson, continued to serve in that role after his appointment to the Court. For most of his time on the Court, according to another justice, "Abe was sitting in Lyndon Johnson's lap."[32] As an adviser, Fortas dealt with some issues that could have come before the Court, and he disclosed to an FBI official information on the Court's deliberations in two cases. Warren Burger, appointed chief justice by President Richard M. Nixon, later discussed pending cases with Nixon.[33]

Since Burger and Nixon, it appears that no justice has engaged in that kind of presidential consultation. However, some justices interact with groups that have positions on issues of legal policy. Scalia and Clarence Thomas occasionally appear at events of the Federalist Society, a conservative legal group. Ruth Bader Ginsburg had ties to Legal Momentum, a group that litigates on women's rights issues, through a lecture series named after her that the group cosponsored. These interactions, like consultation with presidents, have been criticized for potentially compromising the justice's impartiality.[34]

The justices are well known and enjoy high status within the legal community, a status reflected in the frenzy over the bobblehead dolls of the justices that one legal publication gives its subscribers.[35] The mass media also give considerable attention to the justices, especially the ones who are most colorful. Justice Scalia has even been the occasional subject of a comic strip

Justice Antonin Scalia speaks at the University of Connecticut law school in 2006. In this speech, as in others, Scalia argued for the desirability of his approach to legal interpretation.

that appears in weekly newspapers. The cartoonist depicts Scalia as a motorcycle-riding avenger who attacks enemies such as Saddam Hussein and the Florida Supreme Court.[36]

Yet few justices have much visibility among the general public. In a 2005 survey, 27 percent of adults could name Sandra Day O'Connor as a justice, 21 percent Clarence Thomas, and 16 percent John Roberts. All the other justices fell below 15 percent, and Stephen Breyer and John Paul Stevens were at 3 percent.[37] Nor are the faces of most justices widely recognized. According to Justice Breyer, "out of the 10 times somebody asks me 'Are you on the Supreme Court?' nine of them thought I was Justice Souter."[38]

This anonymity is partly a result of the justices' own choices to stay largely out of public view. As one reporter put it, the justices are "glimpsed only rarely, like Bigfoot, crashing through the forest at twilight."[39] One key choice is a refusal to allow televising of the Court's public sessions. The justices have adhered to that position despite some pressure to change it, including a bill—approved by the Senate Judiciary Committee in 2006— that would require the Court's public sessions to be televised as a general rule. This position is part of a broader practice of limiting the disclosure of information about the Court's decision-making processes. By limiting the flow of information about themselves and the Court, the justices may be trying to maintain an impression that the Court is above ordinary politics. Indeed, Barbara Perry has argued that the justices and the Court's staff engage in a careful strategy to give the Court an exalted image among the general public.[40]

If there is such a strategy, it has achieved a degree of success. News coverage of the Court has much in common with coverage of the other branches, but the Court receives more deferential treatment.[41] The Court enjoys a certain "aura" in popular culture,[42] and its public approval ratings are usually more positive than those of the other branches. That high level of approval may provide the Court with some protection from criticism and more concrete attacks by other policymakers.

From this perspective it is interesting that some of the Court's practices have changed recently.[43] Its Web site now provides considerable information, including transcripts of oral arguments posted within a few weeks of the arguments. In a few cases that attracted widespread interest, the Court has allowed immediate release of audiotapes of the arguments. And on the whole, the justices have become more willing to discuss their work in public forums. It may be that the Court collectively sees value in opening itself up a bit. In any event, some of the justices clearly enjoy appearing and expressing themselves in public.

The Court's Schedule

The Court keeps to a constant annual schedule. It holds one term each year, lasting from the first Monday in October until the beginning of the succeeding term a year later.[44] The term is designated by the year in which it begins: the 2006 term began in October 2006. Ordinarily, the Court does its collective work from late September to late June. This work begins when the justices meet to act on the petitions for hearings that have accumulated during the summer and ends when the Court has issued decisions in all the cases it heard during the term.

Most of the term is divided into sittings of about two weeks, when the Court holds sessions to hear oral arguments in cases and to announce decisions, and recesses of two weeks or longer. The justices meet in conference during the sittings and less frequently during recesses. After the Court begins its last sitting in mid-May, it hears no more cases and holds one or more sessions each week to announce decisions. The Court issues few decisions early in the term because of the time required after oral arguments to write opinions and reach final positions. Typically, about one-third of the decisions are announced in June, as the justices scramble to finish their work by the end of the term. According to Justice Scalia, "Toward the end of the term when there are a lot of opinions outstanding that haven't come in yet," Chief Justice Rehnquist was "wont to say, 'Ladies and gentlemen, time to stop thinking and start writing.' "[45] As an associate justice, Rehnquist once wrote to Justice Marshall that "if this were November rather than June, I would prepare a masterfully crafted dissenting opinion exposing the fallacies" of Marshall's majority opinion in a case. "Since it is June, however, I join" Marshall's opinion.[46]

When the Court has reached and announced decisions in all the cases it heard during the term, the summer recess begins. Cases that the Court accepted for hearing but that were not argued during the term are carried over to the next term. In summer the justices generally spend some time away from Washington but continue their work on the petitions for hearings that arrive at the Court. During that time the Court and individual circuit justices respond to applications for special action. When the justices meet at the end of summer to dispose of the accumulated petitions, the cycle begins again.

The schedule of weekly activities, like the annual schedule, is fairly regular. During sittings, the Court generally holds sessions on Monday through Wednesday for two weeks and on Monday of the next week. The sessions begin at ten o'clock in the morning. Oral arguments usually are held during each session except on the last Monday of the sitting. They may be preceded by several types of business. On Mondays the Court announces the filing of its order list, which is a report of the Court's decisions on petitions for hearing and other actions taken at its conference on the preceding Friday. On Tuesdays and Wednesdays, as well as the last Monday of the sitting, justices announce their opinions in cases the Court has resolved. During the last sitting of the term, however, opinions may be announced on any day of the week.

The oral arguments consume most of the time during sessions. The usual practice is to allot one hour, equally divided between the two sides, for arguments in a case. On most argument days the Court hears two cases.

During sittings, the Court holds two conferences each week. The Wednesday afternoon conference is devoted to discussion of the cases that were argued on Monday. In a longer conference on Friday, the justices discuss the cases argued on Tuesday and Wednesday, as well as all the other matters the Court must decide. The most numerous of these matters are the petitions for hearing.

The Court also holds a conference on the last Friday of each recess to deal with the continuing flow of business. The remainder of the justices' time during recess periods is devoted to their individual work: study of petitions for hearing and of cases scheduled for argument, writing of opinions, and reaction to other justices' opinions. That work continues during the sittings.

The Court's History

This book is concerned primarily with the Supreme Court at present and in the recent past, but I frequently refer to the Court's history to provide perspective on the current Court. It is useful at this point to take an overview of that history.

The Court from 1790 to 1865

The framers of the Constitution explicitly created the Supreme Court, but the Constitution says much less about the Court than about Congress and the president. In the Judiciary Act of 1789, which set up the federal court system, the Court's jurisdiction under the Constitution was used as the basis for granting the Court broad powers. Still, what it would do with its powers was uncertain, in part because their scope was ambiguous.

The Court started slowly, deciding only about fifty cases and making few significant decisions between 1790 and 1799.[47] Several nominees rejected offers to serve on the Court, and two justices—including Chief Justice John Jay—resigned to take more attractive positions in state government. The Court's fortunes improved considerably under John Marshall, chief justice from 1801 to 1835. Marshall, appointed by President John Adams, dominated the Court to a degree that no other justice has matched. He used his dominance to strengthen the Court's position and advance the policies he favored.

The Court's most important assertion of power under Marshall was probably its decision in *Marbury v. Madison* (1803), in which the Court struck down a federal statute for the first time. In his opinion for the Court, Marshall argued that when a federal law is inconsistent with the Constitution, the Court must declare the law unconstitutional and refuse to enforce it. A few years later, the Court also claimed the right of judicial review over state acts.

The Court's aggressiveness brought denunciations and threats, including an effort by President Thomas Jefferson to have Congress remove at least one justice through impeachment. But Marshall's skill in minimizing confrontations helped to protect the Court from a successful attack. The other branches of government and the general public gradually accepted the powers that he claimed for the Court and the Court's role in policymaking.

This acceptance was tested by the Court's decision in *Scott v. Sandford* (1857), generally known as the *Dred Scott* case. Prior to that decision, the Court had overturned only one federal statute, the minor law involved in *Marbury v. Madison*. In *Dred Scott*, however, Marshall's successor, Roger Taney (1836–1864), wrote the Court's opinion holding that Congress had exceeded its constitutional powers when it prohibited slavery in some territories. That decision was intended to resolve the legal controversy over slavery. Instead, the level of controversy increased, and the Court was vilified in the North. The Court's prestige suffered greatly, but its basic powers survived without serious challenge.[48]

During this period, the Court was concerned with more than its own position; it was addressing major issues of public policy. The primary area of its concern was federalism, the legal relationship between the national government and the states. Under Marshall, the Court gave strong support to national powers. Marshall wanted to restrict state policy where that policy interfered with activities of the national government, especially its power to regulate commerce. Under Taney, the Court was not as favorable to the national government, but Taney and his colleagues did not reverse the Marshall Court's general expansion of federal power. As a result, the constitutional power of the federal government remained strong; the Court had permanently altered the lines between the national government and the state governments.

The Court from 1865 to 1937

After the Civil War, the Court began to focus its attention on government regulation of the economy. By the late nineteenth century, all levels of government were adopting new laws to regulate business activities. Among them were the federal antitrust laws, state regulations of railroad practices, and federal and state laws concerning employment conditions. Inevitably, much of this legislation was challenged in the courts on constitutional grounds.

Although the Supreme Court upheld a great many government policies regulating business in this period, it gradually became less friendly toward those policies. That position was reflected in the development of constitutional doctrines limiting government power to control business activities. Those doctrines were used with increasing frequency to attack regulatory legislation; in the 1920s the Supreme Court held unconstitutional more than 130 regulatory laws.[49]

In the 1930s the Supreme Court's attacks on economic regulation brought it into serious conflict with the other branches. President Franklin

Roosevelt's New Deal program to combat the Great Depression included sweeping statutes to control the economy, measures that enjoyed widespread support. In a series of decisions in 1935 and 1936, the Court struck down several of these statutes, including laws broadly regulating industry and agriculture, generally by 6–3 and 5–4 margins.[50]

Roosevelt responded in 1937 by proposing legislation under which an extra justice could be added to the Court for every sitting justice over the age of seventy who had served at least ten years, up to a maximum of six extra justices. If the legislation were enacted, Roosevelt could appoint six new justices, thereby "packing" the Court with justices favorable to his programs. While this plan was being debated in Congress, however, the Court weakened the impetus behind it. In several decisions in 1937, the Court reversed direction and upheld New Deal legislation and similar state laws by narrow margins.[51] Some, though not all, observers have concluded that this shift was a deliberate effort by one or two moderate justices to mend the Court's contentious relationship with the other branches.[52] In any event, the Court-packing plan died.

During the congressional debate, one of the conservative justices retired. Several other justices left the Court in the next few years, giving Roosevelt the ideological control of the Court that he had sought through the Court-packing legislation. The new Court created by his appointments fully accepted the economic regulation that had been viewed unfavorably by its predecessor, giving very broad interpretations to the constitutional powers to tax and to regulate interstate commerce.

The Court from 1937 to the Present

Since its retreat in the late 1930s, the Court has continued to uphold major economic policies of the federal government. The Court hears many cases concerning economic regulation, but this field has become less central to its role. Instead, the Court's primary emphasis in the current era is civil liberties. More precisely, the Court gives the most attention to the interpretation of legal protections for freedom of expression and freedom of religion, for the procedural rights of criminal defendants and others, and for equal treatment of disadvantaged groups.

The Court's general position on civil liberties issues has varied considerably during this period, mostly as a result of changes in its membership. The one constant has been the Court's collective interest in addressing these issues.

The Court gave the most support to civil liberties during the 1960s, the latter part of the period when Earl Warren was chief justice (1953–1969). The Court's policies during that period are often identified with Warren, but other liberal justices played roles of equal or greater importance: Hugo

Black and William Douglas, Roosevelt appointees who served through the Warren Court, and Dwight D. Eisenhower's appointee William Brennan.

The most prominent decision of the Warren era was *Brown v. Board of Education* (1954), in which the Court ordered the desegregation of school systems that assigned students to separate schools by race. The Court supported the rights of African Americans in several other policy areas as well. During the 1960s, the Court expanded the rights of criminal defendants in state cases. It issued landmark decisions on the right to counsel (*Gideon v. Wainwright,* 1963), police search and seizure practices (*Mapp v. Ohio,* 1961), and the questioning of suspects (*Miranda v. Arizona,* 1966). The Court supported freedom of expression by expanding First Amendment rights, especially on obscenity and libel. In a line of cases beginning with *Baker v. Carr* (1962), the Court required that legislative districts be equal in population.

When Earl Warren retired in 1969, he was succeeded as chief justice by Warren Burger, President Nixon's first Court appointee. In 1970 and 1971 Nixon made three more appointments. The Court's membership changed much more slowly after that. But each new member until 1993 was appointed by a conservative Republican president—one by Gerald Ford, three by Ronald Reagan, and two by George H. W. Bush. In 1986 Reagan named Nixon appointee William Rehnquist, the most conservative justice on the Court, to succeed Warren Burger as chief justice. The string of Republican appointments was broken with Bill Clinton's two appointments in 1993 and 1994. George W. Bush's first appointments came in 2005 after eleven years without any change in the Court's membership, the longest such period since the 1820s.

The Republican appointments from 1969 through 1991 gradually moved the Court's civil liberties policies in a conservative direction. But the movement was not uniform. For example, the Court continued to give considerable support to freedom of expression. Perhaps the most decisive shift came on issues of criminal procedure, although the Court did not directly overturn any of the Warren Court's landmark expansions of defendants' rights. The Rehnquist Court's interpretations of federal antidiscrimination statutes tended to narrow their impact, with exceptions on issues such as sexual harassment.

The Court's policies in other areas changed as well. Its interpretations of environmental and labor laws became more conservative. Beginning in 1995 it narrowed congressional power to regulate the private sector and especially state governments in some respects, although it interpreted that power broadly in others.[53]

The Supreme Court's policies continue to evolve in complex ways, providing a reminder of how difficult it is to predict where the Court is going. The Court's history also demonstrates that its direction is largely a reflection of its membership, so the selection of justices is a crucial process. I examine that process in the next chapter.

NOTES

1. Examples include *Maryland v. Pringle* (2003); *Thornton v. United States* (2004); and *Illinois v. Caballes* (2005).
2. Alexis de Tocqueville, *Democracy in America*, 2 vols., trans. Henry Reeve, rev. Francis Bowen (New York: Knopf, 1945), vol. 1, 280.
3. This figure is updated from Henry J. Abraham, *The Judicial Process*, 7th ed. (New York: Oxford University Press, 1998), 188.
4. Anne-Marie Carstens, "Lurking in the Shadows of Judicial Process: Special Masters in the Supreme Court's Original Jurisdiction Cases," *Minnesota Law Review* 86 (February 2002): 625–715.
5. Tony Mauro, "Mastering the Court," *Legal Times*, September 29, 2003, 10. The case was *New Jersey v. New York* (1998).
6. *Norfolk & Western Railway Co. v. Ayers* (2003).
7. The Supreme Court's decision was *McConnell v. Federal Election Commission* (2003).
8. David D. Kirkpatrick and Linda Greenhouse, "Memoir Deal Reported for Justice Thomas," *New York Times*, January 10, 2003, A20.
9. The justices' wealth is estimated from their annual financial disclosure reports, which list the approximate values of their investments at the end of each calendar year. The reports for the justices since 2002 are posted at www.politicalmoneyline.com. Justice Robert's 2003 report (as a court of appeals judge) is posted at www.judicialwatch.org/judges/robertsjg.pdf.
10. 28 U.S.C., sec. 455.
11. Charles Lane, "High Court to Consider Pledge in Schools," *Washington Post*, October 15, 2003, A1, A9. The case was *Elk Grove v. Newdow* (2004).
12. Justice Scalia's memorandum is at *Cheney v. United States District Court* (2004).
13. Stephanie Reitz, "Scalia Says He's Proud He Didn't Recuse Himself in Cheney Case," Associated Press State and Local Wire, April 13, 2006.
14. Linda Greenhouse, "Tie Affirms Clean Water Act's Reach," *New York Times*, December 17, 2002, A32. The case was *Borden Ranch Partnership v. U.S. Army Corps of Engineers* (2002).
15. David N. Atkinson, *Leaving the Bench: Supreme Court Justices at the End* (Lawrence: University Press of Kansas, 1999), chap. 2.
16. Joan Biskupic, "Supreme Court Granting Fewer Stays of Execution," *USA Today*, October 28, 2003, 13A.
17. The case was *Spencer v. Pugh* (2004).
18. See Bernard Schwartz, *Decision: How the Supreme Court Decides Cases* (New York: Oxford University Press, 1996), 73–74.
19. See Russell R. Wheeler, "Chief Justice Rehnquist as Third Branch Leader," *Judicature* 89 (November–December 2005): 116–120.
20. "2005 Year-End Report on the Federal Judiciary," January 1, 2006, available at www.supremecourtus.gov/publicinfo/publicinfo.html.
21. The law clerks are discussed in Todd C. Peppers, *Courtiers of the Marble Palace: The Rise and Influence of the Supreme Court Law Clerk* (Stanford, Calif.: Stanford University Press, 2006); and Artemus Ward and David L. Weiden, *Sorcerers' Apprentices: 100 Years of Law Clerks at the United States Supreme Court* (New York: New York University Press, 2006).

22. Tony Mauro, "Clerks Follow New Path to High Court," *Legal Times,* October 21, 2002, 1.

23. Corey Ditslear and Lawrence Baum, "Selection of Law Clerks and Polarization in the U.S. Supreme Court," *Journal of Politics* 63 (August 2001): 869–885.

24. David G. Savage, "Anthony M. Kennedy and the Road Not Taken," in *A Year at the Supreme Court,* ed. Neal Devins (Durham, N.C.: Duke University Press, 2004), 41.

25. See Peppers, *Courtiers of the Marble Palace,* chap. 6, and Ward and Weiden, *Sorcerers' Apprentices,* chap. 6.

26. Charles Lane, "Former Clerks' Signing Bonuses Rival Salaries on the High Court," *Washington Post,* May 15, 2006, A15.

27. This discussion of justices' appearances is based in part on the lists of appearances for which the justices receive reimbursements, part of their annual financial disclosure reports, posted at www.politicalmoneyline.com.

28. Elizabeth Walters, "Breaking Ground with the Justices," *Concord (N.H.) Monitor,* April 9, 2006.

29. Sandra Day O'Connor, *The Majesty of the Law: Reflections of a Supreme Court Justice* (New York: Random House, 2003), xvi.

30. Margaret Talbot, "Supreme Confidence," *New Yorker,* March 28, 2005, 40.

31. Jeffrey Toobin, "Breyer's Big Idea," *New Yorker,* October 31, 2005, 36–43. The book was *Active Liberty: Interpreting Our Democratic Constitution* (New York: Knopf, 2005).

32. Laura Kalman, *Abe Fortas: A Biography* (New Haven: Yale University Press, 1990), 293.

33. Seymour M. Hersh, "Nixon's Last Cover-Up: The Tapes He Wants the Archives to Suppress," *New Yorker,* December 14, 1992, 81.

34. Richard A. Serrano and David G. Savage, "Ginsburg Has Ties to Activist Group," *Los Angeles Times,* March 11, 2004, A1, A20.

35. Tony Mauro, "Scalia Doll: A Wolf, A Lemon, No Ducks," *Legal Times,* April 11, 2005, 11.

36. The comic strip is "Tom the Dancing Bug," by Ruben Bolling.

37. "FindLaw's U.S. Supreme Court Awareness Survey," at www.print.public. findlaw.com/ussc/122005survey.html.

38. "Transcript of Discussion between U.S. Supreme Court Justices Antonin Scalia and Stephen Breyer—AU Washington College of Law, January 13 [2005]," 6, posted at http://domino.american.edu/AU/media/mediarel. nsf/ (under "Media Relations Press Releases").

39. Dahlia Lithwick, "Off the Bench," *New York Times,* August 29, 2004, sec. 4, 11.

40. Barbara A. Perry, *The Priestly Tribe: The Supreme Court's Image in the American Mind* (Westport, Conn.: Praeger, 1999).

41. On coverage of the Court, see Elliot E. Slotnick and Jennifer A. Segal, *Television News and the Supreme Court: All the News That's Fit to Air?* (New York: Cambridge University Press, 1998); and Rorie L. Spill and Zoe M. Oxley, "Philosopher Kings or Political Actors? How the Media Portray the Supreme Court," *Judicature* 87 (July–August 2003): 23–29.

42. That term is from Norman L. Rosenberg, "The Supreme Court and Popular Culture: Image and Projection," in *The United States Supreme Court: The Pursuit of Justice,* ed. Christopher Tomlins (Boston: Houghton Mifflin, 2005), 421.

43. See Tony Mauro, "Glasnost at the Supreme Court," in *A Year at the Supreme Court,* ed. Neal Devins (Durham, N.C.: Duke University Press, 2004), 193–208.
44. The Court's schedule is described in Robert L. Stern, Eugene Gressman, Stephen M. Shapiro, and Kenneth S. Geller, *Supreme Court Practice,* 8th ed. (Washington, D.C.: Bureau of National Affairs, 2002), 9–16.
45. Joan Biskupic, "It's Crunch Time for Some of High Court's Biggest Decisions," *USA Today,* June 6, 2005, 7A.
46. Joan Biskupic, *Sandra Day O'Connor* (New York: HarperCollins 2005), 125.
47. See William R. Casto, *The Supreme Court in the Early Republic: The Chief Justiceships of John Jay and Oliver Ellsworth* (Columbia: University of South Carolina Press, 1995). For another perspective, see Scott Douglas Gerber, ed., *Seriatim: The Supreme Court before John Marshall* (New York: New York University Press, 1998).
48. Robert G. McCloskey, *The American Supreme Court,* 4th ed., rev. by Sanford Levinson (Chicago: University of Chicago Press, 2005), 64–66.
49. This figure was calculated from data in Congressional Research Service, *The Constitution of the United States of America: Analysis and Interpretation* (Washington, D.C.: Government Printing Office, 1987), 1885–2113.
50. The cases included *Carter v. Carter Coal Co.* (1936); *United States v. Butler* (1936); and *Schechter Poultry Corp. v. United States* (1935).
51. The cases included *National Labor Relations Board v. Jones & Laughlin Steel Corp.* (1937); *Steward Machine Co. v. Davis* (1937); and *West Coast Hotel Co. v. Parrish* (1937).
52. See "AHR Forum: The Debate Over the Constitutional Revolution of 1937," *American Historical Review* 110 (October 2005): 1046–1115.
53. See *United States v. Morrison* (2000) and *Gonzales v. Raich* (2005).

Chapter 2

The Justices

Supreme Court decisions are shaped by an array of influences. The most direct influence, and probably the most powerful, is the Court's membership. When the Court decides a case by a 5–4 vote, as it frequently does, that one-vote margin emphasizes how much difference it makes that some people sit on the Court rather than others. And for that reason, it is understandable that people in and out of government give so much attention to the identities of the people who serve as justices.

As of mid-2006, presidents have made 151 nominations to the Supreme Court, and 110 justices have served. Four candidates were nominated and confirmed twice, and eight declined appointments or died before beginning service on the Court. Twenty-nine did not secure Senate confirmation; a few of these nominees dropped out before the Senate could consider them.[1] Table 2-1 lists the forty-four nominations to the Court since 1933 and the thirty-seven justices chosen since that time.

This chapter focuses on that period and primarily on the past few decades. In the chapter's three sections I discuss the selection of justices, the characteristics of the people who are selected, and how and why they leave the Court.

The Selection of Justices

The selection of a Supreme Court justice begins with the creation of a vacancy, when a member of the Court resigns, retires, or dies. Inevitably, vacancies occur at an irregular rate. President Bill Clinton was able to select two new justices in his first eighteen months in office, but none during the rest of his eight-year tenure. On succeeding Clinton, President George W. Bush then had to wait until the first year of his second term to choose his first two justices.

The formal process for selection of justices is simple. When a vacancy occurs, the president makes a nomination. The nomination must then be

TABLE 2-1
Nominations to the Supreme Court since 1933

Name	Nominating president	Justice replaced	Years served
Hugo Black	F.D. Roosevelt	Van Devanter	1937–1971
Stanley Reed	F.D. Roosevelt	Sutherland	1938–1957
Felix Frankfurter	F.D. Roosevelt	Cardozo	1939–1962
William Douglas	F.D. Roosevelt	Brandeis	1939–1975
Frank Murphy	F.D. Roosevelt	Butler	1940–1949
James Byrnes	F.D. Roosevelt	McReynolds	1941–1942
Harlan Fiske Stone (CJ)[a]	F.D. Roosevelt	Hughes	1941–1946
Robert Jackson	F.D. Roosevelt	Stone	1941–1954
Wiley Rutledge	F.D. Roosevelt	Byrnes	1943–1949
Harold Burton	Truman	Roberts	1945–1958
Fred Vinson (CJ)	Truman	Stone	1946–1953
Tom Clark	Truman	Murphy	1949–1967
Sherman Minton	Truman	Rutledge	1949–1956
Earl Warren (CJ)	Eisenhower	Vinson	1953–1969
John Harlan	Eisenhower	Jackson	1955–1971
William Brennan	Eisenhower	Minton	1956–1990
Charles Whittaker	Eisenhower	Reed	1957–1962
Potter Stewart	Eisenhower	Burton	1958–1981
Byron White	Kennedy	Whittaker	1962–1993
Arthur Goldberg	Kennedy	Frankfurter	1962–1965
Abe Fortas	Johnson	Goldberg	1965–1969
Thurgood Marshall	Johnson	Clark	1967–1991

Nominee	President	Seat	Status / Tenure
Abe Fortas (CJ)[a]	Johnson	(Warren)	Nomination withdrawn, 1968
Homer Thornberry	Johnson	(Fortas)	Nomination became moot, 1968[b]
Warren Burger (CJ)	Nixon	Warren	1969–1986
Clement Haynsworth	Nixon	(Fortas)	Defeated for confirmation, 1969
G. Harrold Carswell	Nixon	(Fortas)	Defeated for confirmation, 1970
Harry Blackmun	Nixon	Fortas	1970–1994
Lewis Powell	Nixon	Black	1971–1987
William Rehnquist	Nixon	Harlan	1971–2005
John Paul Stevens	Ford	Douglas	1975–
Sandra Day O'Connor	Reagan	Stewart	1981–2006
William Rehnquist (CJ)[a]	Reagan	Burger	1986–2005
Antonin Scalia	Reagan	Rehnquist	1986–
Robert Bork	Reagan	(Powell)	Defeated for confirmation, 1987
Douglas Ginsburg	Reagan	(Powell)	Withdrew before formal nomination, 1987
Anthony Kennedy	Reagan	Powell	1988–
David Souter	G. H. W. Bush	Brennan	1990–
Clarence Thomas	G. H. W. Bush	Marshall	1991–
Ruth Bader Ginsburg	Clinton	White	1993–
Stephen Breyer	Clinton	Blackmun	1994–
John Roberts (CJ)[c]	G. W. Bush	Rehnquist	2005–
Harriet Miers	G. W. Bush	(O'Connor)	Nomination withdrawn, 2005
Samuel Alito	G. W. Bush	O'Connor	2006–

Note: CJ = chief justice.

a. Nominated as chief justice while serving as associate justice.

b. When Fortas's nomination for chief justice was withdrawn, no vacancy for his seat as associate justice existed.

c. Originally nominated to replace Justice O'Connor, then nominated to replace Chief Justice Rehnquist.

confirmed by the Senate, with a simple majority of participating senators required for confirmation. When the chief justice's position is vacant, the president has two options: to nominate a sitting justice to that position and also nominate a new associate justice, or to nominate a person as chief justice from outside the Court. Presidents usually take the latter course, as President Bush did when he selected John Roberts to succeed William Rehnquist in 2005. But President Reagan elevated Rehnquist from associate justice to chief justice after Warren Burger retired in 1986.

The actual process of selection is more complicated than the simple formal process suggests. The president and the Senate make their decisions surrounded by individuals and groups with a deep interest in these decisions, and the process of nomination and confirmation can be complex. It will be useful to discuss the roles of unofficial participants in the process and then consider how the president and Senate reach their decisions.

Unofficial Participants

Because Supreme Court appointments are so important, a variety of individuals and groups seek to influence the president and Senate. When a vacancy occurs, presidents and their staffs may hear from a wide array of groups, government officials, other prominent people, and ordinary individuals. Apart from members of the president's administration, the most important of these participants fall into three categories: the legal community, other interest groups, and potential justices. The president and Senate also seek to influence each other. The need for Senate confirmation gives the president an incentive to listen to senators, especially when opposition control of the Senate or other conditions weaken the president's position.

The Legal Community. Lawyers have a particular interest in the Court's membership, and their views about potential justices may carry special weight. As the largest and most prominent organization of lawyers, the American Bar Association (ABA) occupies an important position. An ABA committee investigates presidential nominees who await confirmation and evaluates them as "well qualified," "qualified," or "not qualified." Because they believe that the ABA committee is biased against conservative nominees, some Republican senators give little weight to its judgment. Still, the committee's level of enthusiasm for a nominee can affect the confirmation process. (It has never rated a Supreme Court nominee as "not qualified.") A unanimous rating of "well qualified," which both John Roberts and Samuel Alito received, helps to smooth the path to Senate approval. By the same token, when four committee members rated Robert Bork as "not qualified" in 1987 and two gave that rating to Clarence Thomas in 1991, their prospects for confirmation were weakened. Those negative ratings of two conservative Republicans, one of them (Bork) a prestigious legal scholar, fostered the perception of bias in the ABA committee's decisions.

Other legal groups and individual lawyers also participate in the selection process. Law professors and other prominent attorneys often announce their evaluations of nominees the Senate is considering. Such evaluations sometimes have considerable impact. The criticism of President Nixon's nominees Clement Haynsworth and G. Harrold Carswell by prominent attorneys countered the ABA's official judgment that the two nominees were qualified and contributed to their rejection by the Senate. Seven of Samuel Alito's current and past colleagues on the federal court of appeals for the Third Circuit testified on his behalf in the Judiciary Committee.

Occasionally Supreme Court justices participate in the selection process, usually by recommending a potential nominee. Chief Justice Warren Burger went further. Appointed by Richard Nixon in 1969, he was active in suggesting names to fill other vacancies during the Nixon administration. He played an important role in Carswell's nomination and a crucial role in the nomination of his longtime friend Harry Blackmun. Some years later, Burger lobbied the Reagan administration on behalf of Sandra Day O'Connor.[2]

Other Interest Groups. Many interest groups have a stake in Supreme Court decisions, so groups often seek to influence the selection of justices. The level of group activity has grown substantially in the past half century, and it now pervades both the nomination and confirmation stages of the selection process.

At the nomination stage, interest groups would like to influence the president's choice from the large number of potential nominees. The groups that actually exert influence are typically those that are politically important to the president. Democratic presidents usually give some weight to the views of labor and civil rights groups. Republican presidents usually pay attention to groups that take conservative positions on social issues, such as abortion and school religious observances.

The influence of these core groups was underlined in 2005. After Sandra Day O'Connor announced her retirement, conservative groups lobbied publicly and privately in favor of a strong conservative. They even attacked Attorney General Alberto Gonzales, thought to be a candidate for nomination, for his perceived moderation. President Bush criticized those attacks, but his nominee John Roberts was more acceptable to conservatives, in part because the Bush administration had worked for a year to win their support for Roberts.[3] After Bush nominated Roberts to succeed William Rehnquist, he chose his White House counsel Harriet Miers for O'Connor's position. Many conservatives were uncertain that Miers held views similar to their own, and conservative groups and individuals mounted a strong campaign against her. After their campaign secured Miers's withdrawal, President Bush chose Samuel Alito, a judge who was popular with conservative groups.

Once a nomination has been announced, groups often work for or against Senate confirmation. Significant interest group activity at the confirmation stage can be traced back as far as 1881, but it was fairly limited and sporadic until the late 1960s.[4] Its growth since then reflects the increased number of interest groups and the increased intensity of group activity, greater awareness that nominations to the Court are important, and group leaders' increased understanding of how to participate effectively in the confirmation process. Ideological groups have also found that opposition to controversial nominees is a good way to generate both interest in their causes and monetary contributions from their supporters.

Groups that opposed specific nominees achieved noteworthy successes between 1968 and 1970. Conservative groups helped to bring about the defeat of Abe Fortas, nominated for elevation to chief justice by President Lyndon Johnson in 1968, and labor and civil rights groups helped to secure the defeats of Nixon nominees Haynsworth and Carswell. Liberal groups opposed some later nominees between 1971 and 1986 but achieved no more successes, although their opposition helped to narrow William Rehnquist's majorities in his initial confirmation in 1971 and his elevation to chief justice in 1986.

President Reagan's nomination of Robert Bork in 1987 gave rise to an unprecedented level of group activity.[5] Liberal groups feared that the strongly conservative Bork would move an ideologically divided Court to the right. Accordingly, they devoted considerable effort, and an estimated $12 million to $15 million, to achieving his defeat.[6] Their activities ranged from newspaper advertisements to direct lobbying of senators. Groups favorable to Bork's nomination took action as well. The pro-Bork groups did not mobilize as quickly or as fully as the opposition groups, and the higher level of activity against Bork helped to bring about his defeat.[7]

That episode led to an escalation of interest group conflict over confirmations. When it seems possible that a nominee might lose in the Senate, groups on both sides work actively to influence the outcome. Groups played only a limited role in the confirmations of Clinton nominees Ruth Bader Ginsburg and Stephen Breyer, both of whom seemed assured of victory in the Senate. But a heated battle broke out over Clarence Thomas in 1991, and groups were highly active when the Senate considered Samuel Alito in 2006. Those two Republican nominees were confirmed with more than forty negative votes, opposition that resulted in part from the direct and indirect lobbying of Democratic senators by liberal groups.

Interest group activity for and against Alito illustrates the growth of this activity and its level of intensity. Progress for America, a group that was allied with the Bush administration, had Web sites prepared on several possible nominees and activated its site for Alito within an hour after the president announced his nomination. The group also aired television commercials for Alito and mobilized supporters of the nominee to speak on his behalf.[8] For their part, groups such as the Alliance for Justice and People for the American Way worked against Alito, using e-mails and advertisements to publicize positions the nominee had taken on issues. Some anti-Alito ads attacked him in strong terms, and some ads in support of the nominee attacked his opponents in equally strong terms. Not all confirmations feature so fierce a battle, but such battles are likely whenever the stakes seem high and the outcome uncertain.

Candidates for the Court. When presidents make nominations to the Supreme Court, they sometimes choose people who never thought about themselves as potential justices. Some prospective nominees withdraw from consideration, some turn down nominations, and others accept them reluctantly. Among the reluctant justices were Byron White in 1962, Abe Fortas in 1965, and Lewis Powell in 1971. But for many lawyers, the Supreme Court is a long-standing dream. A decade before his appointment to the Court, Clarence Thomas told a reporter, "I want to be on the Supreme Court."[9] For Samuel Alito, that goal apparently came much earlier. According to the 1972 Princeton yearbook, Alito's intent was to "warm a seat on the Supreme Court."[10] Not surprisingly, most people who are offered nominations accept them readily.

Some lawyers with ambition for the Supreme Court conduct concerted private campaigns for nominations. William Howard Taft became chief justice in 1921 after years of efforts that began even when he was president. As an ex-president he had a great deal of influence, and one commentator described Taft as "virtually appointing himself" chief justice.[11] While serving on a federal court of appeals, Warren Burger exerted considerable effort to make himself a candidate for the Supreme Court. When his effort succeeded, President Nixon's attorney general—overlooking Taft's example—said that "Burger's the first guy to run for the job of Chief Justice—and get it."[12] But presidents do not limit themselves to candidates who openly seek nominations, and such campaigns are usually considered counterproductive.

In the current era, the great majority of nominees are judges on the federal courts of appeals. Undoubtedly, most of those judges would be very pleased to win Supreme Court nominations. It is conceivable that in certain cases some judges take positions that they think will improve their prospects. After interviews with administration officials and five days before his nomination in 2005, John Roberts voted for the president's position in a decision upholding the use of military commissions to try detainees at the Guantanamo military base. If Roberts had voted the other way, the president almost surely would have chosen a different nominee. Some people criticized Roberts for participating in the case. But it is very unlikely that his candidacy for the Court affected his vote, a vote that seemed quite consistent with his personal views.[13]

Sitting justices might welcome a promotion to chief justice. During the last few years of the Rehnquist Court, some observers perceived that Anthony Kennedy and Antonin Scalia were trying to improve their chances of promotion through their off-the-Court activities. One magazine speculated that Scalia was engaged in a "charm offensive" to counter his somewhat abrasive image.[14] If either justice was campaigning for promotion, that campaign failed when President Bush nominated a chief justice from outside the Court.

In past eras, nominees typically played little part in the confirmation process. Today, they participate actively in that process. Nominees visit with senators and testify before the Senate Judiciary Committee.

Because so much attention is focused on nominees' testimony, it has become a key to confirmation. As a consequence, administration officials work hard to prepare nominees for the committee hearings. In their testimony nominees seek to present an attractive image and to avoid taking positions on judicial issues that could arouse opposition.

For their part, senators who seek to defeat a nominee look for ways to elicit unpopular positions from nominees. But well-prepared nominees can usually overcome those efforts. They can turn back questions about matters such as abortion or the death penalty on the ground—largely legitimate—that they do not want to "prejudge" issues that might come before the Court. According to one count, John Roberts refused to answer questions on that ground sixty-seven times.[15] Nominees can limit criticism for nonresponsiveness by addressing questions about issues when they know that their answers will be popular or uncontroversial.

In 1987 Robert Bork's testimony weakened his prospects for confirmation because it left liberal and moderate senators with the impression that he was strongly conservative and because it exposed his rough edges. Clarence Thomas's testimony four years later increased opposition to him because what he said about his views on issues raised doubts about his candor. Nominees since then have done better, in part because they have learned from the Bork and Thomas experiences. John Roberts in 2005 impressed senators with his expertise and with his personality, and he adroitly avoided the traps that some Democratic committee members sought to lay for him. Samuel Alito was not quite as effective in putting forth a positive image, but he too avoided traps. One commentator said, "John Roberts charmed his way through the proceedings. Sam Alito has chosen to simply bore his way through"—and he too did well as a result.[16] In particular, he succeeded in turning back questions based on controversial positions he had taken in the past. Frustrated by the performances of Roberts and Alito, Democratic senator Joseph Biden of Delaware sug-

Judge John Roberts testifies in 2005 at the confirmation hearing for his nomination as chief justice. Nominees' testimony has become a focus of attention, and favorable impressions of Roberts's testimony helped to ensure his confirmation.

gested that the Senate should eliminate nominees' testimony and assess the nominees solely on the basis of their prior records.[17]

The President's Decision

For the president, a Supreme Court vacancy provides a valuable opportunity to influence the Court's direction, and presidents seek to make the most of these opportunities. But the individuals and groups for whom nominations are important can subject the president to heavy and conflicting pressures, and the pressures have grown stronger in recent years.

The process of selecting a nominee differs across administrations and sometimes within them.[18] One difference is in the extent to which prospective nominees are identified and considered before a vacancy actually arises. In the current era, administrations typically do a good deal of preparatory work in anticipation of opportunities to select justices. This work went furthest in Lyndon Johnson's administration: in effect, each of his nominees was chosen even before a vacancy existed. George W. Bush's advisers began preparation early in his administration, and prospective nominees had been identified and scrutinized before a vacancy finally arose in 2005. The Clinton administration was less prepared to fill vacancies, largely because Clinton's two opportunities to nominate justices came early in his presidency.

A second difference is in the extent to which presidents participate in the process that produces a nominee. Reagan and George H. W. Bush gave considerable responsibility to officials in the White House and Justice Department, but Clinton exerted far more direct control over the selection process even in its early stages. George W. Bush has been another active participant in the selection of nominees. Before choosing John Roberts, he interviewed Roberts and four other candidates. He also played the key role in making Harriet Miers the focus of the search that led to her nomination. By necessity, however, every president delegates most of the search process to other officials in the executive branch. Roberts's decisive interview was with President Bush, but he had also been interviewed by Vice President Dick Cheney, Attorney General Alberto Gonzales, and five members of the White House staff.[19]

The third and most important difference is in the mix of criteria that presidents and their advisers use to select nominees. The possible criteria fall into several categories: the "objective" qualifications of potential nominees, their policy preferences, rewards to political and personal associates, and the building of political support. Cutting across these criteria and helping to determine their use is the reality that the Senate must confirm a nominee.

"Objective" Qualifications. Presidents have strong incentives to select Supreme Court nominees who have demonstrated high levels of legal competence and adherence to ethical standards. One reason is most presidents' respect for the Court. Another is that highly competent justices are in the best position to influence their colleagues. Finally, serious questions about a candidate's competence or ethical behavior can make confirmation considerably more difficult.

In general, presidents' choices reflect a concern for competence. This does not mean that all nominees are highly skilled in the law, but only in a few cases has a nominee's capacity to serve on the Court been seriously questioned. One of those nominees was Nixon's choice, G. Harrold Carswell, in 1970; Carswell was denied confirmation. Perceptions that Harriet Miers had only limited knowledge of constitutional law, perceptions shared by some senators who talked with her, were one source of the opposition that ultimately led her to withdraw as a nominee.

The ethical behavior of several nominees has been questioned. Abe Fortas (when nominated to be chief justice), Clement Haynsworth, Stephen Breyer, and Samuel Alito were attacked for alleged financial conflicts of interest; Fortas was also criticized for continuing to consult with President Johnson while serving as an associate justice. The charges against Fortas and Haynsworth helped bring about their defeats in the Senate. After Douglas Ginsburg was announced as a Reagan nominee, disclosures were made about a possible financial conflict of interest when he was in the Justice Department and about his past use of marijuana. The latter disclosure was especially damaging, and Ginsburg withdrew his name from consideration. An allegation that Clarence Thomas had sexually harassed an assistant while he was a federal administrator resulted in a special set of Senate hearings on the charge and put his confirmation in jeopardy.

To minimize the possibility of such embarrassments, administrations today give close scrutiny to potential nominees. After its difficulty with Douglas Ginsburg, the Reagan administration wanted to ensure that Anthony Kennedy, its choice as the next nominee, had no problems in his personal life. White House counsel A. B. Culvahouse came to Kennedy with a twenty-one-page list of questions. The FBI, itself embarrassed by its failure to discover Ginsburg's drug use, undertook a massive investigation of its own. Culvahouse stopped Kennedy during a visit to the White House to tell him that the investigation had uncovered a problem: Kennedy's daughter had an unpaid parking ticket. When nothing else turned up, Kennedy was nominated.[20]

Competence and ethics can be considered screening criteria for potential nominees. These criteria may eliminate some people from consideration, but enough candidates survive the screening process to give presidents a wide range of choices for a nomination.

Policy Preferences. By policy preferences, I mean an individual's attitudes toward policy issues. These criteria have always been a consideration in the selection of Supreme Court justices, because presidents recognize that their appointees' impact on the Court's policies is among a president's major legacies.

In the current era every president gives considerable weight to the policy preferences of prospective nominees, because of the Court's prominence as a policymaker and because interest groups associated with both parties care so much about the Court's direction. But presidents continue to differ in the weight they give to this consideration. Understandably, presidents who want to change the Supreme Court's direction give particular emphasis to policy considerations. This was true of both Richard Nixon and Ronald Reagan. Speaking of potential nominees, Nixon told his chief of staff that he did not care "if the guy can read or write, just so he votes right."[21] Policy considerations are also important to George W. Bush. One reason is that he and other conservatives were unhappy that a string of appointments by his Republican predecessors had not changed the Court as much as they hoped. In contrast, Bill Clinton was less concerned with the policy views of his prospective nominees.

It is in relation to this criterion that the Senate's role creates the greatest complications. Most Democratic presidents are distinctly liberal, most Republicans distinctly conservative. If a strongly liberal president chose a nominee whose preferences were also strongly liberal, that nominee's views would be somewhat distant from the views of Senate moderates and quite distant from the views of many Republican senators. A strongly conservative president is in a similar situation with Democratic senators. Thus, presidents often perceive that they must choose between two imperfect options: choose a nominee whose views mirror their own and risk difficulty with confirmation, or choose a more moderate nominee and reduce their ability to reshape the Court. Presidents have responded to this dilemma in different ways, depending in part on their willingness to get into conflicts over nominees.

Presidents who want to put like-minded people on the Supreme Court need to ascertain that their nominees really *are* like-minded. This is one reason that every nominee since 1986 except for Harriet Miers has come from a federal court of appeals. If a judge has a long record of judicial votes and opinions on federal issues, as Samuel Alito did, presidents and their advisers can be fairly confident about the kinds of positions the judge would take as a justice.

Some nominees do not have these long records. Aside from Miers, Sandra Day O'Connor had served only on state courts, and nearly all of David Souter's judicial service was at the state level. Most kinds of issues that come to the Supreme Court are uncommon in state courts. Clarence Thomas had served only one year on a federal court of appeals, John Roberts only two. For candidates such as these, other sources of information can be consulted, such as records of nonjudicial service and people who know a prospective nominee well. In Miers's case, George W. Bush had a good sense of her views from their long association, including her work in the White House. Sometimes presidents or their representatives ask prospective nominees directly about their views. According to one report, presidential advisers questioned John Roberts closely in order to ascertain the strength of his conservatism.[22]

Presidents concerned with confirmation of their nominees might prefer a situation in which the president has a clear sense of a nominee's views but there is little public evidence of those views for opponents to attack. As George W. Bush said about Harriet Miers, who had not served as a judge, "there's not a lot of opinions for people to look at."[23] But the lack of hard evidence that Miers was strongly conservative on judicial issues aroused concern from members of the president's own party. In the case of David Souter, President George H. W. Bush had what he thought was good evidence of Souter's conservatism from people who knew him, but Senate Democrats had little evidence of their own with which to raise questions about Souter. Souter was confirmed without great difficulty, but his record as a justice suggests that he was not nearly as conservative as Bush thought. That record has served as a cautionary tale for conservatives, and fear of another Souter helps to explain the strong opposition to Miers.

Despite prominent examples such as Souter, most justices turn out to be ideologically compatible with the presidents who appoint them. Those who deviate from the appointing president generally fall into two categories. First, some were chosen by presidents who were not especially interested in choosing compatible justices or who were not careful about doing so. Gerald Ford selected John Paul Stevens without regard for his nominee's policy preferences, so the gap between Ford's conservatism and Stevens's liberalism is not surprising. According to a story that is widely circulated but of uncertain accuracy, Dwight Eisenhower cited his appointees Earl Warren and William Brennan as the two mistakes he had made as president.[24] But as a California governor Warren had shown signs of the liberalism he later manifested as chief justice, and Brennan's own liberalism was apparent from his record as a state judge.

Second, some justices shift their ideological positions after reaching the Court. Richard Nixon's one "failure" was Harry Blackmun, who had a distinctly conservative record in his early years on the Court but gradually adopted more liberal positions. Anthony Kennedy also may have shifted in a liberal direction after reaching the Court, albeit to a lesser degree. A conservative publication later referred to Kennedy as "surely Reagan's biggest disappointment."[25]

Presidents cannot be assured of their appointees' support even on cases that affect the president directly. President Clinton's two appointees, Ruth Bader Ginsburg and Stephen Breyer, joined in the unanimous decision in *Clinton v. Jones* (1997) that allowed a lawsuit against him for sexual harassment to go forward, a lawsuit that ultimately resulted in his impeachment. Three of President Nixon's appointees joined in the unanimous decision in *United States v. Nixon* (1974) that required him to yield tape recordings of his conversations as president. (The fourth, William Rehnquist, did not participate, because he had worked in the Justice Department during the Nixon administration.) After learning of the Court's decision, Nixon reportedly "exploded, cursing the man he had named chief justice, reserving a few choice expletives for Blackmun and Powell, his other appointees."[26]

Political and Personal Reward. When George W. Bush nominated Harriet Miers to the Supreme Court in 2005, he had known Miers for a dozen years. In Texas she was general counsel for Bush's transition team after he was elected governor, and she was also his personal lawyer. She joined his presidential administration in 2001, serving in the White House as staff secretary, deputy chief of staff, and counsel to the president.

In choosing Miers, Bush took what had been a common approach for most of the Supreme Court's history. As of the late 1960s, about 60 percent of the nominees to the Court had known the nominating president personally.[27] With the exception of Dwight Eisenhower, all the presidents from Franklin Roosevelt through Lyndon Johnson selected primarily personal acquaintances. For Harry Truman, reward for political associates seemed to be the main criterion for selecting justices.

Some appointments to the Court were direct rewards for political help. Eisenhower selected Earl Warren to serve as chief justice in part because of Warren's crucial support of Eisenhower at the 1952 Republican convention. As governor of California and leader of that state's delegation, Warren had provided needed votes on a preliminary issue, and Eisenhower's success on that issue helped to secure his nomination.

But since 1968, Miers is the only close associate or political ally that a president has nominated to the Court. Indeed, few nominees have had any contact with the president before being considered for the Court. Perhaps the main reason for the decline in the selection of personal acquaintances is that such nominees are vulnerable to charges of "cronyism." That charge was made in 1968 when President Johnson nominated Justice Abe Fortas for elevation to chief justice and nominated Judge Homer Thornberry to succeed Fortas as associate justice; both Fortas and Thornberry were close to Johnson. The charge played a small role in building opposition to Fortas and Thornberry in the Senate. Ultimately, Fortas's confirmation was blocked by a filibuster, and Thornberry's nomination thus became moot. Miers's nomination was also attacked as a case of cronyism, and that charge was one factor in the pressures that led to her withdrawal.

However, one element of political reward has remained strong: about 90 percent of all nominees to the Court—and all those chosen since 1975—have been members of the president's party. One reason is that lawyers who share the president's policy views are more likely to come from the same party, but there is also a widespread feeling that such an attractive prize should go to one of the party faithful.

Building Political Support. If nominations can reward those who helped the president in the past, they can also be used to seek political benefits in the future. Most often, presidents select justices with certain characteristics in order to appeal to leaders and voters who share those characteristics.

The importance of geography and religion as criteria for selecting justices has declined. Geography was a significant consideration for most of the Court's history, as presidents sought to provide each region with representation on the Court. But after 1891 the justices no longer "rode circuit," helping to staff lower federal courts in designated regions, and there was a perceived decline in regional consciousness among voters. Religious affiliations were of some concern during much of the twentieth century, as presidents sought to maintain Catholic and Jewish representation on the Court. But religious affiliations have also become less relevant.

In contrast, representation by race, gender, and ethnicity has become quite important. President George H. W. Bush's nomination of Clarence

Thomas to succeed Thurgood Marshall reflected the pressure he felt to maintain black representation on the Court. According to one scholar, "gender was the primary and decisive factor" in President Reagan's nomination of Sandra Day O'Connor at a time when there was a widespread feeling that a woman should be appointed.[28] When O'Connor announced her retirement in 2005, President George W. Bush felt some pressure—most directly from Laura Bush—to replace her with a woman.[29] That pressure played a part in the selection of Harriet Miers. But before and after Miers, Bush nominated men to succeed her. (As noted earlier, John Roberts was originally nominated to O'Connor's position before William Rehnquist died.) If Ruth Bader Ginsburg leaves the Court before another woman is appointed, the goal of avoiding an all-male Court is likely to have considerable weight in the president's choice.

Demographic characteristics aside, presidents may seek nominees whose positions on judicial issues appeal to political activists and voters. This consideration does not lead in a single direction. Nominees who appear to be moderates might strengthen a president's support among undecided voters. But nominees who seem strongly liberal or conservative are more likely to garner approval from people who are active in the president's party, including financial contributors and leaders of allied interest groups. These activists typically give greater weight to Supreme Court nominations than do ordinary voters, for whom such nominations are generally not a key consideration.

Summary. Presidents make nominations to the Supreme Court on the basis of several criteria. The importance of these considerations changes over time and varies from one nomination to another.

The Court's importance has at least two effects on the criteria for selection of justices. First, it makes presidents and their representatives weigh all the criteria more carefully than they generally do in making nominations to lower courts. Second, it leads to an emphasis on competence and policy preferences rather than the "political" considerations of reward and support building. If Supreme Court justices are better jurists than lower-court judges, and if their policy preferences are more accurate reflections of their nominators' views, it is largely because presidents have a strong incentive to achieve those results.

Senate Confirmation

A president's nomination to the Court goes to the Senate for confirmation. The nomination is referred to the Judiciary Committee, which gathers extensive information on the nominee, holds hearings at which the nominee and other witnesses testify, and then votes its recommendation for Senate action. After this vote, the nomination is referred to the floor, where it is debated and a confirmation vote taken.

A simple majority is needed for confirmation, although a large minority of senators (under the current rules, 41) could block confirmation through a filibuster that uses extended debate to prevent a confirmation vote. That was the fate of Abe Fortas's nomination for chief justice in 1968. In 2006 some Democrats called for a filibuster against confirmation of Samuel Alito, but the Senate voted 75–25 to end debate and proceed to a vote on Alito.

The length of this process varies, in part with the degree of controversy over a nominee. By historical standards, the period from nomination to confirmation vote has been extraordinarily long in the past two decades, typically running between two and three months.[30]

The Senate's Role and Record. When the president nominates someone to any position, the presumption typically is in favor of confirming that nominee. That presumption applies to the Supreme Court. But the Senate gives Supreme Court nominations a collective scrutiny that district court nominations seldom receive, and confirmation is far from automatic.

Indeed, defeats of nominees are hardly rare. Through mid-2006 the Senate has refused to confirm twenty-six nominations to the Supreme Court, either through an adverse vote or nonaction. These twenty-six cases constitute about one-sixth of the nominations that the Senate considered. This proportion of defeats is the highest of any position to which the president makes appointments. For example, presidents have made far more nominations of cabinet members, but only nine have been defeated.

Presidents were more successful with Supreme Court nominations in the twentieth century and the early twenty-first century than in the nineteenth. Since 1900 only five of the sixty-two nominations considered by the Senate have failed: Herbert Hoover's nomination of John Parker in 1930, Johnson's elevation of Abe Fortas to chief justice in 1968 (withdrawn after Fortas's supporters failed to end the filibuster against him), Nixon's nominations of Clement Haynsworth in 1969 and G. Harrold Carswell in 1970 (both for the same vacancy), and Reagan's nomination of Robert Bork in 1987. Only four successful nominees were confirmed by less than a two-thirds margin in the Senate.

This record of success is a bit misleading, however, because the Senate has continued to scrutinize nominations carefully. This has been especially true since the late 1940s. Of the thirty nominees the Senate considered from 1949 through mid-2006, four were defeated, nine others received more than ten negative votes, and others faced serious opposition. And the withdrawals of Douglas Ginsburg in 1987 and Harriet Miers in 2005 came in part because of concerns about their prospects for confirmation. The Senate votes in this period are shown in Table 2-2. As suggested by these votes, nominees have faced especially close scrutiny since 1968.

TABLE 2-2
Senate Votes on Supreme Court Nominations since 1949

Nominee	Year	Vote
Tom Clark	1949	73–8
Sherman Minton	1949	48–16
Earl Warren	1954	NRV
John Harlan	1955	71–11
William Brennan	1957	NRV
Charles Whittaker	1957	NRV
Potter Stewart	1959	70–17
Byron White	1962	NRV
Arthur Goldberg	1962	NRV
Abe Fortas	1965	NRV
Thurgood Marshall	1967	69–11
Abe Fortas[a]	1968	Withdrawn
Homer Thornberry	(1968)	No action
Warren Burger	1969	74–3
Clement Haynsworth	1969	45–55
G. Harrold Carswell	1970	45–51
Harry Blackmun	1970	94–0
Lewis Powell	1971	89–1
William Rehnquist	1971	68–26
John Paul Stevens	1975	98–0
Sandra Day O'Connor	1981	99–0
William Rehnquist[b]	1986	65–33
Antonin Scalia	1986	98–0
Robert Bork	1987	42–58
Douglas Ginsburg	(1987)	No action
Anthony Kennedy	1988	97–0
David Souter	1990	90–9
Clarence Thomas	1991	52–48
Ruth Bader Ginsburg	1993	96–3
Stephen Breyer	1994	87–9
John Roberts	2005	78–22
Harriet Miers	(2005)	No action
Samuel Alito	2006	58–42

Source: Joan Biskupic and Elder Witt, *Guide to the U.S. Supreme Court,* 3d ed. (Washington, D.C.: Congressional Quarterly, 1997), 1099; table updated by the author.

Note: NRV = no recorded vote.

a. Elevation to chief justice; nomination withdrawn after the Senate vote of 45–43 failed to end a filibuster against the nomination (two-thirds majority was required).
b. Elevation to chief justice.

Nominees vary a great deal in the degree of difficulty they face in the Senate, from those who face no opposition to those who fail to win the needed majority. This variation reflects the characteristics of nominees and of the situations in which the Senate considers them.[31]

Nominees and Situations. As noted, the attributes of nominees that affect confirmation the most are their perceived ideological positions and qualifications. Nominees who are thought to be highly liberal or highly conservative have greater difficulty than those who seem to be moderate, simply because extremists are more distant ideologically from the average senator. Nominees who seem less qualified also may arouse opposition. A perceived weakness in legal skills or ethical standards might cause senators who are otherwise favorable to oppose a nominee. More important, senators who are ideologically distant from a nominee often use questions about a nominee's qualifications as an "objective" justification for opposing the nominee.

Whatever a nominee's personal characteristics may be, several aspects of the situation at the time of nomination affect the Senate's action. One is the president's political strength in the Senate. According to one count, presidents whose party holds a Senate majority have had 90 percent of their nominees confirmed, as against 61 percent for presidents who faced an opposition majority.[32] One reason for this difference is that senators of the majority party chair the Judiciary Committee and schedule votes on the floor. Another reason is that a Senate controlled by the opposition has more senators who are politically opposed to the president and who are ideologically distant from a nominee.

Other factors affect the president's strength. Presidents with high public approval have an advantage, because strong public support deters opposition to their nominees. And nominations made late in a president's term are more vulnerable because the president's popularity tends to decline, some presidents are "lame ducks" who will leave office shortly, and partisanship often increases. Nearly half of the nominees selected in the last year of a presidential term were defeated in the Senate.[33]

A second aspect of the situation is the mobilization of activity for and against the nominee. Substantial interest group activity against a nomination can overcome the assumption that a nominee will be confirmed and thus cause senators to consider voting against confirmation. It is also important whether some senators decide to play an active role in mustering votes against a nominee and whether the administration mounts a strong effort to secure confirmation.[34]

Finally, the perceived impact of a nomination helps to determine whether senators feel that efforts to defeat the nominee are worthwhile. Probably the central explanation for the intense scrutiny given to recent nominations is the increased prominence of the Supreme Court in the resolution of controversial policy issues. If a nominee has the potential to change the Court's policies substantially, senators will attach particular importance to that nomination.

Among nominees in the past quarter century, David Souter and Clarence Thomas illustrate the importance of personal characteristics. The two were chosen by President George H. W. Bush a year apart, with the Democrats holding majorities in the Senate. Each would replace a strongly liberal justice and therefore change the Court's ideological balance considerably. Souter won confirmation with only moderate difficulty, but Thomas's margin was only four votes. The difference can be explained primarily by two widespread perceptions: that Souter was a moderate conservative and Thomas a strong conservative, and that Souter was well qualified but Thomas's qualifications might be questioned.

Another pair of nominees illustrates the importance of the situation. President Reagan selected Antonin Scalia in 1986 and Robert Bork in 1987. Both were viewed as highly conservative, and both were former legal scholars who were thought to be well qualified for service on the Court. Scalia was confirmed unanimously, and Bork was defeated. One difference was that the Senate had a Republican majority in 1986 but a Democratic majority the next year. Another was that Scalia would replace another strong conservative, but Bork would replace a moderate conservative on a Court with a close ideological balance. Finally, in 1986, liberal senators and interest groups focused their efforts on defeating William Rehnquist's nomination for chief justice and largely ignored Scalia. In 1987, in contrast, liberals in and out of the Senate gave intense attention to Bork.

These generalizations can be illustrated further by looking at two sets of nominations. The first set includes the four defeats of nominees in the past half century. The second includes the four nominees considered by the Senate since 1993, all of whom won confirmation.

The Defeats. From 1930 to 1967, a long series of Supreme Court nominees won confirmation. Then, in the period from 1968 to 1970, three nominees lost in the Senate. The first was Abe Fortas, a sitting justice nominated to be chief justice by President Johnson in 1968. The Senate had a Democratic majority, but many of the Democrats were conservative, and Fortas's strong liberalism on the liberal Warren Court aroused conservative opposition. Moreover, some Republicans wanted to prevent Fortas's confirmation in order to reserve the vacancy for a new president—expected to be Republican—in 1969. These opponents pointed to two activities that raised doubts about Fortas's ethical fitness: his continued consultation with the president about policy matters while a member of the Court and an arrangement by which he gave nine lectures at American University, in Washington,

D.C., for a fee of $15,000 raised from businesses. The Judiciary Committee approved the nomination by a divided vote, but it ran into a filibuster on the Senate floor. A vote to end the filibuster fell fourteen votes short of the two-thirds majority then required; the opposition came almost entirely from Republicans and southern Democrats. President Johnson withdrew the nomination at Fortas's request.

In 1969 Fortas resigned from the Court. President Nixon selected Clement Haynsworth, chief judge of a federal court of appeals, to replace him. Haynsworth was opposed by labor groups and the National Association for the Advancement of Colored People (NAACP), both of which disliked his judicial record. Liberal senators, concerned about this record, sought revenge for Fortas's defeat as well. Haynsworth was also charged with unethical conduct: he had sat on two cases involving subsidiaries of companies in which he owned stock, and in another case he had bought the stock of a corporation in the interval between his court's decision in its favor and the announcement of the decision. These charges led to additional opposition from Senate moderates. Haynsworth ultimately was defeated by a 55–45 vote, with a large minority of Republicans voting against confirmation.

President Nixon then nominated another court of appeals judge, G. Harrold Carswell. After the fight over Haynsworth, most senators were inclined to support the next nominee. One senator predicted that any new Nixon nominee "will have no trouble getting confirmed unless he has committed murder—recently."[35] But Carswell drew opposition from civil rights groups for what they perceived as his hostility to their interests, and their cause gained strength from a series of revelations about the nominee that suggested an active opposition to racial equality. Carswell was also criticized for an alleged lack of judicial competence. After escorting Carswell to talk with senators, one of Nixon's staffers reported to the president that "they think Carswell's a boob, a dummy. And what counter is there to that? He is."[36] The nomination was defeated by a 51–45 vote; the lineup was similar to that in the vote on Haynsworth.

Robert Bork's 1987 defeat differed from the three that preceded it in that no serious charges were made about Bork's competence or his ethical standards. But liberals were concerned about his strong conservatism on civil liberties issues and his potential to shift the Court's ideological balance. Senator Ted Kennedy and liberal interest groups worked hard to secure votes against Bork. Concern about Bork's views was intensified by his testimony before the Senate Judiciary Committee, in which he discussed in detail his positions on issues such as the right to privacy.

This growing concern, combined with the unprecedented level of interest group activity against Bork, made his defeat possible. Also important was President Reagan's political weakness: not only did the Democrats control the Senate, but Reagan's popularity both inside and outside Congress had declined. Even so, a more effective campaign for Bork by the administration might have secured his confirmation. In any event, confirmation was denied by a 42–58 vote. All but eight senators voted along party lines; the overwhelming and unexpected opposition of southern Democrats made the difference in the outcome.

These four defeats, different though they were, have some things in common. In each instance, many senators were inclined to oppose the nominee on ideological grounds. All but Fortas faced a Senate controlled by the opposite party, and Fortas was confronted by a conservative majority. And each nominee was weakened by a "smoking gun" that could rally opposition: the ethical questions about Fortas and Haynsworth, the allegations of racism and incompetence against Carswell, and the charge that Bork was outside the mainstream in his views about judicial issues. The combination of these problems created a basis for enough opposition to prevent confirmation in each instance.

The Recent Confirmations. The Senate has voted on two nominees put forward by Bill Clinton and (as of mid-2006) two nominees of George W. Bush. All won confirmation, though their paths to victory differed considerably.

When President Clinton nominated Ruth Bader Ginsburg in 1993 and Stephen Breyer in 1994, there remained a good deal of resentment among Republicans over the defeat of Robert Bork. As the fates of Haynsworth and Carswell indicate, such resentment can lead to retaliation. However, the Democrats held a majority in the Senate.

Just as important, Clinton gave greater weight than most other presidents to the goal of avoiding confirmation battles.[37] As a result of this concern, his two nominees were both relatively moderate liberals in contrast with stronger liberals whom Clinton could have chosen. Ginsburg had helped lead the litigation campaign in the Supreme Court on behalf of equal rights for women, but her record as a court of appeals judge was fairly centrist. And neither nominee would change the Court's ideological balance very much.

Ginsburg won confirmation with no serious obstacles and only three negative votes. Breyer had a slightly more difficult time. Some Republican senators argued that he had shown a lack of prudence in investing in an insurance syndicate and that the investment had created conflicts of interest in some cases in which he had participated. Ultimately, nine Republicans cast votes against him, but his nomination was never in real jeopardy.

George W. Bush's nominations of John Roberts and Samuel Alito in 2005 came at a time when increased polarization between the parties and concern over the Supreme Court's future direction made it likely that Senate Democrats would oppose a nominee who seemed to be a strong conservative. Yet interest groups allied with the Republican Party were adamant that the president should choose a strong conservative, and the president's own inclination seemed to be the same. Bush had the advantage of a moderately large Republican majority in the Senate, increasing the chances of a favorable outcome for any nominee. Under the circumstances, he chose two nominees whose records suggested that they were quite conservative. (Harriet Miers, who withdrew before Senate consideration of her nomination, also appeared to be strongly conservative.)

Nothing like a smoking gun emerged for Roberts. Indeed, his testimony in the Judiciary Committee left most observers with a highly positive image of him. Ultimately, he was confirmed by a 78–22 vote, with all the negative votes coming from Democrats. The unusually large number of negative votes indicates that half the Democratic senators were willing to vote against a nominee solely on ideological grounds.

Like Roberts, Alito had demonstrated a high level of legal skills. But he was more vulnerable than Roberts because he had a more extensive record of strongly conservative positions. Some opponents thought they had a smoking gun in two 1985 statements in which Alito said that he was proud of his contributions to the Reagan administration's arguments that the "Constitution does not protect the right to an abortion" and implied that his goal was "the eventual overruling of Roe v. Wade."[38] Alito was also criticized for participating as a judge in one case involving a mutual fund firm that held a substantial investment of his, despite a pledge to recuse himself from such cases when he was nominated to the court of appeals.

Most senators seemed to regard that participation as inadvertent and inconsequential. In contrast, Alito's efforts to reassure senators that he was not an extreme conservative and that he would not necessarily vote to overturn *Roe* had limited success with Democrats. But it was clear early in the process that nearly all Republican senators would vote for him. As the minority party in the Senate the Democrats could block Alito only with a successful filibuster, and many Democratic senators saw a filibuster as inappropriate or at least bad political strategy. After the vote to end debate Alito won by a 58–42 margin, with one Republican and all but four Democrats voting against him.

Summary. The Senate's use of its power over confirmation of Supreme Court nominees has varied a good deal over time. Since 1968 the Senate has taken an assertive role in scrutinizing nominees. One reason for this change is the growth in efforts by interest groups to defeat nominees whose views run counter to group positions. Another spur has been the growing awareness that a single Court appointment can affect national policy in important ways. In both respects one issue—abortion—has been especially important.

Even so, the great majority of nominees since 1968 have been confirmed. There is still a presumption in favor of confirming nominees, and those who vote against a nominee have the burden of justifying their negative votes. Presidents have further improved the chances of confirmation by choosing nominees carefully, sometimes choosing moderates to avoid conflicts and usually looking closely for attributes or past actions of prospective nominees that might provide senators with a basis for opposition.

We are now in an era of strong party polarization in national politics. The confirmation of Samuel Alito illustrates the effects of that polarization. Except for Clarence Thomas, no successful nominee in more than a century has won by a closer margin than Alito. Yet there was never much uncertainty about the outcome. Because of the ideological gap and the bitterness between the parties, a nominee with a strong ideological position is certain to garner negative reactions from the opposition party. For the same reasons, senators from the president's party are strongly inclined to support a nominee.

Thus, if the nominee's objective qualifications are at least reasonably strong and the president's party controls the Senate, confirmation is nearly guaranteed. But if the opposing party has a Senate majority, a nominee like Alito runs a serious risk of defeat, and a president who seeks to avoid that risk will be inclined to choose a nominee with a record of ideological moderation. In the current period, even more than in some past periods, the kinds of people who reach the Supreme Court depend on Senate elections as well as presidential elections.

Who Is Selected

A children's book about Justice O'Connor concludes with a set of suggestions "if you want to be a Supreme Court justice."[39] Although other observers might add or delete specific suggestions, the list underlines an important reality: because of the workings of the selection process, certain kinds of people are more likely to reach the Supreme Court than others.

Career Paths

The kinds of people who become justices can be understood from the paths they take to the Court. These paths have changed over time. In this section I give particular attention to the period from the presidency of Franklin Roosevelt to the present. In that period thirty-five justices were selected. Some characteristics of these justices are listed in Table 2-3. The box on pages 52–53 summarizes the careers of the justices who sat on the Court in 2006.

TABLE 2-3
Selected Characteristics of Justices Appointed since 1937

Justice	Age[a]	State of residence[b]	Law school	Position at appointment[c]	Years as judge	Elective office[d]	Administrative position[e]
Black	51	Ala.	Alabama	Senator	1	Senate	—
Reed	53	Ky.	Columbia	Solicitor general	0	State leg.	Solicitor general
Frankfurter	56	Mass.	Harvard	Law professor	0	—	Subcabinet
Douglas	40	Wash.	Columbia	Chair, Sec. & Exchange Comm.	0	—	Sec. & Exchange Comm.
Murphy	49	Mich.	Michigan	Attorney general	7	Governor	Attorney general
Byrnes	62	S.C.	None	Senator	0	Senate	—
Jackson	49	N.Y.	Albany	Attorney general	0	—	Attorney general
Rutledge	48	Iowa	Colorado	U.S. Ct. App.	4	—	—
Burton	57	Ohio	Harvard	Senator	0	Senate	—
Vinson	56	Ky.	Centre (Ky.)	Sec. of Treasury	5	House of Rep.	Sec. of Treasury
Clark	49	Texas	Texas	Attorney general	0	—	Attorney general
Minton	58	Ind.	Indiana	U.S. Ct. App.	8	Senate	Asst. to president
Warren	62	Calif.	California	Governor	0	Governor	—
Harlan	55	N.Y.	New York	U.S. Ct. App.	1	—	Asst. U.S. attorney
Brennan	50	N.J.	Harvard	State Sup. Ct.	7	—	—
Whittaker	56	Mo.	Kansas City	U.S. Ct. App.	3	—	—
Stewart	43	Ohio	Yale	U.S. Ct. App.	4	City council	—
White	44	Colo.	Yale	Dep. atty general	0	—	Dep. atty general
Goldberg	54	Ill.	Northwestern	Sec. of labor	0	—	Sec. of labor
Fortas	55	D.C.	Yale	Private practice	0	—	Subcabinet

Justice	Age[a]	State[b]	Law school	Highest office[d]	Years		Highest appointive administrative position[e]
Marshall	59	N.Y.	Howard	Solicitor general	4	—	Solicitor general
Burger	61	Minn.	St. Paul	U.S. Ct. App.	13	—	Asst. atty general
Blackmun	61	Minn.	Harvard	U.S. Ct. App.	11	—	—
Powell	64	Va.	Wash. & Lee	Private practice	0	—	State Bd. of Education
Rehnquist	47	Ariz.	Stanford	Asst. atty general	0	—	Asst. atty general
Stevens	55	Ill.	Northwestern	U.S. Ct. App.	5	—	—
O'Connor	51	Ariz.	Stanford	State Ct. App.	6	State leg.	State asst. atty general
Scalia	50	D.C.	Harvard	U.S. Ct. App.	4	—	Asst. atty general
Kennedy	51	Calif.	Harvard	U.S. Ct. App.	11	—	—
Souter	51	N.H.	Harvard	U.S. Ct. App.	12	—	State atty general
Thomas	43	D.C.	Yale	U.S. Ct. App.	1	—	Equal Empl. Opp. Comm.
Ginsburg	60	D.C.	Harvard, Columbia	U.S. Ct. App.	13	—	—
Breyer	56	Mass.	Harvard	U.S. Ct. App.	13	—	—
Roberts	50	D.C.	Harvard	U.S. Ct. App.	2	—	Principal deputy solicitor general
Alito	55	N.J.	Yale	U.S. Ct. App.	15	—	U.S. attorney

Sources: Leon Friedman and Fred L. Israel, *The Justices of the United States Supreme Court, 1789–1969: Their Lives and Major Opinions* (New York: R. R. Bowker, 1969; 1978 supp.); Harold W. Chase and Craig R. Ducat, *Constitutional Interpretation,* 2d ed. (St. Paul: West, 1979), 1361–1376; Joan Biskupic and Elder Witt, *Guide to the U.S. Supreme Court,* 3d ed. (Washington, D.C.: Congressional Quarterly, 1997), 930–962; *Biographical Directory of Federal Judges,* compiled by the Federal Judicial Center, at http://www.fjc.gov.

Note: Dashes = none.

a. Age at time of appointment.

b. Primary state of residence before selection.

c. In this and following columns, positions are federal except where noted otherwise.

d. Highest office.

e. Highest appointive administrative position. Minor positions omitted.

Careers of the Supreme Court ...

John G. Roberts Jr. (born 1955)

Law degree, Harvard University, 1979
Law clerk, U.S. Court of Appeals, 1979–1980
Supreme Court law clerk, 1980–1981
U.S. Justice Department, 1981–1982
White House Counsel's Office, 1982–1986
U.S. Solicitor General's Office, 1989–1993
Private law practice, 1986–1989, 1993–2003
Judge, U.S. Court of Appeals, 2003–2005
Appointed chief justice, 2005

John Paul Stevens (born 1920)

Law degree, Northwestern University, 1947
Supreme Court law clerk, 1947–1948
Private law practice, 1949–1970
Judge, U.S. Court of Appeals, 1970–1975
Appointed to Supreme Court, 1975

Antonin Scalia (born 1936)

Law degree, Harvard University, 1960
Private law practice, 1960–1967
Law school teaching, 1967–1971
Legal positions in federal government, 1971–1977
Law school teaching, 1977–1982
Judge, U.S. Court of Appeals, 1982–1986
Appointed to Supreme Court, 1986

Anthony M. Kennedy (born 1936)

Law degree, Harvard University, 1961
Private law practice, 1961–1975
Judge, U.S. Court of Appeals, 1975–1988
Appointed to Supreme Court, 1988

David H. Souter (born 1939)

Law degree, Harvard University, 1966
Private law practice, 1966–1968
New Hampshire attorney general's office, 1968–1978
Attorney general, New Hampshire, 1976–1978
Judge, New Hampshire trial court, 1978–1983
Justice, New Hampshire Supreme Court, 1983–1990
Judge, U.S. Court of Appeals, 1990
Appointed to Supreme Court, 1990

...Justices (2006)

Clarence Thomas (born 1948)

Law degree, Yale University, 1974
Missouri attorney general's office, 1974–1977
Attorney for Monsanto Company, 1977–1979
Legislative assistant to a U.S. senator, 1979–1981
Assistant U.S. secretary of education, 1981–1982
Chair, U.S. Equal Employment Opportunity Commission,
  1982–1990
Judge, U.S. Court of Appeals, 1990–1991
Appointed to Supreme Court, 1991

Ruth Bader Ginsburg (born 1933)

Law degree, Columbia University, 1959
Federal district court law clerk, 1959–1961
Law school research position, 1961–1963
Law school teaching, 1963–1980
Judge, U.S. Court of Appeals, 1980–1993
Appointed to Supreme Court, 1993

Stephen G. Breyer (born 1938)

Law degree, Harvard University, 1964
Supreme Court law clerk, 1964–1965
U.S. Justice Department, 1965–1967
Law school teaching, 1967–1980
Staff, U.S. Senate Judiciary Committee,
  1974–1975, 1979–1980
Judge, U.S. Court of Appeals, 1980–1994
Appointed to Supreme Court, 1994

Samuel A. Alito Jr. (born 1950)

Law degree, Yale University, 1975
Law clerk, U.S. Court of Appeals, 1976–1977
Assistant U.S. Attorney, 1977–1981
U.S. Solicitor General's Office, 1981–1985
U.S. Justice Department, 1985–1987
U.S. Attorney, 1987–1990
Judge, U.S. Court of Appeals, 1990–2006
Appointed to Supreme Court, 2006

Source: Based chiefly on information in Kenneth Jost, *The Supreme Court Yearbook, 1998–1999* (Washington, D.C.: CQ Press, 2000), 321–339; for Roberts and Alito, based on information in *Biographical Directory of Federal Judges,* Federal Judicial Center (www.fjc.gov/).

Note: With the exception of Justice Breyer's Senate staff service, only the primary position held by a future justice during each career stage is listed.

The Legal Profession. The Constitution does not require that Supreme Court justices be attorneys. In practice, however, this restriction has been absolute. Nearly everyone involved in the selection process assumes that only a person with legal training can serve effectively on the Court. If a president nominated a nonlawyer to the Court, this assumption—and the large number of lawyers in the Senate—probably would prevent confirmation.

Thus, holding a law degree constitutes the first and least flexible requirement for recruitment to the Court. Most of the justices who served during the first century of the Court's history followed what was then the standard practice, apprenticing under a practicing attorney. In several instances, the practicing attorney was a leading member of the bar.[40] James Byrnes (chosen in 1941) was the last justice to study law through apprenticeship; all his successors have taken what is now the conventional route of law school training. A high proportion of justices have graduated from prestigious schools. Of the nine justices sitting in 2006, seven received their law degrees from Harvard or Yale.

High Positions. If legal education is a necessary first step in the paths to the Court, almost equally important as a last step is attaining a high position in government or the legal profession. Obscure private practitioners or state trial judges might be superbly qualified for the Court, but their qualifications would be questioned because of their lowly positions. A high position in government or the legal profession also makes a person more visible to the president and to others involved in the nomination process.

At the time they were selected, the thirty-five justices appointed since 1937 held positions of four types. They were judges, executive branch officials, elected officials, or well-respected leaders in the legal profession.

Eighteen of the justices appointed in this period were appellate judges at the time of selection. Sixteen of them sat on the federal courts of appeals; the other two (Brennan and O'Connor) served on state courts. Six of the sixteen federal judges came from the District of Columbia circuit, which is especially visible to the president and other federal officials.

Ten justices served in the federal executive branch, seven in the Justice Department. The other three justices served as chair of the Securities and Exchange Commission (Douglas), secretary of the Treasury (Vinson), and secretary of labor (Goldberg).

Of the other seven justices appointed since 1937, four held high elective office; three were senators (Black, Byrnes, and Burton) and the fourth was the governor of California (Warren). The other three held positions outside government. Each had attained extraordinary success and respect—as a legal scholar (Frankfurter), a Washington lawyer (Fortas), and a leader of the legal profession (Powell). Frankfurter and Fortas had also been informal presidential advisers.

The Steps Between. The people who have become Supreme Court justices took a variety of routes from their legal education to the high positions that made them credible candidates for the Court. Frankfurter, Fortas, and Powell illustrate one simple route: entry into legal practice or academia, followed by a gradual rise to high standing in the legal profession. Some justices took a similar route through public office. Earl Warren held a series of appointive and elective offices, leading to his California governorship. Clarence Thomas and Samuel Alito each served in several nonelected government positions and then as a judge on a federal court of appeals.

Since 1975 the most common route to the Court has been through private practice or law teaching, often combined with some time in government, before appointment to a federal court of appeals. Antonin Scalia, Ruth Bader Ginsburg, and Stephen Breyer were law professors. John Paul Stevens, Anthony Kennedy, and John Roberts went directly from private practice to a court of appeals. During their careers, all six had held government positions or participated informally in the governmental process.

Justice O'Connor took a unique path to the Court. She spent time in private practice and government legal positions, with some career interruptions for family reasons, before becoming an Arizona state senator and majority leader of the senate. O'Connor left the legislature for a trial judgeship. Her promotion to the state court of appeals through a gubernatorial appointment put her in a position to be considered for the Supreme Court.

Implications of the Career Paths

The paths to the Supreme Court help to explain some significant characteristics of the justices. They also underline the role of chance in determining who becomes a justice.

Age. Since 1937, most Supreme Court justices have been in their fifties at the time of their appointments and the rest in their forties or early sixties. William Douglas was the youngest appointee, at age forty; at the other end of the spectrum, Lewis Powell was sixty-four.

The ages of Court appointees reflect a balance between two considerations. On the one hand, lawyers need time to develop the record of achievement that makes them credible candidates for the Court. The steps that lead to high positions usually take considerable time to complete.

On the other hand, presidents would like their appointees to serve for long periods of time in order to achieve the maximum impact on the Court. Thus, a candidate such as Clarence Thomas, forty-three when George H.W. Bush appointed him, can be especially attractive. Of course, people of the same age can vary considerably in their prospects for future good health. Perhaps it is for this reason that George W. Bush asked at least one prospective nominee about how much he exercised. That candidate, Judge J. Harvie

Wilkinson, reported that the president admonished him for limiting himself to running despite his doctor's advice to engage in cross-training. "He thought I was well on my way to busting my knees," Judge Wilkinson reported. "He warned me of impending doom."[41]

Class, Race, and Sex. The Supreme Court's membership has been quite unrepresentative of the general population in terms of social class; most justices grew up in families that were relatively well off. One study found that one-third of the justices were from the upper class and one-quarter were from the upper middle class. Only one-quarter were from the lower middle class or below.[42]

Since the 1930s an unusually high percentage of appointees to the Court, especially Democrats, have had lower-status backgrounds. Still, the recent justices as a group grew up in better than average circumstances. Among the justices on the 2006 Court the family of John Paul Stevens and perhaps that of John Roberts can be characterized as upper class, Clarence Thomas's family was impoverished, and the other justices' families were divided about evenly between the middle class and upper middle class.

The predominance of higher-status backgrounds can be explained by the career paths that most justices take. First and most important, a justice must obtain a legal education. To do so is easiest for individuals of high status, because of the cost of law school and the college education that necessarily precedes it. Second, individuals of high status have a variety of advantages in their careers. Those who can afford to attend elite law schools, for instance, have the easiest time obtaining positions in successful law firms.

The partial deviation from this pattern since the 1930s reflects the increased availability of legal education. In addition, the larger size of the legal profession, the judiciary, and the federal government has made high positions in these sectors more accessible to individuals with lower-status backgrounds who previously might have been excluded. If these explanations have some validity, the proportion of justices with lower-status backgrounds will remain relatively large and may increase in the future.

Until 1967 all the justices were white men. This pattern is not difficult to understand. Because of various restrictions, women and members of racial minority groups had extreme difficulty pursuing an education in the law. As a result, the number of potential justices from these groups who passed the first barrier to selection was quite small. Moreover, prejudice against women and members of racial minorities limited their ability to advance in the legal profession and in politics. As a result, very few individuals who were not white men could achieve the high positions that people generally must obtain to be considered for nomination to the Court.

Since 1967 two women (O'Connor and Ginsburg) and two African Americans (Marshall and Thomas) have won appointments to the Court. These appointments reflect changes in society that made it somewhat less difficult for people other than white men to achieve high positions. They also reflect the growing willingness of presidents to consider women and members of racial minority groups as prospective nominees. Still, because of the various advantages they enjoy, white men are likely to enjoy disproportionate representation on the Court for some time.

If the Court has been composed primarily of white men with higher-status backgrounds, what has been the effect on its policies? One possible effect concerns the legal claims of racial minority groups and of women. It seems likely that those claims would have been taken seriously at an earlier time if members of these groups had sat on the Court, because these justices would have influenced their colleagues' perceptions of discrimination. As Justice O'Connor pointed out, Thurgood Marshall had that kind of influence once he joined the Court.[43]

Political and social attitudes differ somewhat between people of higher and lower socioeconomic status, so justices' class origins might affect the Court's decisions. But the justices typically are people who have achieved high status themselves even if their origins were humble. The sympathies of people who have "climbed" upward from a low socioeconomic level may differ little from those of people who started out with social and economic advantages. Notably, the justices with humble backgrounds have included such solid conservatives as Warren Burger and Clarence Thomas as well as such liberals as Earl Warren and Thurgood Marshall. Some commentators argue that the Court's decisions generally reflect the values and interests of people who are well off. If so, this may result from the status that the justices achieve in their own lives more than from their origins.

Partisan Political Activity. One characteristic shared by most current justices, like their predecessors, is a degree of involvement in partisan politics. Antonin Scalia, John Roberts, and Samuel Alito each held multiple positions in Republican administrations. Anthony Kennedy drafted a state ballot proposition for California governor Ronald Reagan. Clarence Thomas worked with John Danforth when Danforth was the Missouri attorney general and a U.S. senator, and Thomas later served in the Reagan and George H.W. Bush administrations. Stephen Breyer interrupted his law school teaching twice to work with Democrats on the Senate Judiciary Committee.

This pattern reflects the ways that justices are chosen. Even if nominations to the Court are not used as political rewards, presidents look more favorably on those who have contributed to their party's success. Partisan activity also brings people to the attention of presidents, their staff members, and others who influence nomination decisions. Perhaps more important, it enables people to win the high offices and appointive positions that make them credible candidates for the Court. For instance, lawyers who avoid any involvement in politics are unlikely to win federal judgeships.

The Role of Chance. No one becomes a Supreme Court justice through an inevitable process. Rather, advancement from membership in the bar to a seat on the Court results from luck as much as anything else. This luck comes in two stages. First, good fortune is often necessary to achieve the high positions in government or law that make individuals possible candidates for the Court; it is not necessarily the "fittest" who become cabinet members or federal appellate judges. Second, even after they achieve such positions, whether candidates are seriously considered for the Court and actually win an appointment depends largely on several circumstances.

For one thing, a potential justice gains enormously by belonging to a particular political party at the appropriate time. Every appointment to the Court between 1969 and 1992 was made by a Republican president. As a result, a whole generation of potential justices who were liberal Democrats had no chance to win appointments. Further, someone whose friend or associate achieves a powerful position becomes a far stronger candidate for a seat on the Court. David Souter was fortunate that someone who described Souter as "my closest friend" (Warren Rudman) became a U.S. senator and that a person who knew and admired him (John Sununu) became the president's chief of staff.[44]

More generally, everyone appointed to the Court has benefited from a favorable series of circumstances. Eisenhower's attorney general became aware of William Brennan because Brennan gave a conference address in place of a colleague on the New Jersey Supreme Court who was ill. John Paul Stevens has reported that his pro bono volunteer services for a client led to favorable publicity that later helped him win a judicial appointment.[45]

This does not mean that the effects of presidential appointments to the Court are random. No matter which individuals they choose, Democratic presidents generally nominate people with liberal views and Republicans tend to select conservatives. But it does mean that specific individuals achieve membership on the Court in large part through good fortune. "You have to be lucky," said Sandra Day O'Connor about her appointment,[46] a statement that reflects realism as well as modesty.

Changes in Paths to the Court

The most noteworthy characteristic of the justices' backgrounds in the period since 1937 is the extent to which they have changed. As noted earlier, the numerical dominance of people from privileged backgrounds has declined somewhat. But more striking is the change in justices' pre-Court careers. Put simply, those careers have come to involve less politics

California governor Earl Warren (left) and University of Pennsylvania president Harold Stassen (right) in 1952 with Republican presidential candidate Dwight Eisenhower, who appointed Warren chief justice the next year. In that era, unlike the current era, many justices had held elective office.

and more law. To a degree, this change was gradual, but a fairly sharp dividing line can be drawn between the set of justices chosen before 1969 and those selected since then.

The twenty-one justices appointed to the Court between 1937 and 1968 were reasonably typical of those selected in earlier periods. Ten, about half, had served on a lower court. Nine had held elective office, and eight others had held high positions in a presidential administration.

The fourteen justices who have arrived at the Court since then are a different kind of group. All but two have come directly from lower courts. Only one, Sandra Day O'Connor, ever held elective office. Several spent little or no time in government before winning judgeships. Among these justices, the median proportion of their careers spent in what might be called the legal system—private practice, law-school teaching, and the judiciary—was 88 percent. For the justices from the earlier period, the median was 67 percent.[47] The extent of this change was underlined when John Roberts became chief justice in 2005: every member of the Court had lower-court experience. A few months later, when Samuel Alito joined the Court, every justice had come to the Court from a federal court of appeals.

One reason for this change, perhaps the primary one, is that a prior judicial record helps presidents and their advisers to predict the positions that prospective nominees might take as justices. In an era in which most presidents care a great deal about the Court's direction, any help in making these predictions is valued. There may also be a growing feeling that service on a lower court helps to prepare a judge for the Supreme Court. Harriet Miers, the first nominee since 1971 without judicial experience, was criticized for the absence of that service.

Whether or not lower-court experience is needed as preparation for the Supreme Court, the change in paths to the Court since 1969 may affect the justices' perspectives and their thinking about legal issues. Some commentators argue that justices do not understand government and politics as well as their counterparts in earlier periods and that this lack of understanding reduces their ability to recognize the likely consequences of some decisions.[48] There may be some truth to this argument, and the shift from politics to law in the backgrounds of justices may have other effects on the Court's decisions.[49] But today, as in the past, people who had no contact with the political world would have little chance to reach the Court. None of the current justices fits that description.

Leaving the Court

In the Supreme Court's first century, Congress sometimes increased the Court's size to allow new appointments of justices. Such legislation has become very unlikely, almost unthinkable. Today new members come to the Court only when a sitting justice leaves.

Justices can leave the Court in three ways: through death, voluntary decisions, or external pressure.[50] In contrast with the nineteenth century, justices today seldom stay on the Court until they die. Before William Rehnquist's death in 2005, the last justice to die in office had been Robert Jackson in 1954. Thus, departures from the Court result primarily from voluntary choices and external pressure. Table 2-4 summarizes the reasons for departures since 1965.

Voluntary Departures

After its somewhat rocky start, the Supreme Court became a prestigious body with considerable influence on American life. As a result, justices typically are reluctant to leave the Court.

This reluctance is reflected in the infrequency with which justices leave to take other positions or opportunities. In the past century, only a hand-

TABLE 2-4
Reasons for Leaving the Court since 1965

Year	Justice	Age	Primary reasons for leaving	Length of time from leaving until death
1965	Goldberg	56	Appointment as ambassador to United Nations	24 years
1967	Clark	67	Son's appointment as attorney general	10 years
1969	Fortas	58	Pressures based on possible ethical violations	13 years
1969[a]	Warren	78[b]	Age	5 years
1971	Black	85	Age and ill health	1 month
1971	Harlan	72	Age and ill health	3 months
1975	Douglas	77	Age and ill health	4 years
1981	Stewart	66	Age	4 years
1986	Burger	78	Service on Commission on the Bicentennial of the Constitution, possibly age	9 years
1987	Powell	79	Age and health concerns	11 years
1990	Brennan	84	Age and ill health	7 years
1991	Marshall	83[b]	Age and ill health	2 years
1993	White	76[b]	Desire to allow another person to serve, possibly age	9 years
1994	Blackmun	85	Age	5 years
2005	Rehnquist	80	Death	Same time
2006[a]	O'Connor	75	Spouse's ill health, possibly age	NA

Sources: Joan Biskupic and Elder Witt, *Guide to the U.S. Supreme Court,* 3d ed. (Washington, D.C.: Congressional Quarterly, 1997), 931–954; other biographical sources, newspaper stories.

Note: NA = not applicable.

a. Warren originally announced the intent to leave the Court in 1968, O'Connor in 2005.
b. When they announced their intent to leave the Court, Warren was 77, Marshall 82, White 75.

ful of justices have done so. The most recent was Arthur Goldberg, who resigned in 1965 to become U.S. ambassador to the United Nations.

The primary choice that justices face, then, is when to retire from the Court. Financial considerations once played an important part in those choices: several justices stayed on the Court, sometimes with serious infirmities, to keep receiving their salaries. Congress established a judicial pension in 1869, and it is now quite generous. As long as a justice's age and years of service add up to eighty or more, a justice who is at least sixty-five years old and who has served as a federal judge for at least ten years can retire and continue to receive the salary earned at the time of retirement. Justices can also receive any salary increases granted sitting justices if they are disabled or if they perform a certain amount of service for the federal courts—generally equal to one-quarter of full-time work.

Free from financial concerns, then, older justices weigh the satisfactions of remaining on the Court against the somewhat different satisfactions of retirement and against concern about their capacity to handle their work. The satisfactions are so great that most justices stay well past the usual retirement age. But age and health problems eventually tip the balance in favor of retirement. When justices do retire, they usually cite one or both of those factors. When Harry Blackmun retired from the Court in 1994, he explained that "eighty-five is pretty old. I don't want to reach a point where my senility level reaches unacceptable proportions."[51]

Some justices do stay on the Court past the time at which they can function effectively as justices. One clear case is William Douglas, whose health problems had become so great by 1975 that his colleagues took the extraordinary step of agreeing to set aside for later rehearing any case in which Douglas was part of a 5–4 majority. (Such action was never taken because Douglas retired a few weeks later, before any decisions met this criterion.)[52] Other cases are more ambiguous. One scholar has argued that since World War II, seven justices remained on the Court "years or months" too long after their mental capacities should have led to their departures.[53] William Rehnquist's thyroid cancer weakened him considerably, and he could not fully participate in the Court's work during the last term before his death. His illness brought renewed attention to long-standing concerns about the effects of aging and ill health on justices and the Court.

There were no new justices between 1994 and 2005. For some observers this lack of turnover raised the question of whether justices were staying on the Court too long, whether or not they were capable of doing their work. Some legal scholars even suggested a form of term limits for the justices.[54] But justices in the current era do not stand out from their predecessors for the length of their tenure on the Court or for their ages, and the lack of turnover in one recent period may be an anomaly.[55] In any event, the adoption of such a proposal seems quite unlikely.

The justices are well aware that their departures may change the ideological balance on the Court, and that awareness sometimes affects the timing of retirements. Yet the satisfactions of serving on the Court may outweigh this consideration. Almost surely, Justice O'Connor and Chief Justice Rehnquist preferred that a Republican president choose their successors, but O'Connor waited until George W. Bush's second term to retire, and less than two months before his death Rehnquist said, "I am not about to announce my retirement."[56] However, when O'Connor did retire, one of her sons speculated that uncertainty about "who will be our next president" was one consideration.[57]

One current justice has given very early notice of his retirement. In 1992, a year after he joined the Court, Clarence Thomas told two of his clerks that he would remain on the Court until 2034. He explained, "The liberals made my life miserable for 43 years, and I'm going to make their lives miserable for 43 years."[58]

External Pressure

Although justices make their own decisions whether to resign or retire, Congress and the president can try to influence those decisions. For example, the legislation creating attractive pension rights has had considerable effect. The other branches can also try to persuade specific justices to leave the Court. Presidents have good reason to do so—to create vacancies they can fill. John Kennedy reportedly persuaded Felix Frankfurter to retire after ill health had decreased his effectiveness, but Thurgood Marshall bitterly resisted efforts by the Carter administration to persuade him to retire.[59]

Presidents can also try to lure justices away from the Court by offering them other positions. Lyndon Johnson offered Arthur Goldberg the position of ambassador to the United Nations and then exerted intense personal pressure on him to accept that position. Byron White, however, rejected the idea of becoming FBI director when the Reagan administration sounded him out about it.

As the examples of Marshall and White indicate, justices can resist pressure to give up their positions on the Court, but impeachment is beyond their control. Under the Constitution, justices, like other federal officials, can be removed through impeachment proceedings for "treason, bribery, or other high crimes and misdemeanors."[60] President Thomas Jefferson actually sought to gain control of the largely Federalist (and anti-Jefferson) judiciary through the use of impeachment, and Congress did impeach and convict a federal district judge in 1803. Justice Samuel Chase made himself vulnerable to impeachment by participating in President John Adams's campaign for reelection in 1800 and by making some injudicious and partisan remarks to a Maryland grand jury in 1803. Chase was impeached, an action justified chiefly by his handling of political trials, but the Senate acquitted him in 1805. His acquittal effectively ended Jefferson's plans to seek the impeachment of other justices.

No justice has been impeached since then, but the possible impeachment of two justices has been the subject of serious discussion. Several efforts were made to remove William Douglas (most seriously in 1969 and 1970), motivated by opposition to his strong liberalism. The reasons stated publicly by opponents were his financial connections with a foundation and his outside writings.[61] A special House committee failed to approve a resolution to impeach Douglas, however, and the resolution died in 1970.

Had Abe Fortas not resigned from the Court in 1969, he actually might have been removed through impeachment proceedings.[62] Fortas had been criticized for his financial dealings at the time he was nominated unsuccessfully to be chief justice in 1968. A year later, it was disclosed that he had a lifetime contract as a consultant to the Wolfson Foundation and had received money from that foundation at a time when the person who directed it was being prosecuted by the federal government. Under considerable pressure, Fortas resigned. The resignation came too quickly to determine how successful an impeachment effort would have been, but it almost certainly would have been serious.

The campaigns against Douglas and Fortas came primarily from the Nixon administration, which sought to replace the two liberals with more conservative justices. John Dean, a lawyer on Nixon's staff, later reported that Fortas's resignation led to "a small celebration in the attorney general's office" that "was capped with a call from the president, congratulating" Justice Department officials "on a job well done."[63] In contrast, according to Dean, the unsuccessful campaign against Douglas "created an intractable resolve by Douglas never to resign while Nixon was president."[64]

The Fortas episode seems unlikely to be repeated, in part because it reminded justices of the need to avoid questionable financial conduct. The removal of three federal judges through impeachment proceedings between 1987 and 1989 makes it clear that impeachment is a real option. But it is used only in cases with strong evidence of serious misdeeds, often involving allegations of corrupt behavior.

Thus, the timing of a justice's leaving the Court reflects primarily the justice's own inclinations, health, and longevity. Those who want to affect the Court's membership may have their say when a vacancy occurs, but they have little control over the creation of vacancies.

Conclusion

The recruitment of Supreme Court justices is a complex process. People do not "rise" to the Court in an orderly fashion. Rather, whether they become credible candidates for the Court and whether they actually win appointments depend on a wide range of circumstances. Indeed, something close to pure luck plays a powerful role in determining who becomes a justice.

The recruitment process has evolved over the Court's history. To take one example, the balance of power between president and Senate in selecting justices has shifted back and forth. Further, justices today are drawn from a larger portion of American society than they were during most of the

Court's history, and their backgrounds are more "legal" and less "political" than they once were.

The Court's power and prestige have fundamental effects on its membership. For one thing, presidents take nominations to the Court very seriously, and they have a wide range of prospective nominees to choose from. For another, justices are usually reluctant to give up their positions.

Also consequential is the perception of a strong link between the Court's membership and its decisions. Because of this perception, presidents accord heavy weight to the policy preferences of candidates when they choose a nominee. For the same reason, the Senate gives Court nominees greater scrutiny than it does nominees to any other positions. Interest groups regularly seek to influence president and Senate, and they sometimes engage in massive campaigns over nominees.

This perception is well founded. In later chapters I will discuss how the identities of the justices shape the Court's positions on legal and policy issues.

NOTES

1. The four who were nominated and confirmed twice include three individuals elevated from associate justice to chief justice (Edward White, Harlan Stone, and William Rehnquist) and one (Charles Evans Hughes) who resigned from the Court and was later appointed chief justice. Douglas Ginsburg is counted as a nominee even though he withdrew from consideration in 1987, before he was officially nominated. (Harriet Miers was nominated in 2005 but withdrew before the Senate could consider her nomination.)
2. Joan Biskupic, *Sandra Day O'Connor* (New York: HarperCollins, 2005), 72–73. Burger's role in the Nixon nominations is discussed in John W. Dean, *The Rehnquist Choice* (New York: Free Press, 2001), 19, 52, 179–185.
3. David D. Kirkpatrick, "A Year of Work to Sell Roberts to Conservatives," *New York Times,* July 22, 2005, A14.
4. This discussion is based in part on John Anthony Maltese, *The Selling of Supreme Court Nominees* (Baltimore: Johns Hopkins University Press, 1995); and Gregory A. Caldeira and John R. Wright, "Lobbying for Justice: The Rise of Organized Conflict in the Politics of Federal Judgeships," in *Contemplating Courts,* ed. Lee Epstein (Washington, D.C.: CQ Press, 1995), 44–71.
5. Michael Pertschuk and Wendy Schaetzel, *The People Rising: The Campaign against the Bork Nomination* (New York: Thunder's Mouth Press, 1989); Patrick B. McGuigan and Dawn M. Weyrich, *Ninth Justice: The Fight for Bork* (Washington, D.C.: Free Congress Research and Education Foundation, 1990); Mark Gitenstein, *Matters of Principle: An Insider's Account of America's Rejection of Robert Bork's Nomination to the Supreme Court* (New York: Simon and Schuster, 1992).
6. Richard Hodder-Williams, "The Strange Story of Judge Robert Bork and a Vacancy on the United States Supreme Court," *Political Studies* 36 (December 1988): 628.

7. Gregory A. Caldeira and John R. Wright, "Lobbying for Justice: Organized Interests and the Bork Nomination in the United States Senate" (paper presented at the annual meeting of the American Political Science Association, Chicago, September 1992).
8. Glen Justice and Aron Pilhofer, "Unwavering Bush Ally Acts Quickly on Court Choices and Legislation," *New York Times*, November 14, 2005, A1, A16.
9. Andrew Peyton Thomas, *Clarence Thomas: A Biography* (San Francisco: Encounter Books, 2001), 179.
10. Laura Parker, "College Yearbook Described Goal of Becoming Justice," *USA Today*, November 1, 2005, 2A.
11. Henry J. Abraham, *Justices, Presidents, and Senators: A History of the U.S. Supreme Court Appointments from Washington to Clinton*, rev. ed. (Lanham, Md.: Rowman and Littlefield, 1999), 140.
12. Dean, *The Rehnquist Choice*, 14.
13. Stephen Gillers, David J. Luban, and Stephen Lubet, "Improper Advances," *Slate Magazine*, at www.slate.com, August 17, 2005. The case was *Hamdan v. Rumsfeld* (D.C. Cir. 2005).
14. James Carney and Matthew Cooper, "Justice Scalia: The Charm Offensive," *Time Magazine*, January 31, 2005, 18.
15. Dahlia Lithwick, "More Fun than the Emmys," *Slate Magazine*, at www.slate.com, September 20, 2005.
16. Dahlia Lithwick, "Revenge of the Nerd," *Slate Magazine*, at www.slate.com, January 10, 2006.
17. Bob Dart, "Tears Trump Substance during Alito Hearings," *Atlanta Journal-Constitution*, January 13, 2006, 8A.
18. This discussion draws from David Alistair Yalof, *Pursuit of Justices: Presidential Politics and the Selection of Supreme Court Justices* (Chicago: University of Chicago Press, 1999), esp. 6–7.
19. Joan Biskupic and Toni Locy, "Miers Was Vetted by Few in Administration," *USA Today*, October 19, 2005, 4A.
20. David Savage, *Turning Right: The Making of the Rehnquist Supreme Court* (New York: Wiley, 1992), 180–181.
21. Dean, *The Rehnquist Choice*, 96.
22. Steve Holland, "Bush Defends Pick for Supreme Court," *Toronto Star*, October 5, 2005, A11.
23. Fred Barnes, "Souter-Phobia," *Weekly Standard*, August 1, 2005, 11–12.
24. Alyssa Sepinwall, "The Making of a Presidential Myth" (letter), *Wall Street Journal*, September 4, 1990, A11; Tony Mauro, "Leak of Souter Keeps McGuigan in Plan," *Legal Times*, September 10, 1990, 11.
25. "Justice Anthony Kennedy: Surely Reagan's Biggest Disappointment," *Human Events*, May 31–June 7, 1996, 3.
26. J. Anthony Lukas, *Nightmare: The Underside of the Nixon Years* (New York: Viking Press, 1976), 569.
27. Robert Scigliano, *The Supreme Court and the Presidency* (New York: Free Press, 1971), 95.
28. Barbara A. Perry, *A "Representative" Supreme Court? The Impact of Race, Religion, and Gender on Appointments* (New York: Greenwood Press, 1991), 122.
29. Edwin Chen, "First Lady, Democratic Leader Helped Miers," *Los Angeles Times*, October 4, 2005, A16.

30. Denis Steven Rutkus and Maureen Bearden, "Supreme Court Nominations, 1789–2005: Actions by the Senate, the Judiciary Committee, and the President," report of the Congressional Research Service, January 5, 2006.
31. See Lee Epstein, René Lindstädt, Jeffrey A. Segal, and Chad Westerland, "The Changing Dynamics of Senate Voting on Supreme Court Nominees," *Journal of Politics* 68 (May 2006): 296–307.
32. These percentages are based on figures in Jeffrey Segal, "Senate Confirmation of Supreme Court Justices: Partisan and Institutional Politics," *Journal of Politics* 49 (November 1987): 1008; percentages updated by the author. Percentages differ among sources, chiefly because of differences in assignment of partisan affiliation to some presidents.
33. Based on ibid., updated by the author. Nominations made during a president's fourth year but after the president's reelection are not included.
34. See Maltese, *Selling of Supreme Court Nominees.*
35. "Here Comes the Judge," *Newsweek*, February 2, 1970, 19. Quoted in John Massaro, *Supremely Political: The Role of Ideology and Presidential Management in Unsuccessful Supreme Court Nominations* (Albany: State University of New York Press, 1990), 105.
36. Richard Reeves, *President Nixon: Alone in the White House* (New York: Simon and Schuster, 2001), 161.
37. See George Stephanopoulos, *All Too Human: A Political Education* (Boston: Little, Brown, 1999), 168.
38. Ronald Brownstein, "Alito's Remarks on Roe May Not Be Fighting Words," *Los Angeles Times*, December 12, 2005, A11.
39. Lisa Tucker McElroy, *Meet My Grandmother: She's a Supreme Court Justice* (Brookfield, Conn.: Millbrook Press, 1999), 32.
40. This discussion is based in part on John R. Schmidhauser, *Judges and Justices: The Federal Appellate Judiciary* (Boston: Little, Brown, 1979), 41–100.
41. Elisabeth Bumiller, "An Interview by, Not with, the President," *New York Times*, July 21, 2005, A1.
42. Lee Epstein, Jeffrey A. Segal, Harold J. Spaeth, and Thomas G. Walker, *The Supreme Court Compendium*, 3d ed. (Washington, D.C.: CQ Press, 2003), 255–266. This source was also used to classify the justices sitting in 2006 in the next paragraph, except for John Roberts and Samuel Alito.
43. Sandra Day O'Connor, *The Majesty of the Law: Reflections of a Supreme Court Justice* (New York: Random House, 2003), 132–138.
44. See Warren B. Rudman, *Combat: Twelve Years in the U.S. Senate* (New York: Random House, 1996), 152–194; quotation, 153.
45. Richard C. Reuben, "Justice Stevens: I Benefited from Pro Bono Work," *Los Angeles Daily Journal*, August 11, 1992, 11. See Kenneth A. Manaster, *Illinois Justice: The Scandal of 1969 and the Rise of John Paul Stevens* (Chicago: University of Chicago Press, 2001).
46. Laurence Bodine, "Sandra Day O'Connor," *American Bar Association Journal* 69 (October 1983): 1394.
47. These proportions are based on biographies in the *Biographical Directory of Federal Judges*, compiled by the Federal Judicial Center, at www.fjc.gov.
48. Stuart Taylor Jr., "Remote Control," *Atlantic Monthly*, September 2005, 37–39.
49. See David J. Garrow, "The Once and Future Supreme Court," *American History*, February 2005, 28–36.

50. This discussion of resignation and retirement draws on David N. Atkinson, *Leaving the Bench: Supreme Court Justices at the End* (Lawrence: University Press of Kansas, 1999).

51. Douglas Jehl, "Mitchell Viewed as Top Candidate for High Court," *New York Times,* April 7, 1994, A1.

52. Dennis J. Hutchinson, *The Man Who Once Was Whizzer White: A Portrait of Justice Byron R. White* (New York: Free Press, 1998), 434–436, 463–465. See Bruce Allen Murphy, *Wild Bill: The Legend and Life of William O. Douglas* (New York: Random House, 2003), 481–495.

53. David J. Garrow, "Mental Decrepitude on the U.S. Supreme Court: The Historical Case for a 28th Amendment," *University of Chicago Law Review* 67 (fall 2000): 1085. See also Susan Okie, "Illness and Secrecy on the Supreme Court," *New England Journal of Medicine* 351 (December 23, 2004): 2675–2678.

54. Tony Mauro, "Law Professors Propose Term Limits for Justices," *National Law Journal,* January 3, 2005, 7.

55. Kevin T. McGuire, "An Assessment of Tenure on the U.S. Supreme Court," *Judicature* 89 (July–August 2005): 8–15.

56. Linda Greenhouse, "Despite Rumors, Rehnquist Has No Plans to Retire Now," *New York Times,* July 15, 2005, A10.

57. Anne E. Kornblut, "Personal and Political Concerns in a Closely Held Decision," *New York Times,* July 2, 2005, A12.

58. Neil A. Lewis, "2 Years After His Bruising Hearing, Justice Thomas Still Shows the Hurt," *New York Times,* November 27, 1993, 6.

59. Juan Williams, "Marshall's Law," *Washington Post Magazine,* January 7, 1990, 29; from an interview with Marshall conducted by Carl Rowan, quoted in "The Justice and the President," *Washington Post,* September 11, 1987, A23.

60. U.S. Constitution, art. 2, sec. 4.

61. John Ehrlichman, *Witness to Power: The Nixon Years* (New York: Simon and Schuster, 1982), 122.

62. Laura Kalman, *Abe Fortas: A Biography* (New Haven: Yale University Press, 1990), 359–376; Bruce Allen Murphy, *Fortas: The Rise and Ruin of a Supreme Court Justice* (New York: Morrow, 1988).

63. Dean, *The Rehnquist Choice,* 11.

64. Ibid., 26.

Chapter 3

The Cases

I n the current era, the Supreme Court reaches full decisions in about eighty cases a year. The justices choose those cases from more than seven thousand petitions for hearings. But even that number of petitions is a very small portion of all the actions and events that could become Supreme Court cases. From that perspective, a Supreme Court decision is a very rare event.

This chapter examines the process of agenda setting that produces those rare events. In the first stage of that process, people make the series of decisions that bring their cases to the Supreme Court. In the second stage, the Court selects from those cases the ones that it will fully consider and decide.

Several sets of people and institutions help to set the Court's agenda. In the first stage, litigants play a necessary part by filing cases and bringing them through the legal system to the Court. Most of those litigants are represented by lawyers for at least part of this process, and some receive direct or indirect assistance from interest groups. Although the Court plays no direct part at this stage, predictions of how the Court might respond to a case affect decisions about whether to bring it to the Court. In the second stage, the justices are the sole decision makers. But their choices may be influenced by the litigants, lawyers, and interest groups that participate in cases. And the other branches of government structure both stages by setting the Court's jurisdiction and writing the statutes on which most cases are based.

The two stages of agenda setting in the Court are examined in the first two sections of this chapter. In the first section, I consider how and why cases are brought to the Court. In the second I discuss how and why the justices choose certain cases to decide on the merits. In the final section, I take a different perspective on agenda setting by examining the impact of growth in the Court's caseload.

Reaching the Court: Litigants, Attorneys, and Interest Groups

Litigants, their attorneys, and interest groups are all important in determining which cases get to the Supreme Court, and I will examine the role of each in turn. The federal government is the most frequent and most distinctive participant in Supreme Court cases, and its role merits separate consideration.

Litigants

Every case that comes to the Supreme Court has at least one formal party, or litigant, on each side. For a case to reach the Court, one or more of the parties must have acted to initiate the litigation and move it upward through the court system.

Litigants in the Supreme Court are a diverse lot.[1] Of those who petition the Court to hear cases, the great majority are individuals, and most of these individuals are criminal defendants. Among respondents, the litigants who are brought to the Court by petitioners, the largest category includes the array of governments and government agencies from the federal level to the local level. Individuals are also respondents in many cases. Businesses frequently appear as petitioners or respondents. Other kinds of litigants, such as nonprofit groups and labor unions, participate in Court cases as well.

Perhaps the most important question concerning litigants is why they become involved in court cases and carry those cases to the Supreme Court. The motives of litigants can be thought of as taking two general forms, resulting in two "ideal types" of Supreme Court litigation. Some litigants fit one of these ideal types; others have mixed motives.

The first type of case can be called ordinary litigation because it is so common. Most of the time, parties bring cases to court or appeal unfavorable decisions because they seek to advance a direct personal or organizational interest. For instance, plaintiffs file personal injury suits because they hope to receive money through a court verdict or an out-of-court settlement.

One example of ordinary litigation is *Stewart v. Dutra Construction Co.* (2005).[2] To deal with serious traffic problems in Boston, the federal and state governments carried out a massive project (nicknamed the "Big Dig") in which a major highway was rerouted, a new bridge was built, and a tunnel was constructed between the city and its airport. Willard Stewart was an engineer working on a large dredge in the tunnel project in 1993, when a collision between the dredge and a boat caused him to fall through a hatch and suffer serious injuries. Stewart sued for compensation under the federal Longshore and Harbor Workers' Compensation Act from his employer, Dutra, which operated the dredge. Only workers on "vessels" are covered by this statute, and the Dutra Company challenged Stewart's claim on the ground that the dredge was not a "vessel." The company won that point in the lower federal courts, but the Supreme Court unanimously ruled in Stewart's favor. The case affected a federal policy, and, indeed, the federal government submitted an amicus brief in support of Stewart. But there is no indication that Stewart had any interest in the policy; he simply sought compensation for his injury.

The second ideal type of case may be called "political" litigation. In these cases, litigants seek to advance policies they favor rather than their direct self-interest. Most often, political litigation is aimed at winning a judicial decision that supports the litigant's policy goals.

Van Orden v. Perry (2005) exemplifies political litigation.[3] Thomas Van Orden was a former lawyer who had become homeless and lived in Austin. On his daily walks to the Texas State Law Library, Van Orden passed a monument on the grounds of the state capitol that portrayed the Ten Commandments. One day it occurred to him that the monument should be challenged as a violation of the First Amendment's prohibition of an establishment of religion. He decided to do so himself: "I have time; my schedule is kind of light."[4] He filed a case in federal district court and did his own legal work in the case. After Van Orden lost in the court of appeals he secured representation from a constitutional law scholar, who won a hearing in the Supreme Court and argued the case there. Van Orden lost by a 5–4 vote. His loss had no concrete effect on him, and the same would have been true of a victory; Van Orden was motivated by his views about the separation of church and state rather than any self-interest.

Van Orden's situation was such that his participation was relatively cost free. But political litigation can be costly in multiple ways, and those costs often discourage potential litigants. Justice Souter did not think it remarkable that Van Orden was the first to challenge the long-standing Texas monument: "Suing a State over religion puts nothing in a plaintiff's pocket and can take a great deal out, and … the risk of social ostracism can be powerfully deterrent."[5]

Many cases have large elements of both ordinary and political litigation. Individuals or companies may bring lawsuits to gain something directly, but along the way they become concerned with the larger policy issues that arise from their cases. In cases brought by government agencies, ordinary and political elements may be difficult to separate: prosecutors file criminal cases to advance the specific mission of their agencies, but that mission is linked to the broader political goal of attacking crime.

The proportion of cases that can be classified as fully or partly political increases with each step upward in the judicial system, so political litigation is most common in the Supreme Court. This pattern is not accidental. Ordinary litigation usually ends at a relatively early stage because the parties find it more advantageous to settle their dispute or even to accept a defeat than to fight on. In contrast, political litigants often want to get a case to the highest levels of the judicial system, where a victory may establish a national policy they favor. In addition, political litigation sometimes attracts the support of interest groups that help to shoulder the costs and other burdens of carrying a case through the judicial system.

Even so, the great majority of cases brought to the Supreme Court are best classified as ordinary litigation. A large proportion are criminal cases in which a convicted defendant who wants to get out of prison, or to stay out, seeks a hearing. Other cases come from business corporations whose economic stake in the outcome justifies a petition to the Court. Still other cases concern a variety of individual grievances, big or small; in these cases, the aggrieved party cannot resist going to the Supreme Court in one final effort to obtain redress.

Political litigation is more common in the cases that the Court agrees to hear, because those cases are more likely to concern the broad legal issues that interest the justices. Yet, as the *Stewart* case illustrates, ordinary litigation is by no means absent from the cases that the Court hears. Even in the biggest cases, the ones that attract the attention of large numbers of interest groups, the chief motivation of the litigants is often their own direct interests.

Some Supreme Court litigants play active roles in their cases. A few litigants who were lawyers have gone one step further than Thomas Van Orden and presented oral arguments in the Court. Dudley Hiibel, a Nevada man who challenged a law under which police officers could require people to identify themselves, set up a Web site about his case.[6] But most litigants have limited involvement in their cases. An extreme example is *Rasul v. Bush* (2004), which concerned the jurisdiction of federal courts to review the detention of suspected terrorists at the Guantanamo Bay Naval Station in Cuba. The cases were initiated by relatives of detainees on their behalf; because detainees were kept isolated from the outside world, those still in detention did not know that their cases existed.[7]

Attorneys

In November 2004 the Supreme Court heard arguments in *Howell v. Mississippi* (2005), a case involving a dispute over jury instructions in a murder trial. The attorney for Marlon Howell was Ronnie Mitchell, partner in a North Carolina law firm. James Hood, Mississippi's attorney general, represented the state. Neither lawyer had argued in the Supreme Court before.

That situation was not rare. In each term most of the lawyers who argue cases in the Court are doing so for the first time, and many have not even worked on a Supreme Court brief. One lawyer was making his first appearance in any appellate court.[8] Often these lawyers become involved in a case at its inception, without any thought that it might go as far as the Supreme Court. When the Court does accept their case, they and their clients resist entreaties to turn the case over to a lawyer with experience in the Court. For first-time lawyers, the opportunity to argue before the nation's highest court can be irresistible.

Another set of lawyers participates frequently in Supreme Court litigation and argues substantial numbers of cases. Most prominent are members of the solicitor general's staff, representatives of the federal government in the Supreme Court. Some lawyers for state governments also handle many Supreme Court cases over time. Some attorneys work for interest groups that frequently have cases in the Supreme Court. Others have private practices in which Supreme Court advocacy is a major specialty. The box on pages 74–75 describes several lawyers who are part of this "inner circle." Unlike other attorneys, those who are frequent participants in the Supreme Court usually do not become involved in a case until the appellate level, often not until it reaches the Supreme Court.

It is true today, as in the past, that the great majority of the lawyers who argue before the Court do so only once. However, the number of lawyers who participate frequently in the Court has grown, and they account for a growing share of the arguments before the Court. In part this is because the federal government with its experienced advocates now participates in a higher proportion of cases than it did a quarter century ago. More recently, litigants started to turn more often to Supreme Court specialists in the private sector, many of whom gained experience in the solicitor general's office or as law clerks in the Court.

Table 3-1 shows that when lawyers for the federal government are excluded, a majority of oral arguments are still presented by lawyers who appear only once before the Court over a five-term period. But compared with a decade earlier, lawyers who argued cases in the 2004 term were more likely to have multiple arguments over five years, and a larger share of the arguments was presented by lawyers who appear in the Court with some regularity. Chief Justice John Roberts exemplifies the increased prominence of these advocates. He clerked in the Court and later worked in the solicitor general's office for four years before joining a private law firm in which he regularly represented clients in the Court. Another illustration of this development is the 2006 patent dispute between businesses in which the lawyer for one side was arguing his forty-seventh case before the Court and his opponent was arguing for the forty-ninth time.[9]

Not surprisingly, most arguments by newcomers to the Court are not as strong as those by experienced advocates. One lawyer reported, "I still recall my first appearance at the Court as the worst oral argument I have ever delivered, and one of the worst experiences of my life."[10] But the

Some Lawyers Who Participate . . .

Carter G. Phillips. Phillips clerked for Chief Justice Warren Burger and served on the solicitor general's staff. He then joined the Washington office of a large law firm, and his work includes frequent participation in Supreme Court cases. He handles a wide range of cases for clients that include businesses, local governments, and professional groups. He argued eleven cases in the 2002–2004 terms, on issues that ranged from civil rights to antitrust to maritime law.

Maureen Mahoney. Mahoney argued her first Supreme Court case in 1988 while working in the Washington office of a large firm. Three years later she joined the solicitor general's office, where she gained considerable experience before the Court in two years. Returning to the law firm, she has continued to participate in Supreme Court litigation. She argued for the University of Michigan in *Grutter v. Bollinger* (2003), the case in which the Court upheld the university's affirmative action program. Reflecting her standing, in 2005 she was mentioned as a candidate to succeed Sandra Day O'Connor.

advantage gained by parties with experienced Supreme Court advocates is not overwhelming.

For one thing, newcomers sometimes perform very well. Until Michael Newdow brought his challenge to the inclusion of "under God" in the Pledge of Allegiance recited in schools, he had a law degree but no experience as a lawyer. When he insisted on arguing his own case in the Supreme Court, one civil liberties lawyer complained that "he's in over his head."[11] But his argument won strong praise, with one reporter calling it "spellbinding."[12] More important, although the quality of lawyers' work has some impact, it is only one factor that helps to shape the Court's decisions. As one lawyer put it, the justices "recognize they are deciding questions for the whole country, and they try to avoid having accidents of legal ability affect the outcome."[13]

For both reasons, inexperienced lawyers are often successful in the Court. In the 2003 term, a young Seattle lawyer who had never argued a criminal case in any court (but who had been a Supreme Court law clerk) argued and won two major criminal cases in the Court.[14]

In the legal system as a whole, a relationship exists between the wealth of an individual or institution and the quality of the legal services available to that party. To a considerable degree, this is true of the Supreme Court. The

---

... *Frequently in Cases before the Supreme Court*

Thomas Goldstein. As a young lawyer in the late 1990s, Goldstein decided to develop a Supreme Court practice. Identifying cases that the Court might be inclined to accept, he offered to represent parties for no charge. His successes in these cases helped him achieve a reputation as a Supreme Court advocate. Goldstein argued three cases in both the 2003 and 2004 terms. In contrast with Carter Phillips and Maureen Mahoney, Goldstein was part of a very small firm led by him and his wife, Amy Howe; their law office was in their home. In 2006 Goldstein joined a large law firm.

Edwin Kneedler. Kneedler has worked for the federal government with the Office of the Solicitor General for nearly his entire legal career, dating back to the late 1970s. Like other lawyers in the solicitor general's office, he participates regularly in Supreme Court cases. Along with his work in other roles, he has presented oral arguments in more than eighty cases during his career, typically arguing three or four cases a term. The subjects of his arguments reflect the diversity of cases in which the federal government participates.

Sources: Supreme Court decisions; biographical directories; newspaper and magazine stories.

---

experienced Supreme Court advocates in private practice are most readily available to large corporations and other prosperous organizations that can afford their regular fees. In 2004 one of those lawyers charged clients $775 an hour.[15]

For parties without substantial resources, the picture is mixed. People with low or moderate incomes are seldom represented by the most skilled advocates when they petition for hearings in the Court, and often they have to petition without any lawyer's help. But if the Court accepts a case, the picture changes. The Court appoints attorneys to represent indigent litigants. And because "Supreme Court arguments are highly coveted," one lawyer argues, "a party with limited resources can almost always find one or more seasoned Supreme Court veterans to take the case for a discount— or for free."[16]

Lawyers are eligible to participate in cases if they join the Supreme Court bar, for which the most important requirement is that they have been admitted to practice in a state for at least the last three years. Lawyers who cannot meet this requirement, however, usually are allowed to argue cases they have brought to the Court. Only a minority of the lawyers who belong to the Supreme Court bar ever take cases before the Court; lawyers join primarily for the honor. The Court routinely disbars lawyers after serious dis-

Thomas Goldstein speaks with reporters after arguing before the Supreme Court in 2004. At a relatively young age, Goldstein became a regular participant in litigation at the Court.

TABLE 3-1
Numbers of Oral Arguments over a Five-Term Period
by Lawyers Arguing Cases in the 1994 and 2004 Terms
(Lawyers for Federal Government Excluded)

Number of arguments	1994 (%)	2004 (%)
1	69.2	59.7
2	20.5	12.8
3–5	9.0	14.1
6–10	0.0	4.5
11–15	0.0	5.4
16–20	1.3	3.4

Note: For lawyers who argued cases in 1994, the five-term period is 1990–1994; for lawyers who argued cases in 2004, the period is 2000–2004. Lawyers who argued multiple cases in 1994 or 2004 are counted each time they argued a case. Thus, the 3.4% in the lower-right cell of the table means that, leaving aside arguments by lawyers for the federal government, 3.4% of the oral arguments in the 2004 term were made by lawyers who had 16 to 20 arguments in the 2000–2004 terms.

ciplinary action by their state bars. In 2001 Bill Clinton resigned from the Supreme Court bar to avoid that sanction after he had accepted suspension from the Arkansas bar.[17]

Interest Groups

Leaders of interest groups must decide how to allocate their limited resources. Many groups devote some of their resources to the Supreme Court, and some give a high priority to the Court. One reason is that the Court is highly visible, so groups can publicize themselves to members and others by giving attention to the Court. More fundamentally, the Court's decisions are highly relevant to a wide range of interest groups, so groups have an incentive to try to influence those decisions. As a result, interest groups are important participants in the Court.

Forms of Group Activity. Groups that want to influence congressional decisions often communicate directly with individual members of Congress. In contrast, it is considered highly improper to lobby judges directly. Because of this norm, Supreme Court justices generally try to avoid contact with litigants and the groups that support them.

But interest groups can attempt to influence the Court in other ways. As described in chapter 2, some groups participate in the nomination and confirmation of justices. Groups on both sides of the abortion controversy conduct marches and demonstrations when the Court considers abortion cases, in part to put indirect pressure on the justices.

The primary route used to influence the Court is participation in the litigation process, participation that takes multiple forms. First, groups can initiate litigation or help bring it to the Court. Organizations that exist primarily as interest groups generally lack standing, a legal stake in a case, to bring cases in their own names. But other organizations that may be considered interest groups, especially businesses and governments, are often parties in Supreme Court cases.

A group that is not a party can "sponsor" a case on an issue that concerns it, providing attorneys' services and bearing the costs from the start. Sponsorship entails considerable expense and practical difficulties, and relatively few groups undertake it. Still, a substantial portion of the cases the Court agrees to hear are sponsored by interest groups. Sometimes groups engage in what might be considered a limited sponsorship of cases that have already been initiated, helping to bear the financial costs and supplying legal services and advice.

One recent example of sponsorship was *Kelo v. City of New London* (2005).[18] The Institute for Justice, a conservative public-interest law firm, developed a litigation campaign in which it argued that governments were exceeding their eminent domain powers under the Constitution by taking property (with compensation) for private use rather than public use. New London, a Connecticut city, sought to buy property for a development project; when some homeowners and other property owners balked, the city condemned their property. The Institute for Justice sued the city on their behalf, and it carried the lawsuit forward through a mixed decision in the state trial court, a defeat in the state supreme court, and ultimately a 5–4 defeat in the Supreme Court.

Whether or not it sponsors cases, a group can try to influence the Court's decisions to accept or reject cases and how to decide those that it accepts. If a group effectively controls a case, its attorneys submit a brief that asks the Court to grant or deny a writ of certiorari. If the case is accepted for decision on the merits, the group's attorneys submit new briefs and participate in oral argument.

When a group does not control the case, it still may submit arguments to the Court in what are called amicus curiae, or friend of the court, briefs. With the consent of the parties to a case or by permission of the Court, any person or organization may submit an amicus brief to supplement the arguments of the parties. (Legal representatives of government do not need to obtain permission.) Most of the time, the parties give their consent for the submission of amicus briefs. When the Court's consent is needed, it seldom is denied—only nine times in the 2000–2004 terms. Amicus briefs can be submitted on whether a case should be heard or, after a case is accepted for hearing, directly on the merits.

An amicus can also participate in oral argument if invited or allowed by the Court. The federal government regularly plays this role, as it did thirty times in the 2004 term. Lawyers for states argued as amicus in four cases in that term, reflecting the Court's increasing willingness to give this privilege to the states.

Amicus briefs are by far the most common means by which groups other than parties participate in litigation before the Court. As might be expected, amicus briefs are especially common in cases that the Court has accepted for consideration on the merits. In the 2004 term amicus briefs were submitted in more than 95 percent of the cases decided after oral argument; more than half the cases had at least five briefs, and nearly one-third had at least ten briefs.[19] And because groups or individuals can join in submitting a brief, the number of participants is considerably larger than the number of briefs.

The popularity of amicus briefs has several sources.[20] First, although the costs of preparing them are substantial, they are considerably cheaper than case sponsorship. Second, the logistics of submitting an amicus brief are relatively simple. Third, many lawyers and other people believe that amicus briefs influence the Court's decisions. For this reason, parties to cases often encourage or even orchestrate supportive briefs, and groups whose interests are implicated by a case may feel that they need to have their say. Group leaders can also use amicus briefs as a concrete action with which to impress their members.

The Array of Groups in the Court. Interest group participation in Supreme Court litigation has increased dramatically in the past few decades. Groups are sponsoring more cases, and amicus briefs have proliferated. To take one indicator, in cases with oral arguments the Court received an average of 0.63 briefs per case in the 1956–1965 terms, 4.23 in the 1986–1995 period, and 7.99 in the 2004 term.[21] The growth in amicus briefs is symbolized by the record-breaking eighty-five that were submitted in the Court's 2003 case on affirmative action in law school admissions.[22] This growth has several sources. Throughout government, the number of active interest groups and the level of their activity have increased considerably. The apparent success of some groups in shaping the Supreme Court's policies has encouraged other groups to seek that success. Indeed, "arms races" have developed between groups that compete to influence the Court's decisions in particular fields.[23]

With this growth, hundreds of interest groups participate in Supreme Court cases in some way. Among them are nearly all the groups that are most active in Congress and the executive branch. The box on page 80 provides a sampling of this participation by listing some of the groups that submitted amicus briefs in the 2005 term.

The groups that participate in Supreme Court cases can be placed in four broad categories. The first is economic: individual businesses, trade associations, professional groups, labor unions, and farm groups. Economic

A Sampling of Groups
Submitting Amicus Curiae Briefs
to the Supreme Court in the 2005 Term

Economic Groups: Business and Occupational

AFL-CIO
American Express Company
American Medical Association
Association of Trial Lawyers of America
Ford Motor Company
National Association of Manufacturers
National Treasury Employees Union

Noneconomic Interests

AARP
Disability Rights Education & Defense Fund
National Association of Evangelicals
National Gay and Lesbian Law Association
National Organization for Women

Ideological Groups

Family Research Council
NARAL Pro-Choice America
People for the American Way Foundation
University Faculty for Life
Washington Legal Foundation

Governments and Governmental Groups

City of New York
Members of the Oregon Congressional Delegation
National League of Cities
United States
Virginia School Boards Association

groups are somewhat less prominent in the Court than they are in the other branches, because civil liberties issues occupy a large portion of the Court's agenda. Many of these issues, especially in criminal law, have little relevance to economic groups. But the Court's work in other areas often affects economic interests, and the business community is especially well represented among parties to cases and submitters of amicus briefs.

In the second category are groups that represent segments of the population defined by something other than economics. These groups are based on such characteristics as race and ethnicity, gender, age, and sexual orientation. The prototype for these groups is the NAACP Legal Defense and Educational Fund (sometimes called the NAACP Legal Defense Fund or simply the Fund). Originally an arm of the NAACP, the Fund works through its own staff attorneys and a network of cooperating lawyers throughout the country. It initially focused its efforts on securing voting rights for black citizens and desegregating southern public schools. It later involved itself in other areas, such as employment and criminal justice, giving special attention to the death penalty. The Fund's successes in the Supreme Court encouraged the creation of organizations concerned with discrimination on grounds other than race, groups that proliferated from the 1960s on.

The groups in the third category represent broad ideological positions rather than the interests of a specific segment of society. Here the prototype is the American Civil Liberties Union (ACLU).[24] Established in 1920 to protect civil liberties, the ACLU has always relied heavily on litigation. The ACLU involves itself in virtually every area of civil liberties law. The ACLU also has created special projects to undertake concerted litigation campaigns in specific areas of concern, such as women's rights, capital punishment, and national security. The ACLU frequently submits amicus briefs in cases that it does not sponsor.

The ACLU is one of many ideological groups that work to achieve liberal policy goals. Two others are the Sierra Club, which has a litigation arm devoted to environmental protection, and the Planned Parenthood Federation of America, for which abortion rights are a primary concern. There is also a range of public interest law firms with a liberal perspective. These firms initiate litigation on issues such as consumer rights, civil liberties, and the environment.

Ideological groups that favor conservative positions on legal issues were slower to involve themselves in litigation, but many such groups are now active. For example, Americans for Effective Law Enforcement frequently submits amicus briefs in Supreme Court cases involving criminal justice issues. Several public interest law firms act on behalf of conservative interests. A campaign against affirmative action programs by one firm, the Center for Individual Rights, led to the Supreme Court's split decisions in 2003 on the use of affirmative action in college admissions.[25] As noted earlier, the Institute for Justice, another conservative firm, represented the losing side in the Court's 2005 decision on the taking of property by government. The Institute was more successful in *Swedenburg v. Kelly* (2005), in which it represented one of the successful challengers to state laws that prohibited interstate shipment of wine to consumers.

Several litigating groups represent conservative religious interests.[26] One is the American Center for Law and Justice (ACLJ), established by the religious leader Pat Robertson in 1991. The ACLJ gives some emphasis to assisting people who want to participate in religious activities in schools and other places. Another Christian group, the Rutherford Institute, handles a wide range of cases relating to religious expression and other issues. The Rutherford Institute supported Paula Jones in the lawsuit against President Clinton that ultimately brought about Clinton's impeachment in 1998.

The final category consists of governments, which regularly appear as interest groups in the Court. The federal government is a special case, which is examined separately. State and local governments often come to the Court as litigants, and they file many amicus briefs. It has become standard practice for many or most states to join in a brief to emphasize their strong shared interest in a case. In Michael Newdow's challenge to the inclusion of "under God" in the Pledge of Allegiance, every state signed onto a brief arguing against that challenge.

Group Strategies and Tactics.   Any interest group that engages in litigation must make strategic and tactical decisions. At the strategic level, groups that are not set up solely to litigate must decide how much of their energy and resources to devote to litigation rather than other forms of political action. Groups must also decide what kinds of issues to emphasize in their litigation work and how to coordinate their efforts with other groups that have similar interests. At the tactical level, a group's lawyers consider whether initiating a specific case or supporting a litigant in an existing case would serve their goals.[27] They sometimes have a choice among different regions in which to initiate cases or between federal and state courts. And like other lawyers, they have to choose which arguments to make in the cases in which they participate.

Many considerations affect these decisions, including the views of group members and the availability of resources. Perhaps the most fundamental consideration is a group's perceptions of the courts in general and the Supreme Court in particular. It is not surprising that conservative groups have become more active in Supreme Court litigation since the 1970s as the Court has become more receptive to conservative arguments. Similarly, choices of specific cases and arguments reflect judgments about potential responses from the justices.

Some groups establish long-term litigation strategies in which they seek to shape legal policy over time. The most famous example was the campaign by the NAACP Legal Defense Fund to attack racial inequality and, ultimately, racial segregation in public schools. The Fund won a series of victories that culminated in *Brown v. Board of Education* (1954). The organization had considerable difficulty in coordinating cases and funding its campaign, but its success was noteworthy. The ACLU's Women's Rights Project achieved a less dramatic but significant set of favorable decisions (although it lost some other cases) in the Supreme Court in the 1970s. But few other groups have achieved so much success. Even as the Court becomes more conservative, some conservative groups have been stymied thus far in their campaigns to establish new principles of constitutional law on issues such as affirmative action.

The Significance of Interest Groups. Interest groups can affect what the Supreme Court does in several ways; here, I focus on their effect on whether cases get to the Court. In this respect, cases may be placed in three categories.

The largest category includes the cases that come to the Court without any participation by interest groups. For the most part, these cases constitute what I have called ordinary litigation. The issues in these cases are too narrow to interest any group. They reach the Court because the parties and attorneys have sufficient motivation of their own to seek a Supreme Court hearing and sufficient resources to finance the litigation. These conditions are met when a large business has a substantial financial stake in a case. They are also met when indigent criminal defendants face significant prison terms and need not pay lawyers' fees or other expenses involved in getting a case to the Court.

The second category consists of cases that would have reached the Court without any interest group involvement but in which groups are involved in some way. An interest group may assist one of the parties by providing attorneys' services or financing to ensure that the case does reach the Supreme Court and to gain some control over the position that the party takes. Far more often, a group submits an amicus brief supporting the petition for a hearing by the Court.

The third category includes cases that would not reach the Court without group sponsorship. There are many important legal questions in civil liberties that no individual litigant has the capability or sufficient incentive to take to the Supreme Court. For example, most of the individuals whom the ACLU assists could not go to court without the group's legal assistance.

Because group sponsorship of cases in the Court is relatively rare, only a small proportion of cases brought to the Court fall into this third category. But groups are most likely to sponsor cases that have the potential to be heard by the Court and to produce major legal rulings. Indeed, much of the Court's expansion of legal protections for civil liberties during the twentieth century was made possible by interest group action.[28]

Groups can do more than get cases to the Court; they can help to determine whether those cases are heard and how the Court rules. That influence is discussed later in this chapter and in Chapter 4.

The Federal Government as Litigant

Of all the litigants in the Supreme Court, the federal government appears most frequently. It is a party in a large minority of the cases brought to the Court for consideration. Of the cases actually argued before the Court, the federal government participates as a party or an amicus in a substantial majority. The Court heard arguments in seventy-six cases in its 2004 term; the government presented arguments on its own behalf in twenty-three of those cases and as an amicus in thirty others, for a participation rate of 70 percent. In other recent terms, the rate has been even higher.[29] As a result of its frequent participation, the federal government is the most important interest group in the Court.

In turn, the group of about two dozen lawyers who work for the Office of the Solicitor General in the Justice Department has more impact on the Court than does any other set of attorneys. Those lawyers are primarily responsible for representing the federal government in the Supreme Court. They decide whether to bring federal government cases to the Court; only a few federal agencies can take cases to the Court without the solicitor general's approval. Lawyers in the solicitor general's office also do the bulk of the legal work in Supreme Court cases in which the federal government participates, including petitions for hearings, the writing of briefs, and oral arguments.

The solicitor general's office occupies a complicated position.[30] On the one hand, it represents the president and the executive branch, functioning as their law firm in individual cases. In this role, the office helps to carry out policies of the president. But the office also has developed a unique relationship with the Supreme Court, one in which it serves as an adviser as well as an advocate. As Richard Pacelle put it, the solicitor general's office straddles the line "between law and politics."[31]

The unique relationship of the Office of the Solicitor General with the Court rests on the fact that it represents a unique litigant. For one thing, the executive branch and the Supreme Court are both part of the federal government. In addition, the executive branch is involved in far more potential Supreme Court cases and actual cases than any other entity. As a result, the solicitor general has the opportunity to build a mutually advantageous relationship with the Court.

One way the solicitor general does so is by exercising self-restraint in requesting that the Court hear cases. In the cases acted on by the Court in the 2004 term, the federal government filed 19 petitions for certiorari, compared with 2,220 for its opponents. Although the government loses fewer cases in the courts of appeals than do its opponents, the primary reason for this difference is the solicitor general's willingness to forgo possible petitions for certiorari. The solicitor general's office also seeks to maintain credibility by taking a less partisan stance than other litigants. For example, lawyers in the office try to ensure that the justices can rely on what they say in briefs and in oral argument. On the rare occasions when questions are raised about the accuracy of what the government's lawyers say, those questions get attention because they run counter to the image that the solicitor general seeks to foster.[32] Further, the experience that those lawyers gain allows them to make high-quality arguments to the Court.

In response, the justices give considerable deference to the solicitor general. The office has an extraordinary success rate for its certiorari petitions. The Court frequently "invites" (in reality, orders) the solicitor general to file amicus briefs in cases that do not affect the federal government directly because the justices are interested in the government's views. In the 2004 term, typical in this respect, the solicitor general's office filed amicus briefs in response to thirteen petitions for hearings—all at the Court's invitation.[33] And the solicitor general often participates in oral argument as amicus, a role that is uncommon for other litigants (although the Court increasingly allows state governments to play that role).

The office's special relationship with the Court leads to a degree of independence from the president and attorney general, who understand the value of maintaining that relationship. But the solicitor general usually is someone who shares the president's general point of view about legal policy, and the office operates in a general climate created by the president and attorney general. Moreover, these superiors occasionally intervene in specific cases. It was reported that the solicitor general's office filed a brief supporting display of the Ten Commandments in courthouses after debate within the Bush administration.[34] President Bush himself resolved the 2003 debate over the government's position on affirmative action programs at the University of Michigan and announced the decision to file amicus briefs opposing those programs in a televised address.[35] For all these reasons, an administration's policy views will be reflected in the overall pattern of positions that the office takes in litigation. Between 1965 and 2000, to take one example, Republican administrations took liberal positions about half the time in sex discrimination cases; Democratic administrations, 80 percent of the time.[36]

The linkages between the solicitor general's office and the administration have strengthened in the last quarter century, beginning with the

Reagan presidency. In effect, the political side of the solicitor general's work has become more prominent. In the Clinton administration, for example, solicitors general with liberal points of view took into account Clinton's less liberal views on most civil liberties issues and his desire to avoid being identified with unpopular positions.

This change is symbolized by the backgrounds of the two solicitors general who have served in George W. Bush's administration. Theodore Olson, who served from 2001 to 2004, had been heavily involved in conservative political and legal causes over the years, a role that culminated in his presenting oral argument for Bush in *Bush v. Gore*. Primarily because of this background, Olson was confirmed in the Senate by only four votes. Paul Clement, appointed in 2005, had served as a law clerk for two prominent conservative judges, worked on the staff of Republican senator (and future attorney general) John Ashcroft, and helped to write two amicus briefs supporting Bush in *Bush v. Gore* (2000).[37]

At the same time, the legal side of the solicitor general's work has remained strong. Both Olson and Clement were highly respected appellate lawyers before their appointment as solicitor general. The legal credentials of the other lawyers in the solicitor general's office are impressive. Nor has the office lost its degree of independence. Indeed, in some cases the office has taken positions that run counter to the general tenor of Bush administration policy. The solicitor general's office continues to play a distinctive role, and the federal government as a litigant benefits from that role.

Deciding What to Hear: The Court's Role

In its 2004 term the Supreme Court considered 7,496 petitions for hearings. The Court granted certiorari and full consideration to only 80 of those petitions.[38] Of the thousands of other petitions, the great majority were simply denied, allowing a lower-court decision to become final. Some of those cases involved prominent people or powerful institutions. Some raised issues of national importance. Nonetheless, the Court chose not to hear them. In selecting a few dozen cases from the thousands brought to them, the justices determined which legal claims and policy questions they would address.

Options

In screening petitions for hearings, the Court makes choices that are more complicated than simply accepting and rejecting individual cases. To begin with, petitions are not always considered in isolation from one another. The justices may accept a case to clarify or expand on an earlier decision in the same policy area. They may accept several cases that raise the same issue to address that issue more fully than a single case would allow them to do. They may reject a case because they are looking for a more suitable case on the same issue.

When the Court does accept a case, the justices can choose which issues they will consider. The Court often limits its grant of certiorari to one issue raised by the petitioner, and it sometimes asks the parties to address an issue that neither had raised. No matter what issues the parties raise and address, the Court retains the freedom to determine the issues it actually resolves in its opinion. In *Mapp v. Ohio* (1961), the Court made a landmark decision on police searches and seizures after the parties had argued the case as one about constitutional limits on the regulation of obscenity.

In accepting a case, the Court also determines the kind of consideration it will give that case. It may give the case full consideration, which means that the Court receives a new set of briefs on the merits from the parties and holds oral argument, then issues a decision on the merits with a full opinion explaining the decision. Alternatively, it may give the case summary consideration. This usually means that the case is decided without new briefs or oral argument; the Court relies on the materials that the parties already submitted. In a typical term, a large minority of the cases that the Court accepts receive summary consideration.

In most summary decisions, the Supreme Court issues a "GVR" order— Granting certiorari, Vacating the lower-court decision, and Remanding the case to that court for reconsideration. Most of these orders are issued because some event since the lower-court decision, usually a Supreme Court decision, is relevant to the case. In its 2004 term the Court issued an extraordinary number of GVRs because of its decision in *United States v. Booker* (2005), which struck down the mandatory guidelines for criminal sentencing in federal district courts. By the end of the term the Court had returned more than 750 cases to the federal courts of appeals to reconsider in light of *Booker.*

In other summary decisions, the Court actually reaches a decision on the merits and issues an opinion of several paragraphs or even several pages. This opinion typically is labeled *per curiam,* meaning by the Court, rather than being signed by a justice, but it has the same legal force as a signed opinion. When the Court takes this kind of action, dissenting justices sometimes complain that it should not have decided the case without getting full information from the parties through briefs that directly address the merits of the case and through oral argument.

Even after accepting a case, the Court can avoid a decision by issuing what is called a DIG, or Dismissed as Improvidently Granted.[39] A DIG occurs a few times each term, when the parties' briefs on the merits or the oral arguments suggest to the justices that the case is inappropriate for a decision. In *Howell v. Mississippi* (2005), the Court DIGged a case because it determined that Marlon Howell had not raised his claim under federal law properly in state court, so the Court could not consider that claim.

Congress caused a 2003 case to drop off the Court's agenda. The issue in *Department of Justice v. City of Chicago* was whether a Justice Department bureau must release certain information about gun sales and crimes. A few weeks before oral argument, Congress enacted a budget bill with a provision forbidding the agency from spending money to release the information, apparently to get the case out of the Court. The action was successful; the Court canceled the argument and sent the case back to a lower court for reconsideration.[40]

Screening Procedures

The Court uses a series of complex procedures to screen petitions for hearing, and these procedures are made more complex by two distinctions between types of cases. The first is between the certiorari cases, over which the Court's jurisdiction is discretionary, and the very small number of cases labeled appeals, which the Court is required to decide. Few appeals reach the Court. The Court retains, and uses, the option of deciding them without holding oral argument or issuing full opinions. The second distinction, between paid cases and paupers' cases, requires more extensive discussion.

Paid Cases and Paupers' Cases. In recent years less than one-quarter of the requests for hearings that arrive at the Supreme Court have been "paid" cases, for which the Court's filing fee of $300 has been paid and all required copies of materials have been provided. The remaining cases are brought *in forma pauperis* by indigent people for whom the fee and the requirement of multiple copies are waived. The great majority of the "paupers'" cases are brought by prisoners in federal and state institutions. (A person responding to a petition may also be given pauper status.)

Criminal defendants who have had counsel provided to them in the lower federal courts because of their low incomes are automatically entitled to bring paupers' cases in the Supreme Court. Other litigants must submit an affidavit supporting their motion for leave to file as paupers. The Court has never developed precise rules specifying when a litigant can claim pauper status. In recent years, however, it has denied many litigants the right to proceed as paupers in particular cases on the grounds that they were not truly paupers or that their petitions were frivolous or malicious.[41] The Court has also gone further, issuing a general denial of pauper status in noncriminal cases to some litigants who had filed large numbers of paupers' petitions. Justice Stevens regularly dissents from such denials because of an experience he had before becoming a judge: he had found "unexpected merit" in the allegations of a repetitive and annoying litigant when he led an investigation of judicial corruption in Illinois in 1969.[42]

A very small proportion of paupers' petitions are accepted for full decisions on the merits—about two-tenths of 1 percent in the 2004 term, compared with 4.1 percent of the paid cases in the same term.[43] The lack of inherent merit in many of these cases and the fact that many litigants have to draft petitions without a lawyer's assistance help to account for the low acceptance rate. It may also be that the Court looks less closely at paupers' petitions than at the paid petitions. One study found evidence that in cases that were similar in other respects, the Court was less likely to accept a pauper's petition than a paid petition.[44] But because there are so many paupers' petitions, even the small proportion that are accepted add up to a significant number of cases—an average of about a dozen a term in recent years—and they constitute an important part of the Court's work on issues of criminal procedure.

Prescreening: The Discuss List. Under its "rule of four," the Court grants a writ of certiorari and hears a case on the merits if at least four justices vote at conference to grant the writ. But petitions for hearings are considered and voted on at conference only if they are put on the Court's "discuss list."[45] The chief justice creates the discuss list, but other justices can and do add cases to it. Cases left off the discuss list are denied hearings automatically. This is the fate of a substantial majority of petitions.

The discuss-list procedure serves to limit the Court's workload. But this procedure also reflects a belief that most petitions do not require collective consideration, because they are such poor candidates for acceptance. A great many petitions raise only very narrow issues, and many others make very weak legal claims, so it is easy to reject them.

Action in Conference. In conference, the chief justice or the justice who added a case to the discuss list opens the presentation of views on the case. In order of seniority, from senior to junior, the justices then speak and usually announce their votes. If the discussion does not make the justices' positions clear, a formal vote is taken, also in order of seniority. Despite the prescreening of cases, a substantial majority of the petitions considered in conference are denied.

Most cases receive very brief discussion in conference. Some cases receive more consideration, which sometimes extends beyond the initial discussion. In conference, any justice can ask that a case be "redistributed" for a later conference. This step might be taken to obtain additional information, such as the full record of the case in the lower courts. A justice also might ask for redistribution to circulate an opinion dissenting from the Court's tentative denial of a hearing and thereby try to change the Court's decision. Of the cases in which the Court heard oral arguments in fall 2005, most were redistributed at least once, and *Maryland v. Blake,* a case involving *Miranda* rights, was redistributed five times.

When it accepts a case, the Court also decides whether to allow oral argument or to decide the case summarily on the basis of the available written materials. Four votes are required for oral argument. A case that is not given oral argument may be granted a hearing and decided on the merits at the same conference, so the two stages of decision in effect become one.

The Court does not issue opinions to explain its acceptance or rejection of cases. Nor are individual votes announced. But in a very small proportion of cases justices record their dissents from denials of petitions for hearings or their reasons for voting against granting certiorari. In *Padilla v. Hanft* (2006), a case involving the rights of suspected terrorists who were arrested in the United States, three justices dissented from the denial of certiorari. Justice Ginsburg wrote an opinion explaining the basis for her dissent, and Justice Kennedy wrote an opinion for three of the justices who had voted against granting a hearing. The Court's decision apparently was hard fought: the case was redistributed seven times.

The Clerks' Role.   One of the law clerks' primary functions is to scrutinize requests for hearings. Since 1990 every justice except Stevens has been part of the "certiorari pool." According to one study of law clerks, Stevens does not participate in the pool because he believes that "he and his clerks provide an important check against potential mistakes."[46] Petitions and other materials on each case are divided among the clerks for the other eight justices. The clerk who has responsibility for a case writes a memorandum, one that typically includes a summary of the case and a recommendation that the petition be granted or denied. Some justices then have their own law clerks examine and react to the memo for each case.

The effect of the law clerks' analyses and recommendations on the justices is difficult to ascertain. Because of the press of time, it is clear that the justices rely heavily on law clerks' analyses of cases, which means that the pool memo has considerable importance. Some justices and other observers have expressed particular concern about the justices' collective reliance on the pool memo.[47] One former law clerk argued that this reliance is less problematic than it might appear: clerks typically write their pool memos with care, and justices frequently vote contrary to the memo's recommendation. "Still," he concluded, "any system that depends to a considerable degree on the views of a single novice lawyer is fairly subject to criticism."[48]

The law clerks' impact on certiorari decisions should not be exaggerated, however. For one thing, the great majority of petitions would elicit a denial from any justice or clerk. "I would guess," Chief Justice Rehnquist wrote, "that several thousand of the petitions for certiorari filed with the

Court each year are patently without merit," so no justice "would have the least interest in granting them."[49] And justices hardly cede full control over screening to their clerks. A study found that in the cases the Court accepted in the 1984 and 1985 terms, about half had certiorari pool memos recommending that the petition be denied or that the Court take some action other than accepting the petition at that time.[50]

Criteria for Decision

The Supreme Court's decisions to accept some petitions and deny others certainly are not random. Rather, the justices look for cases whose attributes make them desirable to hear. The Court's Rule 10 lists some of those attributes, which are based on the Court's role in ensuring the certainty and consistency of the law. Rule 10 indicates that the Court is more interested in hearing cases if they contain important legal issues that the Court has not yet decided, if there is conflict between lower courts on a legal question or conflict between a lower court's decision and the Supreme Court's prior decisions, or if a lower court has departed "from the accepted and usual course of judicial proceedings."

The existence of these conditions undoubtedly increases the chances that a case will be accepted, but the list in Rule 10 suggests a conception of the Court's function and of its members' interests that is unrealistically narrow. The Court's pattern of screening decisions and evidence from other sources indicate the significance of several types of considerations.

Technical Criteria. The Court will reject a petition for hearing if it fails to meet certain technical requirements. Some of these requirements are specific to the Court. For example, paid petitions must comply with the Court's Rule 33, which establishes requirements on matters such as the size of print and margins used, type of paper, format and color of cover, and maximum length. These requirements are relaxed for the paupers' petitions, but even paupers' petitions may be rejected if their deviation from the rules is extreme.

The Court also imposes the same kinds of technical requirements for the hearing of cases that other courts apply. One specific requirement is that petitions for hearing be filed within ninety days of the entry of judgment in the lower court, unless the time has been extended in advance. The Court routinely refuses to allow the filing of petitions that are brought after the deadline.

More fundamental are the requirements of jurisdiction and standing. The Court cannot accept a case for hearing that clearly falls outside its jurisdiction. For example, the Court could not hear a state case in which the petitioner raised no issues of federal law in state court.

The rule of standing holds that a court may not hear a case unless the party bringing the case is properly before it. The most important element of standing is the requirement that a party in a case have a real and direct legal stake in its outcome. This requirement precludes hypothetical cases, cases brought on behalf of another person, "friendly suits" between parties that are not really adversaries, and cases that have become "moot" (in effect, hypothetical) because the parties can no longer be affected by the outcome. For this reason, the Court must dismiss a case if the parties have reached a settlement.

The technical requirements sometimes are easy to apply, but their application can be quite ambiguous. *Tory v. Cochran* (2005) involved a dispute between the lawyer Johnnie Cochran, famous for his defense of O. J. Simpson in a 1995 murder case, and a very disgruntled former client. The Supreme Court accepted the case to determine whether an injunction prohibiting the client from certain kinds of expressions against Cochran violated the First Amendment. A week after the case was argued, however, Cochran died. His death would seem to make his case moot. But a majority of the Court ruled that it was not moot because the injunction continued, and the Court allowed Cochran's widow to be substituted for him as a party to the case.

In Michael Newdow's challenge to the inclusion of "under God" in the Pledge of Allegiance, five of the eight participating justices held that Newdow's lack of legal custody over his daughter deprived him of standing to challenge her school's practice. But the other three justices strongly disagreed, arguing that Newdow had standing and concluding that the school's practice did not violate the First Amendment. It may be that some justices in the majority wanted to avoid ruling on the merits of the case and used the standing issue for that purpose.

Conflict between Courts. Justice Breyer heartily agrees with Rule 10 on the importance of conflict among lower courts as a basis for accepting cases. "If the lower courts are in agreement," he asked, "why us?"[51] Other justices have expressed the same view. Justice Ginsburg said that "the overwhelming factor" in the granting of certiorari "is the division of opinions in the Circuits."[52]

The depictions of case selection by Breyer and Ginsburg have considerable accuracy.[53] The existence of legal conflict greatly increases the chances that a case will be accepted. And one expert estimated that 80 percent of the cases that the Court accepts involve conflicts between federal courts of appeals.[54]

The Court does not accept all conflict cases. Indeed, the justices reject substantially more such cases than they accept. In choosing among the conflict cases, they take into account the extent of the conflict and the seriousness of its effects. The Court emphasized the latter criterion in 1995 when it revised its Rule 10 by inserting the word "important" in three places, indicating that it was inclined to hear conflict cases only if they involved important matters or legal questions. But the Court occasionally accepts a case to resolve a conflict even though only two courts are in conflict on a seemingly minor issue. In contrast, the Court sometimes turns down cases involving fairly serious conflicts among several courts. Eventually, however, the Court is likely to resolve a conflict that is persistent and troublesome.

Importance of the Issues. Whether or not a case involves conflict between lower courts, the significance of the issues has considerable influence on the Court's willingness to accept the case. Rule 10 emphasizes this consideration for good reason: the best way for the Court to maximize its impact is to decide the cases that affect the most people and that raise the most important policy issues.

This consideration in itself eliminates most petitions for certiorari, petitions in which the "questions presented" at the beginning are narrow and limited in their impact. Frequently, they ask only whether the case was wrongly decided. The petitioners in these cases may have suffered an injustice, but the justices typically see little reason to address an issue that will have little or no impact beyond the litigants themselves.

Whether a case has sufficient importance for the Court to hear is in part a subjective matter. The justices look for cases in which a decision would have broad effects on courts, government, or society as a whole. In some of the cases that meet this criterion, the issues are dramatic. In others, the issues are technical but nonetheless important. Even the justices may find such cases unexciting. Chief Justice Rehnquist noted in 2003 that the Court hears a steady stream of cases under the federal Employee Retirement Income Security Act (ERISA). "The thing that stands out about them is that they're dreary," he said, and the Court takes such cases as a matter of "duty, not choice."[55]

Just as the Court rejects some cases that involve conflicts between lower courts, it rejects some important cases as well. The primary reason is the same: the number of meritorious cases is considerably larger than the number the Court is willing and able to hear. Justices may have more specific reasons to vote against cases with significant issues. To take two examples, they may agree with the lower-court decision or want to delay before tackling a difficult issue.

Occasionally, an issue is so consequential that the justices are virtually compelled to hear a case on that issue. In *Blakely v. Washington* (2004), the Court ruled that one element of the sentencing guidelines for judges in Washington State was unconstitutional. The effect was to strike down those guidelines in their current form. The federal sentencing guidelines had the same element, and criminal defendants began to challenge their convictions in federal court on the basis of *Blakely*. Many courts ruled in favor of these challenges, creating considerable uncertainty about whether federal judges should still follow the guidelines. Not surprisingly, the Supreme Court quickly accepted two cases in order to provide a definitive ruling on that question, and a few months later it held that the federal guidelines as they stood were unconstitutional.[56]

Some justices doubted the wisdom of the Court's decision to hear *Bush v. Gore* (2000), the case in which the Court ensured the election of President Bush. But for Justice Scalia, looking back five years later, the Court had no choice but to hear the case. "What did you expect us to do? Turn the case down because it wasn't important enough? Or give the Florida Supreme Court another couple of weeks in which the United States could look ridiculous?"[57] A year earlier, Justice Thomas expressed the same idea more simply. "What do you think?" he asked. "Donald Duck is going to decide it?"[58]

Policy Preferences. Rule 10 does not mention justices' personal conceptions of good policy as a criterion for accepting or rejecting cases, but those conceptions have considerable effect on the Court's choices. Because case selection is such an important part of the Court's policymaking, members of the Court could scarcely resist use of the agenda-setting process as a way to advance their policy goals.

Justices can act on their policy goals primarily in two ways. First, they may vote to hear cases because they disagree with the lower-court decision that they are reviewing: seeing what they believe was an error by the lower court, they want to correct it. Second, they may act strategically by voting to hear cases when they think the policy they favor would gain a majority if the Court decided those cases on the merits.

The justices' use of the first approach is made clear by the Court's decisions on the merits. In most terms the Court overturns the lower court altogether or in part in more than two-thirds of its decisions. The comparable rate for the federal courts of appeals, which lack the Court's power to screen the cases brought to it, is under 10 percent.[59] One reason for the Court's reversal rate is that it accepts so many cases in order to resolve conflicts between lower courts; in those cases, there is something like a 50–50 chance that the Court will overturn the decision it hears. But the justices' interest in hearing cases when they have doubts about the validity of the lower court's decision also has a lot to do with the high rate of reversals.

The second, strategic, approach requires justices to predict how the Court would decide a case if it were accepted. Such predictions often can be made with some confidence because the justices have a good sense of each other's positions on legal issues. Considerable evidence suggests that justices engage in this prediction process. One study demonstrated that justices are much more likely to vote to grant certiorari when the Court's decision could be expected to reflect their ideological leanings rather than run contrary to those leanings.[60]

The practice of voting not to hear a case when a justice fears that the Court would make the "wrong" decision is so well established that justices and clerks routinely refer to "defensive denials" of certiorari.[61] Defensive denials are especially appealing to the members of the Court's ideological minority at any given time (such as liberals on the Rehnquist and Roberts Courts) because they have the most reason to fear the Court's prospective decisions.

It is uncertain how these two ways of acting on policy preferences fit together, but research on this question indicates that each is important. Justices respond to both their evaluations of lower-court decisions and their expectations about the Court's decision if a case is accepted.[62] And it is clear that justices' preferences, expressed in these ways, have considerable effect on their choices of cases.

Identity of the Petitioner and Supporting Amici. As a petitioner for certiorari in the Supreme Court, the federal government had an unusually bad year in the 2004 term. The Court considered nineteen petitions filed by the solicitor general's office and accepted ten. That success rate of 53 percent was well below that in other recent terms. Indeed, in 2001 the Court accepted 85 percent of the government's petitions.[63] Yet even 53 percent is remarkably high in comparison with the fates of petitions brought by other parties. And the federal government also does well when it supports another party's petition with an amicus brief

What accounts for this impressive record? It can be ascribed chiefly to the advantages of what Marc Galanter calls a "repeat player"—a litigant engaged in many related cases over time.[64] This status provides the government with at least three advantages.

First, the solicitor general's staff chooses cases to bring to the Court from a large pool of cases that are eligible for Court consideration. As a result, the staff can select those that are the most likely to be accepted. Almost any litigant who could be so selective would enjoy a fairly high rate of success in the Supreme Court.

Second, the solicitor general's selectivity earns some gratitude from the Court and builds credibility as well. If the federal government brought petitions at the high rates that other litigants bring them, the Court's caseload would be much heavier than it is. The justices reciprocate for this restraint by viewing the government's petitions in a favorable light. Further, the justices know that the government takes to the Court only the cases that its lawyers deem most worthy, so the justices also are inclined to view those cases as worthy.

Third, the attorneys in the solicitor general's office handle a great many Supreme Court cases, and they develop an unusual degree of expertise in dealing with the Court. Few other lawyers learn as much about how to appeal to the Court's interests. As a result, the government can do more than most other litigants to make cases appear worthy of acceptance.

It helps that the solicitor general represents the federal government, a litigant with unique status. This status is reflected in the Court's treatment of the solicitor general's office as something of a partner. But it is primarily the status of repeat player that accounts for the remarkable record of the solicitor general as a petitioner for certiorari.

Some other litigants and interest groups also enjoy advantages in securing hearings from the Court because of the expertise of their attorneys or their credibility with the justices—although these advantages fall well short of those held by the federal government. One 2004 case that the Court accepted suggests the importance of credibility. When a Texas inmate challenged his death sentence, the Court received an amicus brief arguing that it should consider the case because of serious procedural errors in the trial. The brief was signed by a former federal prosecutor, two retired judges from the federal courts of appeals, and a former federal judge who had also headed the Federal Bureau of Investigation (FBI). At the least, that unusual lineup of supporters for a criminal defendant must have attracted the justices' attention.[65]

Avoiding Problematic Cases. The Supreme Court agrees to hear a good many cases that involve controversial matters—cases in which the Court's decision may stir up considerable discontent. It accepts cases about abortion, the death penalty, and religious observances in public schools. At least four justices voted to hear *Bush v. Gore* despite their recognition that the Court's intervention in the 2000 presidential election was certain to make many people unhappy.

Yet the justices are always free to reject cases that have the potential to embroil the Court in controversy, and some denials of certiorari suggest that the justices may have had this consideration in mind. Two years after *Bush v. Gore*, the Court turned away another Republican challenge to a state court's interpretation of election law, this one from New Jersey. At least some of the justices may have been leery about the consequences of intervening once again.[66] In 2005 the Court refused to hear three cases challenging President Bush's temporary "recess" appointment of a federal judge whose confirmation had been blocked by Senate Democrats. The justices may have been influenced by the desire to avoid stepping into the heated battle between the parties over the selection of federal judges.[67]

Alabama attorney general William Pryor. President George W. Bush's recess appointment of Pryor to a federal judgeship raised an important legal issue in the context of strong partisan conflict; in 2005 the Supreme Court chose not to address that issue.

One consequential example of the Court's caution was its refusal to rule on whether it was constitutional for the United States to participate in the war in Vietnam without a declaration of war. Few issues brought to the Court have been so important, but the Court refused to hear the cases that raised this question between 1967 and 1972. Undoubtedly, some justices wanted to avoid injecting the Court into the most important and most disputed issue of national policy.

Often the Court's refusal to address a difficult issue is only temporary. It may accept a case on that issue later, when a more appropriate case comes to it or the issue has "percolated" in the lower courts. If an issue recurs often enough and has considerable importance, the justices may feel a degree of pressure to address it at some point.

Summary. When Supreme Court justices vote on petitions for hearings by the Court, their choices reflect their goals and perspectives. Each justice acts on a complex set of considerations. Inevitably, justices with different priorities and perspectives respond differently to petitions. Some give a higher priority to resolving conflicts among lower courts than others. They assess the importance of cases in various ways. And they act on quite different sets of policy preferences.

It follows that the Court's selection of cases to decide fully, like everything else it does, is affected by its membership at any given time. Most cases are unlikely to be accepted no matter who is on the Court. But the composition of the cases the Supreme Court actually accepts in a term strongly reflects the identities of the justices who serve during that term.

Caseload Growth and the Court's Response

During the 2004 term litigants brought nearly 7,500 cases to the Supreme Court. That number was well below the record of 8,255 in the 2002 term, but it was still high by historical standards. The 1961 term was the first one in which the Court received as many as 2,000 cases, and the first term with 4,000 cases was 1979. The growth in the Court's caseload over the years can be seen in the "total petitions" line in Figure 3-1.

The long-term growth in caseload reflects two quite different processes in two different periods. The first was a general growth that culminated in the 1960s. In part, this growth reflected broad developments in American society: a larger population, an apparent increase in "rights consciousness" that led people to bring more legal claims, and the development of interest groups that assist litigants in carrying cases through the courts. Meanwhile, massive growth in the activities of the federal government produced new laws and legal questions.

The Court contributed to this trend by allowing indigent litigants to file paupers' petitions without meeting all the ordinary requirements for filing cases. In addition, the Court showed considerable sympathy for claims that government actions violated civil liberties. This sympathy encouraged those who felt their rights had been violated, whether they were criminal defendants or members of racial minority groups, to bring cases to the Court.

After a period of relative stability in the Court's caseload, a second period of rapid growth began in the late 1980s and continued into the current decade. The number of petitions in the 2000–2004 terms was 72 percent higher than the number in the 1985–1989 terms. As Figure 3-1 shows, this new rise in cases is entirely in the paupers' petitions. The number of paid petitions per term has been remarkably stable, remaining between 1,700 and 2,300 in every term since 1971. In contrast, the number of paupers' petitions, which hovered around 2,000 per term from the late 1960s to the mid-1980s, grew to the point that there was an average of more than 6,000 per term in the 2000–2004 terms—more than three times the number of paid petitions.

The preponderance of paupers' petitions come from prisoners, and the number of adults in prison more than quadrupled between 1980 and

FIGURE 3-1
*Paid and Paupers' Cases Filed in the Supreme Court per Term,
by Five-Year Averages, 1960–2004 Terms*

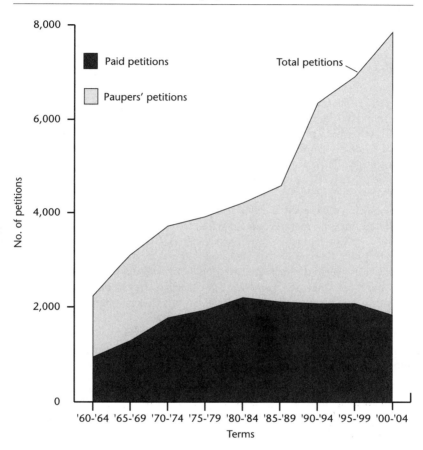

Sources: Gerhard Casper and Richard A. Posner, *The Workload of the Supreme Court* (Chicago: American Bar Foundation, 1976), 34; "Statistical Recap of Supreme Court's Workload During Last Three Terms," *United States Law Week,* various years.

2003.[68] This trend accounts for most if not all of the increase in paupers' cases. Indeed, this growth has occurred even though other factors that affect criminal petitions have worked in the opposite direction. The Court has become much less favorable to the claims brought by criminal defendants since the 1960s, and more recently both Congress and the Court have limited the use of habeas corpus actions to challenge criminal convictions.

After the period of caseload growth that culminated in the 1960s, observers of the Court and the justices themselves argued that the larger number of cases had created problems for the Court and for federal law. For the Court, the perceived problem was that the justices' ability to do their work well was compromised by the increased volume of work. For federal law, the concern was that the Court was accepting a smaller proportion of petitions as their numbers grew, so important issues were going unresolved.

These concerns resulted in proposals to create a new court between the courts of appeals and the Supreme Court as a way to address the problems resulting from caseload growth. Depending on the proposal, this new court would help the Supreme Court to screen petitions for hearings or it would actually decide some cases in place of the Court. Although some justices favored these proposals, the support for them on the Court and elsewhere in government was insufficient for Congress to make such a major change in the structure of the judicial branch.

Beginning in the late 1980s, the Court acted on its own to make an unofficial but major change. After William Rehnquist became chief justice in 1986, the Court began to accept fewer cases. Between the mid-1980s and the late 1990s, the number of decisions with full, signed opinions dropped from 140 per term to 80. Since then the Court has maintained these lower caseloads. Although the justices undoubtedly were aware that they were accepting fewer cases, this decline seems to reflect a combination of several developments, including changes in the Court's membership, rather than a single deliberate choice.[69]

If the Court of the 1970s suffered from a workload problem, that problem apparently has been solved. Because the number of paid petitions for hearings has not risen in the past thirty years, the justices have had ample time to adjust to that number. The continuing growth in paupers' petitions has little impact on the justices, as so few are considered seriously. Meanwhile, the work involved in reaching decisions on the merits was cut essentially in half in the Rehnquist Court.

If the Court of the 1970s was failing to resolve important issues in federal law, however, the reduction in the number of cases it heard aggravated that problem. As long ago as 1987, Chief Justice Rehnquist said that the Court was failing to hear some cases involving important legal questions that it would have heard thirty years earlier.[70] Not everyone agrees that there is a problem. In 2003 Justice Kennedy said that the number of cases heard by the Court "frankly, is too low" but added that the Court was deciding the cases that merited its review.[71] Still, the Court almost surely bypasses more significant legal questions today than it did two decades ago.

In any event, the difficulty of gaining a hearing in the Supreme Court has increased. In its 1985 term, the Court accepted for full consideration about 1 in 12 of the paid petitions filed with it; in the 2004 term that rate dropped to 1 in 24. For paupers' petitions the decline was even more precipitous, from an already low 1 in 108 in 1985 to a spectacularly low 1 in 528 in 2004.[72]

At his confirmation hearing in 2005, Chief Justice Roberts indicated that he was inclined to accept more cases than the Court had heard during the Rehnquist Court. "I think there's room for additional cases on the docket."[73] If the Roberts Court does increase the size of the Court's agenda, petitioners' chances to get a hearing from the Court may improve. But even those who file paid petitions will continue to face steep odds against winning a hearing from the Court.

Conclusion

Like other courts, the Supreme Court can decide only the cases that come to it. For that reason, people and institutions outside the Court have a great effect on the Court's agenda. Ultimately, however, the Court determines which cases it hears. From the wide variety of legal and policy questions brought to the Court, the justices can choose the few that they will address fully. They can also choose which issues in a case they will decide. And the justices help determine which cases are brought to them by suggesting in their opinions what kinds of legal claims they will view favorably in future cases.

The Court is often criticized for its choices of cases to hear and turn aside, and in recent years it has also been criticized for the small number of cases it accepts each term. Whatever the validity of these criticisms may be, the justices employ their agenda-setting powers rather well to serve their purposes. They accept and reject cases on the basis of individual and collective goals, such as avoiding troublesome issues, resolving legal conflicts, and establishing policies that the justices favor. The justices' selection of cases for full decisions helps them shape the Court's role as a policymaker. They also use that process to limit their workloads.

After the Court selects the cases to hear, it decides those cases. In the next chapter, I examine the Court's decision-making process and the forces that shape its choices.

NOTES

1. This summary of the distribution of litigants across categories is based in part on Gregory A. Caldeira and John R. Wright, "Parties, Direct Representatives, and Agenda-Setting in the Supreme Court" (paper presented at the annual meeting of the Midwest Political Science Association, Chicago, April 1989).
2. The description of the *Stewart* case is based on court briefs and opinions.

3. The description of the *Van Orden* case is based primarily on press reports, including Sylvia Moreno, "Supreme Court on a Shoestring," *Washington Post*, February 21, 2005, A1, A7; and Ralph Blumenthal, "An Unlikely Journey Up the Legal Ladder," *New York Times*, March 3, 2005, A18.

4. Moreno, "Supreme Court on a Shoestring," A7.

5. *Van Orden v. Perry*, 162 L. Ed. 2d 607, 657 (2005).

6. The case was *Hiibel v. District Court* (2004). Hiibel's Web site is at www.papersplease.org/hiibel/.

7. Joseph Margulies, "A Prison beyond the Law," *Virginia Quarterly Review* 80 (fall 2004): 39.

8. J. Richard Cohen, "Pretender in Paradise," *Journal of Appellate Practice and Process* 5 (spring 2003): 87.

9. Tony Mauro, "Justices Hear High-Stakes Patent Fight," *Legal Times*, March 29, 2006. Online at www.legaltimes.com. The case was *eBay v. MercExchange* (2006).

10. J. Thomas Sullivan, "Twice Grilled," *Journal of Appellate Practice and Process* 5 (spring 2003): 152.

11. Tony Mauro, "'Under God' Underdog?" *Legal Times,* June 23, 2003, 9.

12. Linda Greenhouse, "Atheist Presents Case for Taking God from Pledge," *New York Times*, March 25, 2004, A1.

13. "Stepping Back from the Fray," *Legal Times*, August 9, 2004, 24.

14. David Feige, "The Supreme Beginner," *Los Angeles Times Magazine*, December 5, 2004, 18–20, 28.

15. Tony Mauro, "Pay Cut," *Legal Times*, April 5, 2004, 3.

16. Walter Dellinger, "Why Me?" *Journal of Appellate Practice and Process* 5 (spring 2003): 95.

17. *In the Matter of Clinton* (2001).

18. This discussion of the *Kelo* case is based in part on materials on the Institute for Justice Web site, at www.ij.org/, accessed October 29, 2005.

19. Figures on amicus briefs in the 2004 term were compiled from docket sheets on the Supreme Court Web site at www.supremecourtus.gov.

20. The discussion in this paragraph is based in part on Marcia Coyle, "Court Hears Many Voices in One Case," *National Law Journal*, May 1, 2000, A1, A12, A13. See Thomas G. Hansford, "Information Provision, Organizational Constraints, and the Decision to Submit an Amicus Curiae Brief in a U.S. Supreme Court Case," *Political Research Quarterly* 57 (June 2004): 219–230.

21. The pre-2004 figures are from Joseph D. Kearney and Thomas W. Merrill, "The Influence of Amicus Curiae Briefs on the Supreme Court," *University of Pennsylvania Law Review* 148 (January 2000): 754n26. See also Ryan J. Owens and Lee Epstein, "Amici Curiae during the Rehnquist Years," *Judicature* 89 (November–December 2005): 127–132.

22. *Grutter v. Bollinger* (2003).

23. Kearney and Merrill, "Influence of Amicus Curiae Briefs," 821–824.

24. See Samuel Walker, *In Defense of American Liberties: A History of the ACLU*, 2d ed. (Carbondale: Southern Illinois University Press, 1999).

25. *Grutter v. Bollinger* (2003); *Gratz v. Bollinger* (2003). See Shira Kantor, "Conservative Crusaders Target Affirmative Action in Court," *Chicago Tribune,* January 19, 2003, sec. 1, p. 10.

26. Steven P. Brown, *Trumping Religion: The New Christian Right, the Free Speech Clause, and the Courts* (Tuscaloosa: University of Alabama Press, 2002);

Hans J. Hacker, *The Culture of Conservative Christian Litigation* (Lanham, Md.: Rowman and Littlefield, 2005).

27. Thomas G. Hansford, "Information Provision, Organizational Constraints, and the Decision to Submit an Amicus Curiae Brief in a U.S. Supreme Court Case," *Political Research Quarterly* 57 (June 2004): 219–230.

28. Charles R. Epp, *The Rights Revolution: Lawyers, Activists, and Supreme Courts in Comparative Perspective* (Chicago: University of Chicago Press, 1998), 44–70.

29. Some of the data on the federal government's participation that are discussed here and later in this section were provided by the Office of the Solicitor General.

30. This discussion is based in part on Richard L. Pacelle Jr., *Between Law and Politics: The Solicitor General and the Structuring of Civil Rights, Gender, and Reproductive Rights Litigation* (College Station: Texas A&M University Press, 2003).

31. Ibid.

32. Marcia Coyle, "New Light on an Old Defense of 'Secrets,' " *National Law Journal*, March 10, 2003, A1, A11; Joan Biskupic, "Conyers Asks Whether Torture Denial Was a Lie," *USA Today*, May 20, 2004, 11A.

33. This information is from the Web site of the Office of the Solicitor General, at www.usdoj.gov/osg/briefs/2004/2004brieftypes.html.

34. Tony Mauro, "Decalogue Defense," *Legal Times*, December 13, 2004, 3. The case was *McCreary County v. American Civil Liberties Union* (2005).

35. Neil A. Lewis, "President Faults Race Preferences as Admission Tool," *New York Times*, January 16, 2003, A1, A24. The cases were *Grutter v. Bollinger* (2003) and *Gratz v. Bollinger* (2003).

36. Pacelle, *Between Law and Politics*, 202.

37. Vanessa Blum, "Point Man," *Legal Times*, January 12, 2004, 1, 11, 12.

38. "Statistical Recap of Supreme Court's Workload during Last Three Terms," *United States Law Week* 74 (August 2, 2005): 3076.

39. See Michael E. Solimine and Rafael Gely, "The Supreme Court and the DIG: An Empirical and Institutional Analysis," *Wisconsin Law Review* 2005 (2005): 1421–1478.

40. Nick Anderson, "New Law Hurts Chicago Case in Gun Industry Suit," *Los Angeles Times*, February 27, 2003, A17.

41. See Cristina Lane, "Pay Up or Shut Up: The Supreme Court's Prospective Denial of In Forma Pauperis Petitions," *Northwestern University Law Review* 98 (2003): 335–366.

42. John Paul Stevens, foreword to Kenneth A. Manaster, *Illinois Justice: The Scandal of 1969 and the Rise of John Paul Stevens* (Chicago: University of Chicago Press, 2001), xi.

43. "Statistical Recap of Supreme Court's Workload," 3076.

44. Wendy L. Watson, "The U.S. Supreme Court's Selection of Petitions *In Forma Pauperis*" (Ph.D. diss., Ohio State University, 2004), chap. 5.

45. This examination of the discuss list and of the conference is based in part on H.W. Perry Jr., *Deciding to Decide: Agenda Setting in the United States Supreme Court* (Cambridge: Harvard University Press, 1991), 43–51, 85–91.

46. Artemus Ward and David L. Weiden, *Sorcerers' Apprentices: 100 Years of Law Clerks at the United States Supreme Court* (New York: New York University Press, 2006), 126.

47. Tony Mauro, "Roberts May Look to Stay Out of the Pool," *Legal Times*, August 15, 2005. Online at www.legaltimes.com.

48. Sean Donahue, "Behind the Pillars of Justice: Remarks on Law Clerks," *Long Term View* 3 (spring 1995): 80.
49. William H. Rehnquist, *The Supreme Court,* new ed. (New York: Alfred A. Knopf, 2001), 233.
50. Barbara Palmer, "The 'Bermuda Triangle?' The Cert Pool and Its Influence Over the Supreme Court's Agenda," *Constitutional Commentary* 18 (2001): 111.
51. Tom Miller, "Breyer Speaks to Bar Convention," *Alaska Bar Rag,* May–June 2001, 10.
52. "Judicial Conference, Second Judicial Circuit of the United States," 178 *Federal Rules Decisions* 210, 282 (1997).
53. This discussion draws from Arthur D. Hellman, "Never the Same River Twice: The Empirics and Epistemology of Intercircuit Conflicts," *University of Pittsburgh Law Review* 63 (fall 2001): 81–157.
54. Thomas Goldstein, "One Plugged, Thousands to Go," *Legal Times,* November 18, 2002, 68.
55. Tony Mauro, "Court Aces," *Legal Times,* July 14, 2003, 11.
56. The cases were *United States v. Booker* and *United States v. Fanfan* (2005).
57. "What You Might Hear if Scalia Held Court," *New York Daily News,* November 23, 2005, at www.nydailynews.com.
58. John Hanna, "Justice Thomas Hopes for Smooth Election," *The State* (Columbia, S.C.), October 28, 2004, at www.thestate.com.
59. The proportion for the Supreme Court is based on data in the Supreme Court Database, compiled by Harold Spaeth, archived at www.as.uky.edu/polisci/ulmerproject/sctdata.htm. The proportion for the courts of appeals is based on data in Administrative Office of the United States Courts, *Judicial Business of the United States Courts: Report of the Director, 2004* (Washington, D.C.: Administrative Office of the U.S. Courts, n.d.), 100, and the same report for earlier years.
60. Gregory A. Caldeira, John R. Wright, and Christopher J.W. Zorn, "Sophisticated Voting and Gate-Keeping in the Supreme Court," *Journal of Law, Economics, and Organization* 15 (October 1999): 549–572.
61. Perry, *Deciding to Decide,* 198–207; quotation, 200.
62. Caldeira, Wright, and Zorn, "Sophisticated Voting and Gate-Keeping"; Charles M. Cameron, Jeffrey A. Segal, and Donald Songer, "Strategic Auditing in a Political Hierarchy: An Informational Model of the Supreme Court's Certiorari Decisions," *American Political Science Review* 94 (March 2000): 101–116; Sara C. Benesh, Saul Brenner, and Harold J. Spaeth, "Aggressive Grants by Affirm-Minded Justices," *American Politics Research* 30 (May 2002): 219–234.
63. These data were provided by the Office of the Solicitor General.
64. Marc Galanter, "Why the 'Haves' Come Out Ahead: Speculations on the Limits of Legal Change," *Law and Society Review* 9 (fall 1974): 97–125.
65. Lee Hockstader, "Ex-FBI Chief, Judges Take Interest in Texas Execution," *Washington Post,* March 10, 2003, A2. The case was *Banks v. Dretke* (2004).
66. *Forrester v. New Jersey Democratic Party* (2002).
67. Charles Lane, "Court Declines to Wade into Battle on Judge," *Washington Post,* March 22, 2005, A15. The cases were *Evans v. Stephens* (2005), *Miller v. United States* (2005), and *Franklin v. United States* (2005).
68. Ann L. Pastore and Kathleen Maguire, eds., *Sourcebook of Criminal Justice Statistics,* (Bureau of Justice Statistics, U.S. Department of Justice) at www.albany.edu/sourcebook, table 6.1.

69. David M. O'Brien, "A Diminished Plenary Docket," *Judicature* 89 (November–December 2005): 134–137, 182.
70. "Chief Justice Urges National Appeals Court, Repeal of Court's Mandatory Jurisdiction," *Third Branch,* July 1987, 1, 5.
71. "U.S. Representative Frank Wolf (R-Va.) Holds Hearing on FY 2004 Supreme Court Budget Request," FDCH Political Transcripts, April 9, 2003, at http://web.lexis-nexis.com/universe. See Tony Mauro, "Money Matters and Mandatory Minimums," *Legal Times,* April 14, 2003, 14.
72. These figures are based on data in "Statistical Recap of Supreme Court's Workload during Last Three Terms," *United States Law Week,* various years.
73. "Transcript: Judge John G. Roberts Jr. Hearing, Day Three," *Pittsburgh Post-Gazette,* September 15, 2005, at www.post-gazette.com.

Chapter 4

Decision Making

O nce the Supreme Court determines which cases to hear, the justices
get to the heart of their work: decision making in the cases they hear.
Ultimately, the Court's impact on government and on the nation as a whole
depends on the content of its decisions on the merits. How and why the
Court makes those decisions is the subject of this chapter.

Components of the Court's Decision

A Supreme Court decision on the merits has two components: the immediate outcome for the parties to the case and a statement of general legal
rules. In cases that the Court fully considers, it nearly always presents the
two components in an opinion. In the great majority of cases, at least five
justices subscribe to this opinion. As a result, it constitutes an authoritative statement by the Court.

The Court's opinions vary in form, but an opinion usually begins by
describing the background of the case. The opinion then turns to the legal
issues in the case, discussing the opposing views on those issues and indicating the Court's conclusions about them. The end of the opinion summarizes the outcome for the parties.

Except in the few cases the Court hears under its original jurisdiction,
the Court describes the outcome in relation to the lower-court decision it
is reviewing. The Court can affirm the lower-court decision, leaving that
court's treatment of the parties undisturbed. Alternatively, it can modify
or reverse the lower-court decision. The terms "modify" and "reverse" are
imprecise. In general, a reversal overturns the lower-court decision altogether or nearly so, and modification is a more limited, partial overturning.
The Court may also vacate (make void) the lower-court decision, an action
whose effect is similar to that of reversal.

When the Court does disturb a lower-court decision, it sometimes
makes a final judgment. More often, it remands the case to the lower court,

sending it back for reconsideration. The Court's opinion provides guidance on how the case should be reconsidered. For example, the opinion in a tax case may say that a court of appeals adopted the wrong interpretation of the federal tax laws and that the court should reexamine the case on the basis of a different interpretation. The Court's opinion in a 2005 case used typical language: "The judgment of the Court of Appeals is reversed, and the case is remanded for further proceedings consistent with this opinion."[1]

The outcome for the parties in *Bush v. Gore* affected the whole country. In most cases, however, the outcome has little impact beyond the parties themselves. Rather, what makes most decisions consequential is the statement of general legal rules that apply to the nation as a whole. When the Court's opinion resolves the legal issues in a case, it is not just providing guidance to a specific lower court in a specific case. It is also laying down rules that any court must follow in a case to which they apply and that can affect the behavior of people outside of court.

As a result, decisions that directly affect only a few people may have a substantial indirect effect on thousands or even millions of other people. In *Kelo v. City of New London* (2005), the Court ruled against the challenge of nine homeowners to one city's development plan that would have required them to sell their properties to the city. But the decision established a rule on the use of eminent domain powers that potentially affected all cities and every property owner in those cities.

The Court has choices about which legal rules it establishes in a case, just as it does about the outcome for the parties. A ruling for one of the parties often could be justified on any of several grounds, and the ground chosen by the Court helps to determine the long-term impact of its decision. If the Court overturns the death sentence for a particular defendant, it might base that decision on an unusual type of error in the defendant's trial. This decision would have a narrow impact. Or the Court could declare that the death penalty is unconstitutional under all circumstances and thereby make a fundamental policy change.

The Decision-Making Process

When the Court accepts a case for a decision on the merits, it initiates the decision-making process for that case. That process varies from case to case, but it typically involves several stages.

Presentation of Cases to the Court

The written briefs that the Court receives when it considers whether to hear a case usually discuss the merits of the case. Once a case has been accepted for oral argument and decision, attorneys for the parties submit new briefs that focus on the merits. In the preponderance of cases that reach this stage, interest groups submit amicus curiae briefs stating their own arguments on the merits.

Most of the material in these briefs concerns legal issues. The parties muster evidence to support their interpretations of relevant constitutional provisions and statutes. In their briefs they frequently offer arguments about policy as well, seeking to persuade the justices that support for their position constitutes not only good law but good public policy.

Material in the briefs is supplemented by attorneys' presentations in oral argument before the Court. Attorneys for the parties to a case sometimes share their time with the lawyer for an amicus, usually the federal government. In most cases, each side is provided half an hour for its argument. Occasionally, the Court grants more time, and in 2003 the parties in the constitutional challenges to the McCain-Feingold campaign finance law were given a total of four hours for argument.[2] When time expires a red light goes on at the attorneys' lectern. Lawyers and the justices who question them typically use all the time available. But in one 2005 case that went over much of the same ground as another case that the Court had recently decided, the argument ended twelve minutes early.[3]

Lawyers' presentations are often interrupted by questions and comments from members of the Court. As one observer said, "The lawyers show up with a big notebook full of speaking points, and the justices make it their business to make sure they never get to the second one."[4] In the 2005 term, the first with Chief Justice Roberts, the justices interrupted the lawyers (and each other) less frequently than in the recent past.[5] But it continues to be the justices who control the flow of argument.

Justices differ in how much they participate in the give-and-take of oral argument. During the Court's first sitting of the 2005 term, Antonin Scalia spoke most often, followed by Ruth Bader Ginsburg and John Roberts.[6] Scalia is typically the Court's most active questioner. At the other end of the spectrum, Clarence Thomas asked no questions during the eight arguments in that sitting, and it is uncommon for him to participate. One reason, he has said, is that "these people only have 30 minutes. Let them talk a little bit. We're not there to debate with them."[7]

Oral argument gives attorneys an opportunity to strengthen their cases by supplementing and highlighting the material in their briefs. For the justices, the argument has two broad functions. First, it allows them to gather information about the strengths and weaknesses of the parties' positions and about other aspects of the case that interest them. In part to serve this function, justices often raise new issues and arguments in their questions to the lawyers.[8]

Second, oral argument provides a forum in which justices try to shape their colleagues' perceptions of a case. Justices may introduce new matters into a case in order to strengthen the side they favor. They may also try to

Stanford law professor Jenny Martinez, a former Supreme Court law clerk, argues before the Court in 2004. Oral argument gives justices an opportunity to probe issues in a case and to try to influence their colleagues' views of the case.

expose weaknesses in the arguments of the other side. One study that examined justices' questions in relation to the positions they ultimately took in a case concluded that "the Justices simply give the side they disagree with a harder time."[9]

Justice Scalia stands out for his active use of oral argument to support the side he favors. Reporter Dahlia Lithwick wrote after one argument that her "choice for best oral advocate *ever* to appear before the U.S. Supreme Court is Associate Justice Antonin Scalia. While Scalia is a distinguished jurist, I'm not sure he always gets the credit he deserves on those days, like today, when he actually finds himself both hearing and arguing a case at the same time." After describing Scalia as "co-counsel" to one of the lawyers in a case, Lithwick reported that at one point the lawyer "actually begins to look toward Scalia for backup before responding" to a question.[10]

Tentative Decisions

After oral argument the Court discusses each case in one of its conferences later the same week. The conference is a closed session attended only by the justices. One might expect a freewheeling discussion of cases, with justices speaking at length and arguing back and forth. Under some chief justices, that has been the practice. Others, such as William Rehnquist, have imposed limits on discussion. Justice O'Connor described the discussion: "You go around the table in order of seniority with the chief justice beginning the discussion and it isn't a debate. Each justice just says, well, this is how I think this case ought to be resolved and why."[11]

Rehnquist's limits on conference discussion of cases reflected his view that such discussion would have little impact, since the justices typically come to the conference with strong views about the cases. He concluded that "it is very much the exception" for justices' minds to be changed in conference.[12] Chief Justice Roberts seems to have a different view, and his colleagues report that he allows more extensive discussion of cases in conference.[13] His practice may increase the effect of the conference on the Court's decisions.

After each two-week sitting, the writing of the Court's opinion in each case is assigned to a justice. If the chief justice voted with the majority, the chief assigns the opinion. In other cases, the most senior justice in the majority makes the assignment. Because so many conference votes are lopsided, the chief justice is usually among the majority. If the Court is divided, the senior justice in the minority assigns the primary dissenting opinion.

Reaching Final Decisions

The justice who was assigned the Court's opinion writes an initial draft, guided by the views expressed in conference. The justice's clerks often do most of the drafting. Once this opinion is completed and circulated, justices in the original majority usually sign on to it.[14] (Like other communications in the decision process, these responses nearly always are in writing rather than delivered in person.) Sometimes, however, they hold back, either because they have developed doubts about their original vote or because they disagree with some of the language in the draft opinion. Members of the original minority also read the draft opinion for the Court. Some might decide to sign on to the opinion because their view of the case has changed, or they might see a possibility of signing on if the opinion is modified.

Justices who do not immediately sign on may indicate fundamental disagreement with the opinion. Exaggerating somewhat, Justice Thomas has described such responses: "Dear Clarence, I disagree with everything in your opinion except your name. Cheers."[15] But justices often indicate that they would be willing to sign on if certain changes are made. Justices who voted with the majority are especially likely to ask for changes. Their memos initiate a process of explicit or implicit negotiation in which the assigned justice tries to gain the support of as many colleagues as possible. At the least, that justice wants to maintain the original majority for the outcome supported by the opinion and to win a majority for the language of the opinion, so that it becomes the official statement of the Court.

In this effort, the justice who was assigned the Court's opinion often competes with other justices, who write alternative opinions supporting the opposite outcome or arguing for the same outcome with a different

TABLE 4-1

Selected Characteristics of Supreme Court Decisions, 2004 Term

Characteristic	Number	Percentage
Number of decisions	80	NA
Vote for Court's decision[a]		
Unanimous	30	38
Nonunanimous	50	62
Support for Court's opinion		
Unanimous for whole opinion	23	29
Unanimous for part of opinion	3	4
Majority but not unanimous	49	61
Majority for only part of opinion	4	5
No majority for opinion	1	1
One or more dissenting opinions[b]	49	61
One or more concurring opinions[c]	42	53
Total number of opinions		
Dissenting	66	NA
Concurring	58	NA

Note: NA = not applicable. The decisions included are those listed in the front section of *Supreme Court Reports, Lawyer's Edition,* vols. 160–162, and information on cases is taken from that source.

a. "Decision" refers to the outcome for the parties. Partial dissents are not counted as votes for the decision.

b. Opinions labeled "concurring and dissenting" are treated as dissenting opinions.

c. Some concurring opinions are in full agreement with the Court's opinion.

rationale. Most of the time, assigned justices succeed in winning a majority for their opinions, although sometimes with very substantial alterations. More often than not, however, they fail to win the unanimous support of their colleagues. Table 4-1, which lists several characteristics of the Court's decisions in the 2004 term, shows that such unanimity was achieved only 29 percent of the time.

Occasionally, no opinion gains the support of a majority. As shown in Table 4-1, this occurred only once in the 2004 term. In that case, *Van Orden v. Perry* (2005), there were seven different opinions. In four other cases an opinion had majority support only in part. Without a majority opinion, there is no authoritative statement of the Court's position on the legal issues in the case. The opinion on the winning side with the greatest support— the "plurality opinion"—may, however, specify the points for which majority support exists.

On rare occasions the justices find themselves unable to reach a final decision in a case before the term ends. They then schedule the case for a second set of oral arguments, usually in the following term. The Court took this route in both *Brown v. Board of Education* and *Roe v. Wade*. It also heard rearguments in three cases that were originally heard early in the 2005 term. Most observers inferred that Justice O'Connor's retirement before the Court completed the decision process left the Court in a 4–4 tie in each case. Rescheduling the cases would allow her successor, Samuel Alito, to participate in the decision and thus ensure there would be no tie votes.[16]

Concurring and Dissenting Opinions

In most cases, an opinion gains a majority but lacks unanimous support. Disagreement with the majority opinion can take two forms. First, a justice may cast a dissenting vote, which expresses disagreement with the result reached by the Court as it affects the parties to a case. If a criminal conviction is reversed, for example, a justice who believes it should have been affirmed will dissent. Second, a justice may concur with the Court's decision, agreeing with the result in the specific case but differing with the rationale expressed in the Court's opinion. Both kinds of disagreement are common. Dissenting votes are especially common, appearing in a majority of decisions.

A justice who disagrees with the majority opinion generally writes or joins in a dissenting or concurring opinion. Because they are individual expressions rather than statements for the Court, both types of opinions can vary a great deal in length, form, and tone. For the same reason, they usually reveal more about the author's views, and often express those views in more colorful language, than do majority opinions.

When a justice writes a dissenting opinion after conference, one aim often is to persuade enough colleagues to change their positions that a minority becomes a majority. After the Court reaches its final decision, this aim is no longer relevant, but issuing a dissenting opinion can serve several purposes.

For one thing, dissenting opinions give justices who disagree with the result in a case the satisfaction of expressing unhappiness with that result and justifying their disagreement. Dissenting opinions sometimes have more concrete purposes as well. Through their arguments, dissenters may try to set the stage for a later Court to adopt their view. In the short term, a dissenting opinion may be intended to subvert the Court's decision by pointing out how lower courts can interpret it narrowly or by urging Congress to overturn the Court's reading of a statute. This is one reason that majority opinions sometimes respond to dissents. In *Stogner v. California* (2003), Justice Breyer used nearly half his opinion to refute Justice Kennedy's dissent.

When more than one justice dissents, the dissenters usually join in a single opinion—most likely the opinion originally assigned by the senior dissenting justice. But often there are multiple dissenting opinions, each expressing the particular view of the justice who wrote it although sometimes indicating agreement with another opinion.

As noted earlier, a concurring opinion can disagree with the majority opinion on the rationale for a decision. This kind of opinion is labeled a "special concurrence." Sometimes this disagreement on doctrine is virtually total. In *Smith v. City of Jackson* (2005), the majority opinion ruled that an individual could bring a lawsuit for age discrimination in employment on the ground that an employer's practice had a "disparate impact" on older workers, but it held that the plaintiffs in this case had not demonstrated a disparate impact. In contrast, Justice O'Connor's concurring opinion argued that older workers could not bring disparate impact cases. Sometimes the disagreement is more limited. In *Thornton v. United States* (2004), O'Connor joined the whole majority opinion except for a footnote.

Another type of concurring opinion, a "regular concurrence," is written by justices who join the majority opinion, indicating that they agree with both the outcome for the litigants and the legal rules that the Court establishes. Under those circumstances, why would justices write separate opinions? Most often, they offer their own interpretation of the majority opinion as a means to influence lower courts and other audiences as well as the Court itself in future cases. "While I join the Court's opinion," a concurrence may say, "I do so on the understanding that ...." [17] Occasionally, as in two 2005 decisions, a regular concurrence addresses the arguments in a dissenting opinion. [18]

Announcing the Decision

The decision-making process for a case ends when all the opinions have been put in final form and all justices have determined which opinions they will join. In contrast with the great majority of other courts, the Supreme Court announces its decisions in a court session, in what one commentator called "ceremonial showtime." [19] Typically, the justice who wrote the majority opinion reads a portion of the opinion. Occasionally, the authors of dissenting opinions also read their opinions.

The length of time required for a case to go through all the stages from filing in the Court to the announcement of a decision can vary a good deal. The cases that the Court decided after full consideration in June 2005 were filed as early as March 2004 and as late as November of that year.

After the Court decides a case—or declines to hear it—the losing party may petition for a rehearing. Such petitions are rarely granted. But after the Court struck down the mandatory federal sentencing guidelines in *United*

States v. Booker (2005), it granted rehearings in more than a dozen cases that it had declined to hear, remanding each case to a lower court for reconsideration in light of *Booker.*

Influences on Decisions: Introduction

Of all the questions that might be asked about the Supreme Court, the one that has intrigued people most is why the Court reaches the decisions that it hands down. Cases present the justices with choices: which party to support, what rules of law to establish. How can these choices be explained?

This question is difficult to answer. Like policymakers elsewhere in government, Supreme Court justices act on the basis of several intermixed considerations. It is not surprising that people who study the Court differ sharply in their explanations of the Court's decisions.

The rest of this chapter is devoted to this question. No conclusive answer is possible, but some insight into the bases for the Court's decisions can be gained by looking at four broad forces that shape those decisions: the state of the legal rules the Court interprets, the justices' personal values, interaction among the justices, and the Court's political and social environment. The sections that follow consider each of these forces.

The State of the Law

Every case requires the Supreme Court to interpret the law, usually in the form of constitutional provisions or federal statutes. In this sense a justice's job is different from that of a legislator: justices interpret existing law rather than write new law. For this reason, the state of the existing law is a good starting point for an explanation of the Court's decisions.

The Law's Significance in Decisions

Judges and justices are servants of the law, not the other way around. Judges are like umpires. Umpires don't make the rules; they apply them. The role of an umpire and a judge is critical. They make sure everybody plays by the rules. But it is a limited role. Nobody ever went to a ball game to see the umpire.[20]

In his opening remarks before the Senate Judiciary Committee in 2005, Chief Justice nominee John Roberts articulated one view about the role of the law in Supreme Court positions. In effect, Roberts was saying that the law is the *only* explanation of what the Court does, that its decisions simply reflect the provisions of law it is called upon to interpret and the appropriate rules for interpreting those provisions. That position has been expressed by other justices as well, but it does not accord with two realities about the Court.

One reality is what might be called the legal ambiguity of the cases the Supreme Court decides. In at least the great majority of cases the Court chooses to hear, the proper interpretation of the Constitution or a federal statute is uncertain. A justice who intended only to interpret the law properly would still have to make choices.

A second reality is that justices care about more than the law. In particular, they often hold strong preferences about the policy issues involved in cases. Understandably, they would be happier if their position in a case was consistent with their policy preferences than if their position conflicted with their conception of good policy.

Justices may act consciously to make good policy. Justice Breyer said, "If you see the result is going to make people's lives worse, you'd better go back and rethink it. The law is supposed to fit together in a way that makes the human life of people a little bit better."[21] The legal ambiguity of cases allows such justices to provide legal justification for the decisions they prefer. Presumably, baseball umpires do not have "rooting interests" in victory for one side. Justices' policy preferences often give them such interests.

Even if justices consciously seek only to interpret the law properly, they will tend toward the interpretation that is most consistent with their policy preferences. One of Justice Frankfurter's law clerks described that process well in talking about Frankfurter.

He felt very intensely about lots of things, and sometimes he didn't realize that his feelings and his deeply felt values were pushing him as a judge relentlessly in one direction rather than another. I'm sure that you can put these things aside consciously, but what's underneath the consciousness you can't control.[22]

Thus, it is understandable that in most decisions the justices disagree about the outcome for the litigants, the appropriate legal rules, or both. The primary reason for those disagreements is that the ambiguity of the law causes justices with different preferences to reach different conclusions.

Because of this ambiguity, it can be argued that the state of the law is irrelevant to the justices. Federal judge Richard Posner said that "from a practical standpoint, constitutional adjudication by the Supreme Court is also the exercise of discretion—and that is about all it is."[23] But legal considerations can still play a part in decisions. Even if decisions on either side could be justified under the law, the law may weigh more heavily on one side than the other. If the justices care about making good law, they would be drawn toward the side that seems to have a stronger legal argument.

And there is excellent reason to think that justices do care about making good law. They have been trained in a tradition that emphasizes the law as a basis for judicial decisions. They are evaluated informally by a peer group of judges and legal scholars who care about their ability to reach well-founded interpretations of the law. Perhaps most important, they work in the language of the law. The arguments they receive in written briefs and oral arguments are primarily about the law. The same is true of arguments they make to each other in draft opinions and memoranda.[24]

It is impossible to specify just how much the state of the law affects justices, and scholars have heated disagreements about this issue.[25] But the law does exert an influence. This influence is clearest when justices take positions that seem to conflict with their conceptions of good policy. Sometimes the justices in the majority are sufficiently unhappy with their interpretation of a statute that they ask Congress to consider rewriting the statute to override their decision—to establish a policy that they feel powerless to adopt themselves because of their reading of the law.[26]

Means of Interpretation

Judges can use an array of techniques to interpret provisions of law, but most of these techniques fit into a few broad approaches. Discussion of those approaches provides a way to consider the role of law in the Court's decisions.

"Plain Meaning." In the most basic approach, judges analyze the literal meaning of the words in the law. Nearly everyone agrees that interpretation of a legal provision should begin with a search for plain meaning, and many possible interpretations of the law are ruled out because they are inconsistent with plain meaning. For example, the Twenty-second Amendment to the Constitution states, "No person shall be elected to the office of the President more than twice." It is difficult to imagine how the Supreme Court could justify a ruling that a twice-elected person can be elected to a third term.

The Court seldom faces such easy issues, however. Most of the Court's decisions involve ambiguous provisions such as the Fourteenth Amendment's protection of "due process of law," which has no plain meaning. And even a provision that may seem to have a plain meaning can be interpreted in multiple ways. The First Amendment states that "Congress shall make no law ... abridging the freedom of speech," but justices and commentators have disagreed about the meaning of "freedom of speech" and even of "speech."

Federal statutes typically are less vague, but they often leave large gaps. One commentator complained that Congress "cannot or will not be specific."[27] And even specific language can be quite ambiguous. In extreme instances, as in a 2004 case, the Court confronts a statute that is "awkward," "ungrammatical," and containing "apparent legislative drafting error."[28]

The justices are not always bound by the apparent plain meaning of the law. Over time the Court has accepted interpretations of the Constitution that depart from the language of its provisions. The due process clause of the Fifth Amendment requires only that the federal government follow proper procedures in taking "life, liberty, or property," but the Court interprets it to prohibit discrimination.[29] It interprets the same language in the Fourteenth Amendment as a protection of freedom of expression and freedom of religion.[30] And for more than a century the Eleventh Amendment's prohibition of lawsuits against states "by citizens of another state" has been read to prohibit lawsuits by a state's own residents as well.[31]

Intent of Framers or Legislators. When the plain meaning of a legal provision is unclear, justices can seek to ascertain the intentions of those who wrote the provision. Evidence concerning legislative intent can be found in congressional committee reports and floor debates, which constitute what is called the "legislative history" of a statute or a constitutional amendment. For provisions of the original Constitution, similar evidence is found in records of the Constitutional Convention of 1787.

Sometimes the intent of Congress or the framers of the Constitution is fairly clear. Frequently, however, it is not. The body that adopted a provision may not have spoken on an issue; the members of Congress who wrote the broad language of the Fourteenth Amendment could hardly indicate their intent concerning all the issues that have arisen under that amendment. And evidence about intent may be contradictory, in part because of conflicting efforts to influence the courts. Some evidence of legislative intent comes from sources, such as committee reports, that may represent the views of congressional staff more than those of the members.

The use of intent in constitutional interpretation has long been the subject of controversy. Some people argue that the Court should adhere to the intent of the framers of each provision as closely as possible; others believe it should interpret the Constitution according to the current meaning of its language and its underlying values. To a considerable extent this is an ideological debate, with liberals wanting the freedom to adopt broad interpretations of constitutional rights. The debate has been especially heated on capital punishment. The Court's decisions prohibiting the death penalty for people who are mentally retarded (in 2002) and for murders committed when the defendant was not yet eighteen years old (in 2005) were based on the majority's view that the prohibition of "cruel and unusual punishments" in the Eighth Amendment should be interpreted on the basis of current values, but the dissenters gave greater emphasis to the meaning of that expression when the Eighth Amendment was written.[32]

There has been a somewhat different kind of debate about the use of legislative intent in interpreting statutes. The leading opponent is Justice Scalia, who views legislative history as illegitimate: it is the laws, not the intentions of legislators, that govern. Further, he sees legislative history as an uncertain and easily distorted guide to congressional intent. Accordingly, Scalia does

Senator Don Nickles, R-Okla., speaks on the floor of the Senate in 2004. Supreme Court justices disagree about whether it is appropriate to use speeches and other forms of "legislative history" to interpret federal statutes.

not refer to legislative history himself and sometimes distances himself from its use by his colleagues. In a 2004 decision, for instance, he did not join the Court's opinion because it was based largely on legislative history. Instead, he concurred "because the statute—the only sure expression of the will of Congress—says what the Court says it says."[33]

Scalia has gained some support for his view from colleagues, primarily other conservatives, and the Court's use of legislative history declined after he joined the Court.[34] But some justices—most vocally, Justice Stevens—continue to favor the use of legislative history. In a 2004 decision, three concurring opinions and a dissenting opinion expressed differing views about the extent to which the Court should make use of evidence about legislative intent, underlining the continuing disagreement about this issue.[35]

Precedent. The Supreme Court's past decisions, its precedents, provide another guide to decision making. A basic doctrine of the law is *stare decisis* (let the decision stand). Under this doctrine a court is bound to adhere to the rules of law established by courts that stand above it. No court stands above the Supreme Court, but *stare decisis* includes an expectation that courts will generally adhere to their own precedents.

Technically, a court is expected to follow not everything stated in a relevant precedent but only the rule of law that is necessary for decision in that case—what is called the holding. As Justice Souter said in a 1999 case, "a line of argument unnecessary to the decision of the case remains dictum,"[36] and "dictum" has no legal force. In *Halbert v. Michigan* (2005), the Court ruled that indigent criminal defendants who plead guilty or no contest in Michigan have the right to be provided with a lawyer if they later seek to appeal their convictions. The Court also said that the state could not require a defendant to waive that right. Because such a requirement was not involved in this case, the Court's statement about it was dictum.

The rule of adhering to precedent would not eliminate ambiguity in legal interpretation even if the justices followed it strictly. Most cases before the Supreme Court concern issues that are at least marginally different from those decided in past cases, so precedents do not lead directly to a particular outcome. Indeed, justices often "distinguish" a precedent, holding that it does not govern the current case. They may also narrow a precedent without overturning it altogether. Through both methods, the Burger and Rehnquist Courts limited the reach of major Warren Court decisions on the rights of criminal defendants.

The Court explicitly abandons some precedents, and it has done so at an unusually high rate since 1960. By one count, the Court has overturned an average of three precedents a year in this period, although the pace has slowed in recent years.[37] Justices are sometimes willing to overturn not just individual precedents but whole lines of Court doctrine. This is especially true of Justice Thomas. Justice Scalia said of him that "he does not believe in *stare decisis,* period."[38] Indeed, in one eight-day period in 2005, Thomas voiced his fundamental objections to major constitutional doctrines concerning the commerce clause of Article I, the takings clause of the Fifth Amendment, and the due process clause of the Fourteenth Amendment.[39]

Inevitably, justices' reactions to precedents are affected by their evaluations of those precedents as legal policy. Most of the time, justices continue to reject a precedent that they opposed when it was originally established.[40] In a 2003 decision, for instance, three justices who had dissented from a 1996 decision establishing constitutional limits on punitive damages reiterated their disapproval of that decision.[41] Moreover, the Court is most likely to weaken or overturn precedents after changes in its membership shift its collective point of view.[42] Many of the precedents overturned by the Rehnquist Court had been issued by the more liberal Warren and Burger Courts that preceded it.

All this may suggest that precedents carry no weight. Yet justices have a degree of reluctance—some more than others—to overturn precedents directly. The Court as a whole adheres to a good many precedents that no longer accord with the majority view among the justices. Further, there is evidence that justices modify their analyses of issues such as freedom of speech to fit new precedents that establish frameworks for those analyses.[43]

If the Court is not fully bound by its own precedents, it is not at all bound by interpretations of law from other courts. However, the justices frequently cite lower-court decisions in support of their positions. In recent years several justices have also cited decisions of courts outside the United States, most often in rulings that broaden constitutional rights. Justice Scalia and Justice Thomas have argued against this practice. It has also attracted criticism from conservatives outside the Court as well as a Web site posting that urged the murder of Justices Ginsburg and O'Connor for their citing of foreign sources.[44]

As for the Court's own precedents, the extent of their influence on the justices' positions in cases is uncertain and a matter of dispute among commentators. However, precedents clearly exert some impact. The rule of *stare decisis* does not control the Court's decisions, but it does structure and influence them. The same is true of the law in general: it channels the justices' choices, often in subtle ways, but it also leaves them considerable freedom in making those choices.

Justices' Values

When he likened judges to umpires, chief justice nominee John Roberts was taking a common position. Speaking to the Senate and the nation, nominees to the Court often say that their own judgments about what is good policy would be irrelevant to their choices on the Court.

Yet others involved in the selection of justices indicate by their actions that they do not share this conception of decision making on the Court. Presidents and their advisers work hard to identify nominees who share the administration's views on major issues of legal policy. Interest groups support or oppose nominees on the basis of their perceived values. And senators ask questions intended to ferret out nominees' attitudes toward issues that they would face as justices. All these people act on the assumption that justices' policy preferences have a fundamental impact on the votes they cast and the opinions they write.

The Influence of Policy Preferences

For the reasons I have already described, the position expressed by some nominees to the Court does not depict reality as accurately as the implicit position of other participants in the selection of justices. Because the state of the law leaves justices with considerable discretion, their choices must be based largely on other considerations. Because the Court has considerable freedom from external pressures, the most powerful of these other considerations are the justices' policy preferences.

It is difficult to ascertain the relationship between justices' preferences and their behavior as decision makers, simply because their preferences cannot be observed directly. But some evidence is highly suggestive. There is considerable consistency between the justices' expressions of personal views outside the Court and their votes and opinions in cases. Certainly this is true of the justices who speak and write most frequently about judicial issues, such as Stephen Breyer, Antonin Scalia, and Clarence Thomas. Similarly, the justices' positions on the Court tend to be consistent with those they took on similar issues before their appointment. To take one specific example, John Paul Stevens's opinion for the Court in *Rasul v. Bush* (2004) held that federal courts could review the detention of noncitizens at Guantanamo Bay Naval Base. More than fifty years earlier, as a law clerk to Justice Wiley Rutledge, Stevens had contributed language to a Rutledge dissent that followed similar lines.[45]

Some scholars argue that the justices' policy preferences are essentially a complete explanation of the Court's decisions.[46] In contrast, I think that the justices' preferences exert their effects in combination with other important forces, such as the political environment—and, for that matter, the law. But policy preferences certainly provide the best explanation for differences in the positions that the nine justices take in the same cases, because no other factor varies so much from one justice to another.

Justices' attitudes on policy issues result from the same influences that shape political attitudes generally. Family socialization, religious training, and career experiences all shape the values of people who become Supreme Court justices. Because justices have different backgrounds and learn different things from those backgrounds, each brings a particular set of attitudes to the Court.

The justices' behavior on the Court could reflect their policy preferences in two different ways. Justices might simply take the positions that best reflect their views of good policy. Or they might act strategically, adjusting their positions where doing so might advance the policies they favor. In Chapter 3, I discussed strategy in decisions whether to accept cases: to a degree, justices vote whether to hear cases on the basis of their predictions about how the Court would rule on those cases. In decisions on the merits, strategic justices might write opinions that do not fully reflect their own views in order to win the support of other justices. Or the Court collectively could modify its position on an issue to reduce the chances that Congress will override the Court's decision and substitute a policy that most justices would want to avoid.

It is not clear to what extent the justices behave strategically and what forms their strategies take.[47] But it appears that strategic considerations seldom move justices very far from the positions they most prefer. For this reason, the impact of justices' policy preferences can be considered initially without taking strategy into account. In the next two sections, I consider strategy aimed at other justices and at the Court's political environment.

The Ideological Dimension

On most issues that come to the Court, the opposing positions can be labeled as liberal and conservative. For this reason justices' preferences, and the votes and opinions that reflect those preferences, may be understood in ideological terms.

Defining Liberal and Conservative Positions. The positions from which justices can choose are most easily defined on civil liberties issues. In this field the position more favorable to legal protection for liberties is typically considered liberal. Thus, the liberal position gives relatively great weight to the right to equal treatment by government and private institutions, procedural rights of criminal defendants and others who deal with government, and substantive rights such as freedom of expression and privacy. In contrast, the conservative position gives relatively great weight to values that compete with these rights, such as the capacity to fight crime effectively and to maintain national security.

On economic issues, liberal and conservative positions are often more difficult to define. But the liberal position is basically more favorable to economic "underdogs" and to government policies that are intended to benefit underdogs. In contrast, the conservative position is more positive toward businesses in conflicts with labor unions and toward efforts by businesses to limit government regulation of their practices.

Some cases that come before the Supreme Court, such as boundary disputes between two states, do not have obvious liberal and conservative sides. On some other issues, ideological lines in American society and thus in the Court have become more complicated. Still, most issues that the Court decides do have clearly defined conservative and liberal sides.

Ideology and Decisions. If opposing positions in most cases can be identified as liberal or conservative, the justices' voting patterns can be described in terms of the frequency with which they support the conservative side and the liberal side. Table 4-2 shows the ideological patterns of votes for the justices in the 1994 through 2004 terms, the long period when the same nine justices sat on the Court. The table shows that every justice cast a good many votes on both sides. But the justices also differed considerably in their ideological tendencies: the three most liberal justices (Stevens, Ginsburg, and Souter) supported the liberal side more than twice as often as their two most conservative colleagues (Scalia and Thomas).

When justices respond differently to the same cases, the primary reason is differences in their policy preferences. Thus one can conclude from Table 4-2 that Justice Thomas is considerably more conservative than Justice

TABLE 4-2
*Percentages of Liberal Votes
Cast by Justices, 1994–2004 Terms*

Justice	Liberal votes
Stevens	67.1
Ginsburg	61.9
Souter	61.7
Breyer	57.9
O'Connor	42.3
Kennedy	41.9
Rehnquist	33.9
Scalia	30.9
Thomas	28.7

Source: U.S. Supreme Court Database, compiled by Harold Spaeth, Michigan State University, at www.as.uky.edu/polisci/ulmerproject/sctdata.htm.

Note: Cases are included if they were decided on the merits with full opinions and if votes could be classified as liberal or conservative. Criteria for classifying votes are those used in the database.

Stevens. This is especially true because the relative positions of the justices on a liberal-conservative scale tend to remain fairly stable from term to term. It is also true that the justices' relative positions tend to be similar across different issues. This similarity, however, is far from absolute. A justice who has one of the most liberal voting records on conflicts between business and labor may have a relatively conservative record on criminal justice.

Within specific areas of policy, the degree of consistency is somewhat greater but typically quite imperfect. The degree of consistency can be measured by what is called a scalogram. If the nine justices can be ranked from most liberal to most conservative in the same way for all the issues that arise in a category, such as criminal cases, the result would be a distinctive pattern of votes on cases in that category. Each time the most conservative justice votes for the liberal position in a case, every other justice should do so as well; each time the second most conservative justice casts a liberal vote, the seven more liberal justices should also do so; and so on. Any deviation from that pattern represents an ideological inconsistency. Scalograms, limited to nonunanimous decisions, lay out the actual pattern of liberal and conservative votes to show how closely they follow this expected pattern.

A scalogram depicting a relatively high level of ideological consistency is presented in Figure 4-1, which shows votes in criminal cases during the

FIGURE 4-1
Scalogram of Justices' Votes in Nonunanimous Decisions Arising from Criminal Prosecutions, 2003 Term

Case citation[a]	Justices' votes									Liberal votes
	So	St	Gi	Br	Ke	O'C	Sc	Re	Th	
540-668	+	+	+	+	+	+	-	+	-	7
542-274	+	+	+	+	+	+	-	-	-	6
542-600	+	+	+	+	+	-	-	-	-	5
542-296	+	+	+	-	-	-	+	-	+	5
541-652	+	+	+	+	-	-	-	-	-	4
542-406	+	+	+	+	-	-	-	-	-	4
542-177	+	+	+	+	-	-	-	-	-	4
542-649	+	+	+	+	-	-	-	-	-	4
542-348	+	+	+	+	-	-	-	-	-	4
542-630	+	+	+	+	-	-	-	-	-	4
540-419	+	+	+	-	-	-	-	-	-	3
541-386	+	+	-	-	+	-	-	-	-	3
541-615	+	+	-	-	-	-	-	-	-	2
541-193	+	-	-	-	-	-	+	-	-	2
542-225	-	-	+	+	-	-	-	-	-	2
541-27	-	+	-	-	-	-	-	-	-	1
Total liberal votes	14	14	12	10	4	2	2	1	1	

Note: Cases are those arising from criminal prosecutions that were decided on the merits. Liberal votes (favoring defendants) are designated +; conservative votes (opposing defendants) are designated –. The stepped vertical line divides votes into groups; – signs to the left of the line and + signs to the right of the line may be interpreted as votes inconsistent with the ideological ordering of the justices.

Key: So = Souter; St = Stevens; Gi = Ginsburg; Br = Breyer; Ke = Kennedy; O'C = O'Connor; Sc = Scalia; Re = Rehnquist; Th = Thomas.

a. Numbers refer to volumes and pages of citations in the *United States Reports*.

Court's 2003 term. The justices varied a good deal in their support for criminal defendants. Stevens and Souter each cast votes for defendants in all but two of the decisions, whereas four of their colleagues cast only one or two votes for defendants in those cases. The scalogram shows that to a considerable extent the divisions among the justices in individual cases followed the same ideological lines as the overall rankings of justices. For example, in all six cases in which the Court divided 5–4 in a conservative direction, the dissenters were Souter, Stevens, Ginsburg, and Breyer. Yet there were still nine inconsistent votes. (That number could have been reduced to seven by putting some cases and justices out of order.)

Imperfect though it is, the scalogram in Figure 4-1 is less messy than most. In the 2004 term the proportion of inconsistent votes in criminal cases was considerably higher. And in most other areas of policy, ideological divisions are not as sharp. The inconsistencies revealed by scalograms result chiefly from the complexity of justices' attitudes. To take an example from the figure, in *Blakely v. Washington* (542 U.S. 296), the three most liberal justices and two of their most conservative colleagues agreed that one feature of a state's sentencing guidelines violated the rights of defendants and thus struck down the guidelines. The four dissenters were primarily moderates who wanted to preserve guideline systems that they saw as highly desirable.

Observers of the Court regularly label the justices not just in relative terms but in absolute terms as well: Justice Thomas is called a conservative, Justice Stevens a liberal. Because the justices' votes in cases reflect several different forces, this conclusion does not follow directly from the patterns of votes. This is especially true because the proportions of liberal and conservative votes that a justice casts in a particular period reflect the mix of cases that the Court decides in that period. A justice who had a strongly liberal voting record in one era might not have as liberal a record in a different era.

Still, the role of the justices' policy preferences in their votes and opinions is sufficiently strong that those labels seem appropriate. A justice who casts a preponderance of votes that can be characterized as conservative almost surely holds conservative views on most issues. Indeed, most justices who were perceived as strongly liberal or strongly conservative at the time of their appointment establish records on the Court that are consistent with those perceptions.[48]

Patterns of Agreement. Analysis of patterns of agreement among justices provides another perspective on the Court's ideological divisions. For each pair of justices who served in the 2003 and 2004 terms, Table 4-3 shows the average percentage of the time that they supported the same opinion in the two terms. Table 4-2 and Figure 4-1 focus on votes, but Table 4-3 focuses on doctrine; justices who voted for the same outcome but who could not support the same opinion are treated as disagreeing.

The table shows that some pairs of justices agreed with each other much more often than other pairs. Not surprisingly, the rates of agreement were highest between pairs of justices who are ideologically close to each other. The three justices who cast liberal votes most often (Stevens, Souter, and Ginsburg) all agreed with each other more than 80 percent of the time, and the three justices with the most conservative records

TABLE 4-3
Average Percentage of Cases in Which Pairs of Justices
Supported the Same Opinion, 2003 and 2004 Terms

Justice	Justice							
	So	Gi	Br	O'C	Ke	Re	Sc	Th
Stevens	82	81	73	61	59	49	44	43
Souter		87	78	65	63	54	51	47
Ginsburg			86	66	62	56	51	45
Breyer				77	68	64	51	48
O'Connor					78	83	64	64
Kennedy						82	65	66
Rehnquist							72	78
Scalia								78
Thomas								

Sources: "The Supreme Court, 2003 Term," *Harvard Law Review* 118 (November 2004): 499; "The Supreme Court, 2004 Term," *Harvard Law Review* 119 (November 2005): 421.

Note: Numbers are the average of the percentages for the two justices for the two terms. Both unanimous and nonunanimous cases are included.

(Rehnquist, Scalia, and Thomas) had agreement rates of greater than 70 percent. For the same reasons, the lowest rates of agreement were between justices at opposite ends of the ideological spectrum. The four most liberal justices each agreed with Justice Thomas less than half the time. In contrast, Justice O'Connor—standing in the ideological center of the Court—had an agreement rate of more than 60 percent with every colleague.

Patterns of agreement among the justices do not necessarily reflect self-conscious alliances or blocs of justices. The justices certainly are aware of those patterns, and like-minded justices sometimes work closely with each other. But ideological allies do not always form close friendships or working relationships. When alliances do develop, they are chiefly the result of agreement about judicial issues rather than the source of that agreement. Shared preferences, not concerted action, best explain the tendency for certain justices to agree on opinions.

Preferences and Policy Change

The ideological mix of Supreme Court decisions varies from term to term. In some terms the most visible decisions are primarily conservative, in others primarily liberal. For example, in the 2002 term, 57 percent of the decisions were liberal; in 2003 the proportion was 46 percent. Observers of the Court often make a good deal of those changes, but they are usually just a product of the particular mix of cases that the Court decides each term rather than a shift in the Court's collective position.

Sometimes, however, that collective position does change, in the sense that the Court would decide the same cases differently. As a result, there is change in the Court's policies in a specific policy area or a broader field, such as civil liberties. The primary source of such a change is a shift in the policy preferences of the justices as a group. These shifts could come from change in the preferences of people already serving on the Court or from change in the Court's membership. In practice, both are significant.

Changes in Individual Preferences. Close observers of the Supreme Court often try to predict how the Court will decide a pending case; typically, they do rather well in their predictions. The primary reason is that individual justices tend to take stable positions on the issues that arise in various policy areas, positions that reflect their policy preferences. The views that a justice expressed in past cases about when cars can be searched or when mergers of companies violate the antitrust laws are a good guide to the justice's stance in a future case. In turn, the Court's collective position on such issues generally remains stable as long as its membership remains unchanged.

But as members of the Court, justices are exposed to new influences and confront issues in new forms. As a result, their policy preferences may be modified. Small changes are common, and more fundamental changes sometimes occur.

A justice who serves on the Court for several years is likely to shift positions on some specific issues, usually because of experience with cases that concern those issues. In his opinion in a 2000 case, Justice Souter took the position that a city seeking to prohibit nude dancing establishments must provide evidence of negative "secondary effects" to meet its burden under the First Amendment. "Careful readers," Souter said,

will of course realize that my partial dissent rests on a demand for an evidentiary basis that I failed to make when I concurred in [a 1991 decision]. I should have demanded the evidence then, too, and my mistake calls to mind Justice Jackson's foolproof explanation of a lapse of his own, when he quoted Samuel Johnson, "'Ignorance, sir, ignorance.'" I may not be less ignorant of nude dancing than I was nine years ago, but after many subsequent occasions to think further about the needs of the First Amendment, I have come to believe that a government must toe the mark more carefully than I first insisted. I hope it is enlightenment on my part, and acceptable even if a little late.[49]

Individual issues aside, most justices retain the same basic ideological position throughout their career. A justice who begins as a liberal, such as Ruth Bader Ginsburg, generally remains a liberal; the same is usually true of a conservative, such as Clarence Thomas. When a justice's position shifts relative to that of the Court as a whole, it is usually because new appointments have shifted the Court's ideological center while the justice has retained the same general views. According to law professor Dennis Hutchinson, John Paul Stevens "has stayed in the center as the court has moved to the right."[50]

Justice Harry Blackmun was one of the few justices whose basic views seemed to shift fundamentally. Blackmun came to the Court in 1970 as a Nixon appointee, and early in his tenure he aligned himself chiefly with the other conservative justices. He and Chief Justice Warren Burger, boyhood friends from Minnesota, were dubbed the "Minnesota Twins." In the 1973 term, Blackmun agreed with Burger on opinions in 84 percent of the decisions, and with liberal William Brennan in only 49 percent.[51] Blackmun gradually moved toward the center of the Court, and from the 1980 term on he usually had higher agreement rates with Brennan than with Burger — in 1985, Burger's last term, 30 percentage points higher. In the last few terms before his 1994 retirement, Blackmun had become one of the two most liberal justices on the Court.

This shift to the Court's left resulted in part from the replacement of liberal colleagues with conservatives, but Blackmun's own positions clearly became more liberal. Although the reasons for this change are uncertain, it appears that his experiences in dealing with cases that came to the Court—especially *Roe v. Wade,* in which he wrote the Court's opinion— were important.[52]

Perhaps more common than individual ideological shifts are changes in the views of the justices as a group on a particular issue. These shifts typically result from developments in American society that shape the views of the justices along with other people.

One example concerns the legal status of women. The liberal Warren Court gave unprecedented support to the goal of equality under the law, but it did not strike down legal rules that treated women and men differently. In contrast, the more conservative Burger and Rehnquist Courts handed down a series of decisions promoting legal equality for men and women. Today, even the most conservative justices use a fairly rigorous standard to evaluate laws that treat women and men differently, a standard that no justice supported in the 1960s. The most fundamental cause of this change was the direct and indirect effect of the feminist movement on the Court's agenda and, even more, on justices' views about women's social roles. This example underlines the potential for significant changes in justices' collective views on policy issues.

Membership Change. Although shifts in the positions of sitting justices can produce changes in the Court's positions, change in the Court's membership is probably the most important source of policy change. If Supreme Court policies are largely a product of the justices' preferences, and if those preferences tend to be stable, then change will come most easily through the replacement of one justice with a successor who has a different set of policy preferences.

Change in the Court's membership often alters its positions on specific issues. As discussed earlier, the overturning of a recent precedent usually results from the replacement of justices who helped create that precedent with others who disagree with it. Even when the Court maintains a precedent, a critical shift in membership may ensure that it is extended no further.

More broadly, shifts in the Court's overall ideological position through new appointments typically lead to change in the general content of its policies. The Court's civil liberties policies since the 1950s demonstrate this effect of membership change. Table 4-4 shows the proportions of decisions favorable to parties with civil liberties claims during successive periods in the 1958 to 2004 terms. Because changes in the content of civil liberties cases can make these proportions misleading, the table also shows civil liberties support with an adjustment for the content of cases based on a statistical technique.

The early Warren Court was closely divided between liberals and conservatives; from 1958 until 1961 there was a relatively stable division between a four-member liberal bloc and a moderate to conservative bloc of five. By the standards of the 1920s and 1930s, the Court's decisions were quite liberal, but the table shows that parties with civil liberties claims won only a little more than half their cases between 1958 and 1961.

President Kennedy's 1962 appointments created a liberal majority; a law clerk during the 1962 term referred to it as "a turning point in the modern history of the Supreme Court."[53] The Johnson appointments later in the decade maintained that majority. The years from 1962 to 1968 were probably the most liberal in the Court's history. The Court established strikingly liberal positions in a variety of policy areas, and the proportion of pro–civil liberties decisions increased substantially.

Between 1969 and 1992, every appointment to the Court was made by a Republican president, and all but Ford sought to use their appointments to make the Court more conservative. Thus, the Court gained a distinctly more conservative set of justices. The impact of these membership changes on the Court's civil liberties policies was somewhat ambiguous. The Court adhered to some policies of the Warren Court and even took new liberal directions on such issues as women's rights. Yet, on the whole, the Burger Court was distinctly less supportive of civil liberties than was the Court of the 1960s, and the early Rehnquist Court was even less supportive than the Burger Court.

TABLE 4-4

Proportions of Supreme Court Decisions Favoring Parties with Civil Liberties Claims and Changes in Court Membership, 1958–2004 Terms

Terms	Proportions of pro– civil liberties decisions		New justices (appointing presidents) and justices leaving the Court
	Actual	Adjusted[a]	
1958–1961	60.1	60.1	NA
1962–1968	75.3	77.6	*New:* White, Goldberg (Kennedy); Fortas, Marshall (Johnson). *Leaving:* Whittaker, Frankfurter, Goldberg, Clark.
1969–1974	48.8	55.9	*New:* Burger, Blackmun, Powell, Rehnquist (Nixon). *Leaving:* Warren, Fortas, Black, Harlan.
1975–1980	42.0	51.6	*New:* Stevens (Ford). *Leaving:* Douglas.
1981–1985	40.0	51.5	*New:* O'Connor (Reagan). *Leaving:* Stewart.
1986–1989	42.4	46.1	*New:* Scalia, Kennedy (Reagan). *Leaving:* Burger, Powell.
1990–1992	42.7	35.4	*New:* Souter, Thomas (Bush). *Leaving:* Brennan, Marshall.
1993–2004	46.6	43.9	*New:* Ginsburg, Breyer (Clinton). *Leaving:* White, Blackmun.

Source: Based on data in U.S. Supreme Court Database, compiled by Harold Spaeth of Michigan State University, at www.as.uky.edu/polisci/ulmerproject/sctdata.htm.

Note: NA = not applicable.

a. Adjusted using a statistical technique to control for changes in the content of civil liberties cases decided by the Court. The technique is described in Lawrence Baum, "Measuring Policy Change in the U.S. Supreme Court," *American Political Science Review* 82 (September 1988): 905–912.

Table 4-4 shows the impact of these Republican appointments on the proportion of decisions favorable to civil liberties. The Nixon appointments reduced that proportion from about three-quarters to about one-half. The replacement of the highly liberal William Douglas with the moderately liberal John Paul Stevens further reduced the level of support for civil liberties. If the content of cases is taken into account, another major decline in support occurred after David Souter and Clarence Thomas replaced the Court's two remaining strong liberals in the early 1990s.

Ruth Bader Ginsburg and Steven Breyer were the first appointees of a Democratic president since 1967. Best characterized as moderate liberals, they did not change the Court's ideological balance a great deal. The proportion of pro–civil liberties decisions did increase somewhat after they joined the Court, but the Rehnquist Court remained distinctly more conservative in its decisions and doctrines than the Warren and Burger Courts.

President Bush's appointments of John Roberts and Samuel Alito may shift the Court's ideological balance somewhat to the right. Whether or not that occurs, it remains true that presidents have the greatest power to bring about ideological change in the Court through their selection of nominees.

Role Values

Policy preferences are not the only values that can affect the Court's decisions. Justices may also be influenced by their role values, their views about what constitutes appropriate behavior for the Supreme Court and its members. In any body, whether it is a court or a legislature, members' conceptions of how they should carry out their jobs structure what they do and affect their policy decisions.

A variety of role values can shape the justices' behavior. Their views about the desirability of unanimous decisions help determine the extent of dissent in the Court's decisions. Their judgments about the legitimacy of "lobbying" colleagues on decisions may determine the outcomes of some cases. But the role values that could have the greatest impact concern the considerations that justices take into account in reaching their decisions and the desirability of active intervention in the making of public policy.

It is clear that several different forces shape the justices' votes and opinions. The relative weight of these forces depends in part on what justices think they ought to do. In particular, justices have to balance their strong policy preferences on many issues with the expectation of others (and themselves) that they will seek to interpret the law accurately.

Some evidence suggests that justices differ in the relative weight they give to these legal and policy considerations.[54] However, these differences are not as sharp as they sometimes appear. For example, at any given time, some justices are more willing than others to uproot some of the Court's precedents. But the justices' attitudes toward precedent in itself are less important than their attitudes toward the policies embodied in particular precedents. In the past decade the Court has abrogated a mix of liberal and conservative precedents, along with some that are not easily classified ideologically. When justices dissent from decisions that abrogate precedents, it is generally liberals who seek to maintain liberal precedents and conservatives who want to protect conservative precedents.

Active intervention in policymaking is often viewed negatively. Justices who seem eager to engage in that intervention are criticized as "activists," and those who seem less prone to do so are praised as "restrained." But activism, like the treatment of precedent, does not seem to differ all that much among justices.

The most visible form of active intervention in policymaking is striking down federal statutes, a form that is often controversial as well. The historical patterns are illuminating. During the 1920s and early 1930s, the laws that the Court struck down were primarily government regulations of business practices. Conservative justices were the most willing to strike down such laws, and liberals on the Court and elsewhere argued for judicial restraint. In contrast, in the 1960s and 1970s, the Court struck down primarily laws that conflicted with civil liberties. Liberals were most likely to act against these laws and conservatives to call for judicial restraint.

Since the 1980s the Court has overturned a wide variety of federal laws. No justice has stood out for a willingness to strike down laws or an unwillingness to do so. Rather, the justices have responded to the ideological content of the statutes in question. In a series of decisions since the mid-1990s that limited congressional power to protect civil liberties against state violations, the Court's liberals have regularly dissented.[55] But in decisions that struck down statutes limiting civil liberties, the dissents have come from the Court's conservatives.[56]

All this is not to say that the justices' role values have no impact on their behavior. Undoubtedly, such values help to structure the ways in which justices perceive their jobs. But justices' conceptions of good public policy have a more fundamental impact on their choices.

Group Interaction

In the preceding section, I treated the justices as individuals who act on their own. But when justices make choices, they do so as part of a Court that makes collective decisions and as part of American government and society. Justices who seek to make good policy might act strategically by taking their colleagues and other institutions into account. Whether or not justices act strategically, they can be influenced in a variety of ways by other justices and by their political and social environment. This section examines the justices as a group, and the next section considers the Court's environment.

A Quasi-Collegial Body

In historical accounts of the Supreme Court, some of the most dramatic events concern interactions among the justices in major cases. Newly appointed chief justice Earl Warren, engaging in what Justice Douglas called "a brilliant diplomatic process," moved the Court from sharp division to a unanimous decision in *Brown v. Board of Education* (1954).[57] The Court's decision in *Planned Parenthood v. Casey* (1992) reflected the close collaboration among three justices on a joint opinion that determined the Court's position, with one of the three shifting position after the Court's initial vote and thereby preventing the Court from overturning *Roe v. Wade.*[58] In *Bush v. Gore* (2000), which ensured that George W. Bush would become president, the Court's decision came after intense interplay among the justices over the short period in which the Court considered the case.[59]

Those episodes are consistent with the image of the Court that many people hold, one in which justices constantly lobby each other over the cases before them and decisions reflect the persuasive powers of certain justices. For the most part, however, that image is false. For one thing, except for oral argument and conferences, there is only limited face-to-face interaction among the justices in the decision-making process. According to Justice Breyer, "Things take place in writing because that is a mode through which appellate judges are most comfortable communicating."[60]

More fundamentally, the justices do influence each other, but that influence occurs within constraints—constraints that result from their strongly held views on many issues. When they apply their general positions on an issue to a specific case, the resulting judgment about that case may be too firm for colleagues to sway. As Justice Rehnquist wrote early in his tenure, when justices who have prepared themselves "assemble around the conference table on Friday morning to decide an important case presenting constitutional questions that they have all debated and written about before, the outcome may be a foregone conclusion."[61] Thus, he concluded some years later, the Court is dominated chiefly "by centrifugal forces, pushing toward individuality and independence."[62]

But the justices' independence should not be overstated. They have powerful incentives to work with each other, even if doing so requires that they adopt positions that depart from those they most prefer. One reason is institutional: justices want to achieve opinions that at least five members endorse so that the Court is laying down authoritative legal rules. And to give more weight to the Court's decisions, they generally would like to reach greater consensus. According to Justice O'Connor, "Neither my colleagues nor I make a practice of joining opinions with which we do not agree." Unanimity "does not overwhelm our other goals." Still, "we all greatly prefer the Court to be unanimous or almost so whenever possible, and we work to make that happen."[63]

The justices' interest in the legal rules that the Court collectively establishes is an even stronger incentive to work together. Justices would like to win the support of colleagues for the rules they prefer, so they have good reason to engage in efforts at persuasion. They also have reason to be flexible in the stances they take in cases, because flexibility may help them to win colleagues' support for rules that are at least close to the ones they prefer.

These incentives are reflected in the negotiation that was described in the first section of this chapter.[64] The most common course of events in a case is for a justice to write a draft opinion for the Court and then gain the support of a majority for that opinion with no difficulty. But a draft opinion frequently attracts requests from colleagues for changes in the opinion, and most of the time justices who make these requests indicate that they cannot join the opinion unless the changes are made. The opinion author usually makes these changes. During the seventeen years of the Burger Court, requests for changes in the draft opinion occurred in 32 percent of all cases, and more often in important cases. Seventy percent of the time, the opinion was modified to make the requested change.[65]

Whether or not colleagues request changes in opinions for the Court, those opinions frequently are revised during the decision process. In the Burger Court, slightly more than half of all cases had at least three drafts of the Court's opinion circulated by the author.[66] Although successive drafts may differ only on minor matters, they sometimes differ substantially— and occasionally with important consequences for legal policy.

Beyond the content of opinions, the votes of individual justices on the case outcome can shift during the decision process. During the seventeen years of the Burger Court, 7.5 percent of the justices' individual votes to reverse or affirm switched from one side to the other, and at least one such switch occurred in 37 percent of the cases. Most vote switches increase the size of the majority, as the Court works toward consensus. During the Burger Court, the justices who initially voted with the majority switched their votes 5 percent of the time, but those who initially voted with the minority switched 18 percent of the time.[67] Occasionally, however, shifts of position turn an initial minority into a majority. This occurred in about 7 percent of the cases decided by the Burger Court.[68]

The effects of interactions among the justices should not be exaggerated. After all, in the great majority of cases, the side that won in the Court's first vote on the merits of the case wins in the final vote as well. Most of the majority opinions that the Court issues look similar to the original drafts of those opinions. But votes and opinions do change; the Court's decisions are often more than simply an adding together of the positions with which each justice begins.

The group life of the Court has effects on its decisions that are broader and more subtle than shifts of position in individual cases. Interactions among the justices create general patterns of influence within the Court, and the Court's ability to reach consensus is affected by the extent of conflict among its members. Both of these effects merit consideration.

Patterns of Influence

If the justices are largely independent of each other, then the capacity of any justice to exert influence over colleagues is inherently limited. Justice O'Connor said, "I work with eight very strong-willed colleagues. I don't think that any of us exerts much power over the others."[69]

Still, the justices do influence each other within those limits. It follows that some are more influential than others. At the broadest level, the requisites for influence are the same as in any other group: an interest in exerting influence and skill in doing so.

Justice William O. Douglas, who served for a record thirty-six years between 1939 and 1975, had relatively little influence because he did little to achieve it. Certainly, he devoted some efforts to winning support for his positions, especially in the cases that concerned him most. But in contrast with some other justices, whom he called "evangelists," he generally preferred to go his own way.[70] According to William Rehnquist, "At the Court conferences we sometimes had the impression that he was disappointed to have other people agree with his views in a particular case, because he would therefore be unable to write a stinging dissent."[71] Douglas's isolation was symbolized by his speedy departures from Washington at the end of the Court terms or, on occasion, even earlier.

Douglas's long-time colleague Felix Frankfurter actively sought influence over his colleagues, and his eminence as a legal scholar seemingly put him in a good position to persuade his colleagues to his position. But his weak interpersonal skills worked against him. Justice Potter Stewart said that Frankfurter "courted" him, but "Felix was so unsubtle and obvious that it was counterproductive."[72] Further, Frankfurter's arrogance caused him to lecture to colleagues, and he reacted sarcastically to opinions with which he disagreed. At one Court conference he "had taken a printed draft opinion by Justice Tom Clark and first verbally and then physically torn it to shreds, contemptuously tossing the sheets of paper all over the ornate private room."[73] Such behavior tends to alienate colleagues, and it had an inevitable impact on Frankfurter's influence within the Court.

William Brennan, who served from 1956 to 1990, had both an interest in exerting influence and a high level of skill in working with his colleagues. As a liberal he worked hard to gain support from more conservative colleagues, both in individual cases and over the long term. For example, he engaged in what one of Harry Blackmun's law clerks called a "courtship" of Blackmun.[74] In his commitment to winning support from his colleagues and his careful consideration of how to do so, Brennan was among the most strategic-minded justices ever to sit on the Court.[75]

Unlike Frankfurter, Brennan had a warm personal style. "Everybody got along with him," according to one observer, "even those who bitterly opposed him from a doctrinal view."[76] Brennan was also perceptive about how to win majorities; one commentator said that he could "accurately judge his colleagues and figure out what is doable."[77] These qualities helped Brennan in his efforts to forge a liberal majority for the expansion of civil liberties in the Warren Court and to limit the Court's conservative shift in the Burger Court.

These three justices illustrate the wide range of roles that justices can play in the Court's decision making. It is often difficult to ascertain the influence that particular justices exert, and this is especially true of those who have served recently. For instance, John Paul Stevens has been depicted as genial but quite individualistic; according to one observer in 1993, he "makes little effort to win over other members of the Court."[78] More recently, however, evidence from the justices' papers suggests that Stevens plays an active role in forging majorities for positions he favors.[79]

Antonin Scalia's personal style would seem likely to reduce his influence. In oral argument he is highly active, sometimes domineering. Like Frankfurter, he has a tendency to lecture colleagues. When Justice Kennedy shifted away from Scalia's side in *Planned Parenthood v. Casey* (1992), it was reported that Scalia "walked over to Kennedy's nearby house . . . to upbraid him."[80] Scalia's concurring and dissenting opinions sometimes criticize other justices' opinions in harsh tones. In 2002 the Indiana Supreme Court suspended a lawyer from practice for a strongly worded attack on the opinion from which he was appealing. To make his point that judges sometimes use equally strong language to attack each other, a justice who did not think the lawyer should be suspended quoted two Scalia opinions.[81]

Scalia's behavior sometimes creates frictions with other justices.[82] Yet he is a gregarious person who has close relationships with some colleagues, and he seems to exert substantial influence on the Court through the strong expression of his views about how the law should be interpreted. The best example is the support he has attracted for his view that the Court should give no weight to legislative history in interpreting statutes.[83]

Among the justices who have served in recent years, Sandra Day O'Connor is especially interesting. For most of her tenure as a justice, O'Connor's policy preferences put her at the middle of the Court. As a result, she was part of the majority in the preponderance of cases that closely divided the Court, including major decisions on issues such as abortion and affirmative action. Primarily for this reason, she was depicted as quite powerful. Reaching the same conclusion as some other observers, the journalist David Broder wrote in 2003 that "the most influential single public official in this land may not be anyone in elective office but Justice Sandra Day O'Connor."[84] One law professor's concern with what he saw as the disproportionate power exerted by O'Connor helped impel him to propose expanding the Court to nineteen members, an expansion that he saw as reducing the chances that a single justice could be so influential.[85]

The reality is not necessarily that simple. A "swing justice" such as O'Connor will be part of the majority more often than her colleagues, but success in that sense is not the same as power. Every justice in a 5–4 majority contributes to that result with one vote.

Yet swing justices do have a degree of influence because their positions are seen as relatively unpredictable and their support as crucial to the outcome of many cases. Thus, lawyers before the Court gave special attention to devising arguments that they hoped would appeal to O'Connor. Further, a swing justice is in an especially good position to shape the content of the Court's opinion. As her biographer Joan Biskupic has described her, O'Connor made the most of this advantage, possessing both the determination and the skills that had marked William Brennan. As a result, it appears, she *was* one of the most influential justices.[86]

The Chief Justice

As head of the Supreme Court, the chief justice would seem to be in a good position to influence other justices. In reality, the chief has both advantages and limitations in seeking to exercise influence. One limitation stems from administrative duties, which reduce the time that the chief can spend on cases. More fundamental is the difficulty of leading colleagues who strongly resist control. As Chief Justice Rehnquist wrote, the chief "presides over a conference not of eight subordinates, whom he may direct or instruct, but of eight associates who, like him, have tenure during good behavior, and who are as independent as hogs on ice. He may at most persuade or cajole them."[87] Balanced against these limitations are the chief's formal powers, which provide at least a moderate advantage in exerting influence.

The Chief Justice's Powers. The chief presides over the Court in oral argument and in conference. In conference the chief can direct discussion and frame alternatives, which can shape the outcome of the discussion. Most important, the chief ordinarily speaks first on a case in conference. Another power involves the discuss list, the set of petitions for hearing that the Court considers fully. The chief, aided by clerks, makes up the initial version of the discuss list. This task gives the chief the largest role in determining which cases are set aside without group discussion.

Opinion Assignment. The power to assign opinions is important and complicated. By custom, the chief justice assigns the Court's opinion whenever the chief is in the majority on the initial vote in conference. (In other cases, the senior justice in the majority makes the assignment.) As a result, the chief justice assigns the great majority of opinions, a little over 80 percent in the period from 1953 to 1990.[88]

In making assignments, chief justices balance different considerations.[89] Administrative considerations relate to spreading the workload and opportunities among the justices. Chief justices generally assign about the same number of opinions to each colleague, taking into account assignments from senior associate justices and the workload of opinion writing that a justice already faces at a given time. These considerations were especially important to Chief Justice Rehnquist. He wrote in 2001, "As the term goes on I take into consideration the extent to which the various justices are current in writing and circulating opinions that have previously been assigned."[90]

Other considerations relate to the substance of the Court's decisions. The legal rules proclaimed by the Court may depend in part on who writes its opinion. For this reason, chief justices tend to favor themselves and colleagues who have similar ideological positions when assigning opinions in important cases.

The selection of the opinion writer may help to determine whether the initial majority remains a majority. When the initial majority is slim, the chief justice is likely to assign opinions to a relatively moderate member of that majority, even if the assigned justice is ideologically distant from the chief. This practice stems from the belief that a moderate typically has the best chance to write an opinion that will maintain the majority and perhaps win over justices who were initially on the other side.

Because chief justices favor ideological allies in assigning important opinions, in effect they reward the justices who vote with them most often. They might also use the assignment power more directly to reward and punish colleagues, as Chief Justice Burger apparently did. Justice Blackmun said that a justice who was "in the doghouse" with Burger might be assigned one of the "crud" opinions "that nobody wants to write."[91]

Under any chief justice, the assignment power gives other justices something to think about. Asked why he joined Rehnquist in singing carols at the Court's Christmas party, David Souter said, "I have to. Otherwise I get all the tax cases."[92] Souter was joking, but he touched on an important reality.

Variation in Leadership. What particular chief justices make of their formal powers and the strength of their leadership varies a good deal. These differences result from several conditions, including the chief's interest in leading the Court, the chief's skill as a leader, and the willingness of the associate justices to be led.

The two chief justices who preceded William Rehnquist—Earl Warren and Warren Burger—are of particular interest. Earl Warren could not compete with some colleagues as a scholar. He presided over a Court that had several skillful and strong-minded members, such as Douglas and Frankfurter, and that was closely divided between liberals and conservatives during most of his tenure. Under these conditions, Warren could hardly dominate the Court.

But Warren possessed excellent leadership skills, a product of his personality and his experience as a political leader. He had a good sense of how to build majorities for his positions, and he was effective at persuasion: several of his colleagues told one observer "how hard it had been to withstand the Chief Justice when he was able to operate in a one-on-one setting."[93] These attributes gave Warren considerable influence on the Court's direction.

Warren Burger was ambitious for leadership. He achieved some success in securing administrative changes in the federal courts and procedural changes in the Court itself. Simply by being chief justice, he exerted considerable influence over the Court's decisions. But he was far less effective than Earl Warren.

To a considerable extent, Burger's limited impact on the Court's decisions stemmed from his own qualities and predilections. Colleagues chafed at what they considered a poor style of leadership in conference, and they disliked Burger's practice of casting "false" votes so that he could assign the Court's opinion.[94] He was also accused of bullying his colleagues. One scholar concluded that Potter Stewart "loathed" Burger,[95] and other colleagues also disliked his leadership style. Apparently, they were not alone; Justice Marshall's messenger said that when Burger retired, "it was just like Christmas morning."[96]

But Burger also faced obstacles that were beyond his control. Perhaps most important, as a strong conservative he had the disadvantage of standing near one end of the Court's ideological spectrum. In any case, his example shows that even a chief justice who wants to be a powerful leader does not always achieve that goal.

William Rehnquist became chief justice in 1986 after serving on the Court for fifteen years. He brought important strengths to the position, especially his well-respected intellectual abilities and a pleasant manner of interaction with people. For these reasons, his promotion was welcomed by colleagues and other Court personnel.[97]

Rehnquist appears to have been a very effective chief justice, and his leadership was widely praised even by justices who did not share his conservative views on most judicial issues.[98] Reflecting his preferences, the Court's discussions of cases at conference were shorter and tighter than in the recent past. His leadership was one source of the sharp decline in the number of cases accepted by the Court. In decision making he enhanced his influence by taking strong positions with an affable style.

John Roberts's effectiveness as chief justice will become clear only with time. However, as Justice Stevens noted in his welcoming remarks at Roberts's first Court session, the new chief began with the "respect and admiration" of his colleagues for his skills as an advocate before the Court.[99] Roberts's affable and confident personal style also should work in his favor as he seeks to exert leadership within the Court. Indeed, the evidence from Roberts's first term suggests that he is an effective leader. He seems to be the primary source of the changes in oral argument and Court conferences that were discussed earlier. He has also worked to achieve greater consensus in decisions. Justice Breyer said that as a result, "people are trying to get more agreement."[100] According to former solicitor general Ted Olson, "one of the justices told me, 'I think that he could be one of our greatest chief justices.' "[101] As Rehnquist noted, however, even the most effective chief justice can achieve only limited influence over a set of notoriously independent colleagues.

Harmony and Conflict

As the justices describe it, the Supreme Court today is a harmonious group. Stephen Breyer said in a television interview, "I have never heard a voice raised in anger in that conference room. I have never heard one member of the court say something insulting about another even as a kind of joke."[102] Sandra Day O'Connor acknowledged that in some past times there had been some "animosity" among justices. "Happily, that has not been the situation during my time here."[103]

Observers of the Court do not necessarily agree with this description of its life as a group. Unlike Justice O'Connor, some think that there is considerable animosity among members of the Court. According to a legal scholar in 2002, "It is abundantly clear that the Rehnquist Court is divided into hostile blocs; that the blocs do not trust each other; that there is at times a good deal of anger and vitriol on all sides."[104]

The reality lies somewhere between these two depictions of the Court. On the one hand, a degree of conflict is inevitable. All the sources of strife that exist in other groups can operate in the Court as well. And the high stakes that justices have in many of the Court's decisions, combined with the pressures under which they work, seem certain to produce personal conflicts. As a result, some justices come to dislike some colleagues. The harsh language that sometimes appears in dissenting opinions may be a rhetorical device more than anything else, but it can also reflect frictions among the justices. The box on page 141 provides some examples from the last two weeks of the 2004 term.

At the same time, the justices have strong incentives to limit such frictions. Harmony makes the Court a more pleasant place to work, and it also helps the justices to achieve consensus in decisions. And justices who seek the support of colleagues for the positions they favor want to maintain good relations with those colleagues. For all those reasons, the justices generally

Excerpts from Dissenting Opinions in Decisions Announced June 20–27, 2005

Instead of heeding what Congress actually said, the Court relies on flawed textual analysis and dubious inferences from legislative silence to impose the Court's view of what it thinks Congress probably wanted to say.

—Justice Anthony Kennedy, in *Mid-Con Freight Systems, Inc. v. Michigan Public Service Commission,* 162 L. Ed. 2d 418, 438

[The Court] fails, however, to ground its analysis in any particular provision of the Constitution or in this Court's precedents.

—Justice Clarence Thomas, in *Halbert v. Michigan,* 162 L. Ed. 2d 552, 569

Three flaws in the Court's rather superficial analysis of the merits highlight the unwisdom of its decision to answer the state-law question *de novo.*

—Justice John Paul Stevens, in *Town of Castle Rock v. Gonzales,* 162 L. Ed. 2d 658, 683

I shall discuss first, why the Court's oft repeated assertion that the government cannot favor religious practice is false; second, why today's opinion extends the scope of that falsehood even beyond prior cases; and third, why even on the basis of the Court's false assumptions the judgment here is wrong.

—Justice Antonin Scalia, in *McCreary County v. American Civil Liberties Union,* 162 L. Ed. 2d 729, 762

It is a sadness that the Court should go so far out of its way to make bad law.

—Justice Antonin Scalia, in *National Cable & Telecommunications Association v. Brand X Internet Services,* 162 L. Ed. 2d 820, 862 work to minimize conflict and develop good relationships with each other. Justice O'Connor, for instance, engaged in a long and ultimately successful effort to get the justices to eat lunch together after oral arguments.[105] Justices organize betting pools on issues ranging from the depth of the snow at the Court building to the state-by-state outcome of the 1992 presidential election.[106] And justices socialize with each other a good deal outside the work setting.

It is difficult to assess the overall balance between harmony and conflict from outside the Court. But one conclusion appears to be safe: the current Court is more harmonious than several past Courts, in which some pairs of justices were actually unable to work with each other. The absence of such deep conflicts undoubtedly improves the functioning of the Court.

The Court's Environment

Compared with Congress, the Supreme Court is more isolated from the world around it and more insulated from the influence of that world. The isolation is reflected in the relatively limited contact between the justices and other participants in politics, such as members of Congress and representatives of interest groups. The insulation is primarily a result of the justices' life terms: no matter whom they displease, they can be removed from office only through impeachment proceedings, a very unlikely occurrence.

But the Court's isolation and insulation are far from total. The justices interact regularly with people outside the Court, and they are aware of events and developments in American society. Moreover, they have reasons to care about what people think of them and their Court, reasons that range from concern about the Court's efficacy as a policymaker to an interest in their personal standing among their friends. As a result, the Court's environment can shape the justices' thinking about cases and issues, and the potential influence of that environment merits consideration.

Mass Public Opinion

In one of the first decisions of the Supreme Court's 2005 term, the Court ruled unanimously that a defendant in a civil case could remove the case from state court to federal court "if there is complete diversity between all named plaintiffs and all named defendants, and no defendant is a citizen of the forum State. It is not incumbent on the named defendants to negate the existence of a potential defendant whose presence in the action would destroy diversity."[107]

It is doubtful that many people knew of this case or would have cared about the Court's decision had they known of it. On the issue in this case, as on many issues that come before the Court, there is no public opinion to speak of.

But many other Court decisions address issues that much of the public does care about, issues such as crime and civil rights. And some individual decisions, such as the Court's major rulings on abortion, are highly visible and controversial. On these issues and cases, it is possible that public opinion or potential public reactions influence the justices.

Such influence may seem unlikely, because the justices do not depend on public approval to keep their jobs. But at least some justices see public support for the Court as a resource, strengthening its position in conflicts with the other branches and improving compliance with its decisions. And even though most justices are fairly obscure, they still might seek public approval for its own sake.

Indeed, some justices clearly care about the public. Sandra Day O'Connor, who had held elective office and who was the best-known justice, wrote books for a general audience and made frequent appearances before groups other than lawyers and judges. She received a great deal of mail from the public, and early in her tenure on the Court she tried to answer it all.[108]

If the justices seek public support for personal or institutional reasons, their interest in that support might affect their decisions. It is true that the justices' votes and the Court's decisions generally have limited impact on their individual and collective public approval. That reality is reflected in the fact that the Court's controversial decision in *Bush v. Gore* did not change its public standing appreciably.[109] But the justices still might want to avoid actions that could jeopardize this standing.

If so, one possible effect is that the justices avoid highly unpopular decisions. The Court certainly does make some decisions on controversial issues that conflict with majority views in the public. Examples include the Court's rulings limiting religious exercises in public schools and the display of the Ten Commandments in public places, striking down state and federal laws against flag burning, and holding that states could not establish term limits for members of Congress. But perhaps concern with public opinion keeps some justices from acting contrary to public views even more often. For instance, liberal and moderate justices might have been deterred from ruling against the inclusion of "under God" in the Pledge of Allegiance in 2004 by their recognition that such a ruling would have aroused strong public opposition.[110]

Another possible effect of public opinion is to move the Court's overall ideological stance. As the public moves to the political left or right, so may the Court. Scholars have disagreed about whether the Court's mix of liberal and conservative decisions or the mix of votes by individual justices tracks ideological trends among the public, but some have found evidence of this relationship.[111]

Even if the justices refrain from making highly unpopular decisions or track public opinion, it is not necessarily the case that they are responding directly to the public. The kinds of decisions that most people strongly dislike usually run contrary to the justices' own values. And the same social forces that move public opinion to the left or right may have a similar effect on the justices. Since the 1980s the Court has addressed a wide range of cases involving conflicts between the government's interest in controlling illegal drugs and individual liberties. With some noteworthy exceptions, it has approved the government policies in question. Perhaps the justices have sought to align themselves with a public that was highly supportive of the government's "war on drugs." But it may be that most justices simply shared the views of the public.

Perhaps the primary effect of public opinion is to reinforce tendencies in the Court's decision making that already exist by helping to shape the justices' values and perceptions of reality. That effect could be substantial. But the justices' absence of worries about reelection undoubtedly reduces the influence of the public on them, giving them greater freedom to follow their own course than elected officials enjoy.

Elite Opinion: Friends and Acquaintances, the Legal Community, and the News Media

Although the justices may respond to the views of the general public, they can also be influenced by more specific sets of relevant people. One set is the justices' personal friends and acquaintances. We would expect the justices, like other people, to give attention to the perspectives and reactions of the people who are most important to them. Two other groups that may be relevant are the legal community and the mass media.

The legal community is important as a professional reference group. Justices draw many of their acquaintances from this community. Most justices interact a good deal with practicing lawyers, law professors, and lower-court judges, and most of the justices' public appearances are before legal groups. Lawyers are also the primary source of expert evaluations of the Court, often presented in the law reviews that law schools publish. Scrutiny by the legal community helps to make legal considerations important to the justices in reaching decisions. And if a particular view of legal issues is dominant among lawyers or in a segment of the bar with which a justice identifies, that justice may be drawn toward the dominant view.

The law reviews can have another kind of impact as well. Because law review articles are often discussed in briefs and may be read by justices and law clerks, they constitute one source of the information that enters into the Court's decisions. Justices frequently cite law review articles in support of their positions, and on occasion articles may help to determine their positions.

Most justices maintain a degree of distance from the news media. They talk to reporters less than do their counterparts in the other branches of government, and they give relatively few on-the-record interviews about their work. But there have always been some justices who interacted a good deal with reporters, and in recent years the justices have become more willing to give interviews.

Whether or not the justices talk with reporters, the news media are important to the Court. The media are the public's primary source of information about the Court, so they can shape public attitudes toward the justices. And whether or not reports in the media affect the public, justices understandably prefer to be depicted positively rather than negatively in news reports. For these reasons, justices pay attention to coverage of the Court. Justice Thomas, with a "near-photographic memory," "can recall the dates of unflattering articles written about him, and the names of the reporters who wrote them."[112] In 2006 Justice Kennedy criticized newspaper editorial writers for their coverage of the Court, asking members of a legal group to suggest "that they read the opinions before they write their editorials."[113]

Justices' personal circles, the legal community, and the news media are all composed primarily of people from elite groups in American society. To the extent that these elites have a distinctive point of view, they may move justices toward that point of view. Indeed, in the current era some conservatives have argued that the justices' positions on social issues are shaped by the liberalism of elites on those issues. President Nixon worried that his appointees' interactions with the "Georgetown crowd" in Washington might pull them in a liberal direction.[114] More recently, conservative commentators have argued that the desire to win praise from legal scholars, reporters who write about the Court, and other elites causes some Republican appointees to the Court to become more liberal over time, among them Harry Blackmun and Anthony Kennedy. Some conservatives call this process the "Greenhouse Effect," after Linda Greenhouse, the longtime Court reporter for the *New York Times*.[115] Whether or not something like a Greenhouse Effect exists, almost surely the justices are influenced more by those people who are especially salient to them than by the public as a whole.

Litigants and Interest Groups

Simply by bringing cases to the Supreme Court, litigants, interest groups, and the lawyers that represent them have an effect on the Court's policies. Once the Court has accepted a case, litigants and interest groups may influence its decision on the merits. Because communications to the Court must go through formal channels, any such influence comes primarily through advocacy in written briefs and oral arguments.

Certainly, justices pay attention to the material provided by litigants and interest groups. Opinions for the Court address the arguments raised by the parties to the case, and they often refer to amicus briefs. Controlling for other factors, the number of amicus briefs on each side has a small but meaningful effect on the outcome of cases. One reason is probably that the new arguments raised by amici sometimes persuade the justices.[116] When justices question lawyers closely during oral argument, they are often looking for responses to strong arguments by the other side. Therefore, the way lawyers frame arguments in a case can affect the justices' thinking and ultimately their decisions.

Further, the quality of advocacy on the two sides of a case has an impact. Justice Blackmun graded the performance of attorneys in oral argument. Using those grades, one study found that the relative strength of the arguments for the two sides affected their likelihood of victory.[117]

Justices may react to the identities of the litigants or amici themselves rather than just the arguments they present. The federal government enjoys a high rate of success in the Court's decisions on the merits, 63 percent in the 2004 term.[118] One source of that success is the expertise of the advocates in the solicitor general's office. But another might be the justices' sympathies for the government's interests.

Individual justices can also have positive or negative attitudes toward such groups as the ACLU or toward particular companies. In the 2003 cases on affirmative action in university admissions, what one commentator called "the range and sheer weight of the establishment voices on the affirmative action side" may have influenced some justices.[119]

Thus, the identities of the participants in cases may influence the Court, and the arguments they make certainly have an effect. But neither influence is as strong as the justices' preexisting attitudes toward the issues they address. The federal government enjoys greater success than any other participant in Supreme Court litigation, but the government wins the justices' support far more often when its arguments accord with their ideological positions than when the two conflict.[120]

Congress and the President

Several sets of policymakers affect the Court and its policies. Because of this effect, the justices may take those policymakers into account when they reach decisions. The president and Congress are especially important to the Court, so they have the greatest potential for influence on the Court's decisions.

Congress. Congressional powers over the Court range from reversing the Court's interpretations of statutes to control over salary increases for the justices. Because of this array of powers, the justices have reason to think about congressional reactions to their decisions. Relations with Congress can affect their prestige and their comfort. And justices who think strategically in a broad sense, who care about the impact of the Court's policies, want to avoid congressional actions that undercut those policies.

If the justices do act strategically toward Congress, the most likely form of strategy involves decisions that interpret federal statutes. These decisions are more vulnerable than the Court's interpretations of the Constitution because Congress and the president can override them simply by enacting a new statute. Indeed, such overrides are fairly common.

For this reason, justices might try to calculate whether their preferred interpretation of a statute would be sufficiently unpopular in Congress to produce an override. If so, justices would modify their interpretation to avoid that result. By making this implicit compromise with Congress, the justices could get the best possible result under the circumstances: not the interpretation of a statute that they favor most, but one that is closer to their preferences than the new statute that Congress would enact to override the Court's decision.

It may be, however, that most justices do not care that much whether Congress overrides their decisions. Or justices might find it so difficult to predict overrides and their content that there is little to be gained by trying to make those predictions. In any case, it is not yet clear how often justices pursue this strategic approach.[121]

Occasionally, the Court gets into conflicts with Congress that go much deeper than disagreement over the meaning of statutes. During a few periods in the Court's history, its general line of policy aroused so much dissatisfaction in Congress that it generated a serious threat of concrete action against the Court itself. In those periods, some justices may have acted to reduce that threat.

The first such period was the early nineteenth century, when John Marshall's Court faced congressional attacks because of its policies. Marshall, as the Court's dominant member, was careful to limit the frequency of decisions that would further anger its opponents. As discussed in Chapter 1, the Court's shift from opposition to support of New Deal legislation in the late 1930s may have reflected the effort by one or two justices to avoid a serious confrontation with the other branches. In the late 1950s, members of Congress reacted to the Court's expansions of civil liberties by seeking to override its policies and limit its jurisdiction; the Court reversed some of its own positions and thereby helped to quiet congressional attacks on the Court.

There have been no clear retreats of this sort since the 1950s. Indeed, the Court has engaged in considerable resistance to congressional pressures. Members of Congress have attacked the Court for its positions on a variety of civil liberties issues, including school desegregation, legislative districting, abortion, school prayer, and flag burning. On each of these issues, members have tried to overturn the Court's decisions, to limit its jurisdiction over the issue, or both. Yet in the face of these attacks, the Court has adhered to many of its unpopular policies, and it changed others only when new appointments made the Court more conservative. Recent history is thus a reminder that the justices do not automatically shy away from decisions that create conflict with Congress.

The President. Presidents have multifaceted relationships with the Supreme Court, and these relationships provide several sources of potential influence. Two of these sources, discussed in earlier chapters, are the power to appoint justices and the government's major role in Supreme Court litigation. The appointment power gives presidents considerable ability to determine the Court's direction. The president helps to shape the federal government's litigation policy and affects the Court's decisions through appointment of the solicitor general and occasional intervention in specific cases.

Presidents may have other ways to influence the justices. One stems from personal relationships between justices and presidents. Some members of the Court were close associates of the presidents who later selected them. Justices may also interact with presidents while serving on the bench. A few, such as Abe Fortas with President Johnson, have been frequent visitors to the White House for advisory or social purposes. Such relationships hardly compel justices to support the president's position in litigation, but they might affect a justice's responses to cases that concern the president.

Another potential source of influence derives from the president's impact on other institutions. Because of their visibility and prestige, presidents might shape the public's view of the Court and its decisions. They also affect responses to the Court's decisions by Congress and the federal bureaucracy. For these reasons, justices have an incentive to keep the peace with the president.

Even with all these means to exert influence, presidents frequently suffer defeats in the Supreme Court cases they care most about. And as one scholar has argued, there are signs that the Court has become less deferential to the president in the past two decades.[122] During that time the Court has favored presidential power in some decisions. But it also allowed lawsuits against presidents to proceed during their time in office and allowed the appointment of independent counsels to investigate charges against presidents; together, the two decisions led to the impeachment of President Clinton. The Court struck down the statute that gave the president power to veto individual items in budget bills. And two of its rulings have overruled presidential policies relating to the procedural rights of suspected terrorists.[123] Clearly, the president's influence over the Court, like that of Congress, has limits.

Conclusion

Of all the considerations that could influence the Supreme Court's decisions, I have given primary emphasis to the justices' policy preferences. The application of the law to the Court's cases is usually ambiguous, and constraints from the Court's environment are generally weak. As a result, the justices have considerable freedom to take positions that accord with their own conceptions of good policy. For this reason, the Court's membership and the process of selecting the justices have the greatest impact on the Court's direction.

If justices' preferences explain a great deal, they do not explain everything. The law and the political environment rule out some possible options for the Court, and they influence the justices' choices among the options that remain. The group life of the Court affects the behavior of individual justices and the Court's collective decisions. In particular, the justices regularly adjust their positions to win support from colleagues and help build majorities. These forces are reflected in results that might seem surprising: strikingly liberal decisions from a conservative Court and the maintenance of precedents even when most justices no longer favor the policies they embody.

Thus, what the Court does is a product of multiple, intertwined forces. These forces can be discussed one at a time, but ultimately they operate together in complicated ways to shape the Court's decisions. Those who want to understand why the Court does what it does must recognize the complexity of the process by which justices make their choices.

NOTES

1. *Arthur Andersen LLP v. United States,* 161 L. Ed. 2d 1008, 1019 (2005).
2. *McConnell v. Federal Election Commission* (2003).
3. Charles Lane, "Sentencing Rules Get Hearing," *Washington Post,* October 5, 2004, A3. The case was *United States v. Booker* (2005).
4. Joe Bob Briggs, "Joe Bob Briggs Goes to the Supreme Court," *Washingtonian,* December 2003, 63.
5. Linda Greenhouse, "In the Roberts Court, More Room for Argument," *New York Times,* May 3, 2006, A1, A17.
6. Numbers of participations were counted from the official transcripts of oral argument at the Supreme Court's Web site, www.supremecourt us.gov/. When justices asked consecutive questions, as they frequently do, that set of questions was counted as one participation.
7. Charles Lane, "A Private Hearing, of Sorts, for Anti-War Activists," *Washington Post,* May 6, 2002, A19.

8. Timothy R. Johnson, *Oral Arguments and Decision Making on the United States Supreme Court* (Albany: State University of New York Press, 2004).

9. Sarah Levien Shullman, "The Illusion of Devil's Advocacy: How the Justices of the Supreme Court Foreshadow Their Decisions during Oral Argument," *Journal of Appellate Practice and Advocacy* 6 (fall 2004): 292.

10. Dahlia Lithwick, "Nino's Chain Gang," *Slate*, at www.slate.com, April 17, 2002.

11. "This Week with George Stephanopoulos," ABC News, July 6, 2003, transcript.

12. William H. Rehnquist, *The Supreme Court*, new ed. (New York: Knopf, 2001), 258.

13. Tony Mauro, "After Just Six Months, Roberts Makes His Mark," *National Law Journal*, March 20, 2006, 14.

14. The process of responding to draft majority opinions is described in Forrest Maltzman, James F. Spriggs II, and Paul J. Wahlbeck, *Crafting Law on the Supreme Court: The Collegial Game* (New York: Cambridge University Press, 2000), 62–72.

15. Kevin Merida and Michael A. Fletcher, "Thomas v. Blackmun: Late Jurist's Papers Puncture Colleague's Portrait of a Genteel Court," *Washington Post*, October 10, 2004, A15.

16. Charles Lane, "Justices to Rehear Speech Case from October," *Washington Post*, February 18, 2006, A15.

17. *Rhines v. Weber*, 161 L. Ed. 2d 440, 453 (2005).

18. *Rompilla v. Beard*, 162 L. Ed. 2d 360, 379–381 (2005); *National Cable & Telecommunications Association v. Brand X Internet Services*, 162 L. Ed. 2d 820, 852–853 (2005).

19. Walter Dellinger, "Showtime for the Supremes," *Slate Magazine*, at www.slate.com, June 28, 2004.

20. John Roberts, in opening remarks at confirmation hearings, Senate Judiciary Committee, September 12, 2005.

21. Tony Mauro, "Solicitor General Has Subpar Season," *Legal Times*, September 4, 1995, 9.

22. Norman I. Silber, *With All Deliberate Speed: The Life of Philip Elman* (Ann Arbor: University of Michigan Press, 2004), 51.

23. Richard A. Posner, "Foreword: A Political Court," *Harvard Law Review* 119 (November 2005): 41.

24. Walter Murphy, *Elements of Judicial Strategy* (Chicago: University of Chicago Press, 1964), 44n*. See Jack Knight and Lee Epstein, "The Norm of *Stare Decisis*," *American Journal of Political Science* 40 (November 1996): 1018–1035.

25. Jeffrey A. Segal and Harold J. Spaeth, *The Supreme Court and the Attitudinal Model Revisited* (New York: Cambridge University Press, 2002), chap. 2; Howard Gillman, "What's Law Got to Do with It? Judicial Behavioralists Test the 'Legal Model' of Judicial Decision Making," *Law and Social Inquiry* 26 (spring 2001): 465–504; Robert M. Howard and Jeffrey A. Segal, "An Original Look at Originalism," *Law and Society Review* 36 (2002): 113–138; Stefanie A. Lindquist and David E. Klein, "The Influence of Jurisprudential Considerations on Supreme Court Decisionmaking: A Study of Conflict Cases," *Law and Society Review* 40 (March 2006): 135–161.

26. Lori Hausegger and Lawrence Baum, "Inviting Congressional Action: A Study of Supreme Court Motivations in Statutory Interpretation," *American Journal of Political Science* 43 (January 1999): 162–185.

27. Fred Barbash, "Congress Didn't, So the Supreme Court Did," *Washington Post*, July 5, 1998, C1.
28. *Lamie v. United States Trustee*, 540 U.S. 526, 534, 530 (2003).
29. *Bolling v. Sharpe* (1954).
30. *Gitlow v. New York* (1925); *Cantwell v. Connecticut* (1940).
31. *Hans v. Louisiana* (1890).
32. The decisions were *Atkins v. Virginia* (2002) and *Roper v. Simmons* (2005).
33. *Intel Corporation v. Advanced Micro Devices, Inc.*, 542 U.S. 241, 267 (2004).
34. James J. Brudney and Corey Ditslear, "The Decline and Fall of Legislative History? Patterns of Supreme Court Reliance in the Burger and Rehnquist Eras," *Judicature* 89 (January–February 2006): 220–229.
35. *Koons Buick Pontiac GMC, Inc., v. Nigh* (2004).
36. *Reno v. American-Arab Anti-Discrimination Committee*, 525 U.S. 471, 511 (1999).
37. Congressional Research Service, *The Constitution of the United States of America: Analysis and Interpretation* (Washington, D.C.: Government Printing Office, 2004), 2392–2399; *2004 Supplement* (Washington, D.C.: Government Printing Office, 2004), 63.
38. Ken Foskett, *Judging Thomas: The Life and Times of Clarence Thomas* (New York: Morrow, 2004), 281.
39. The decisions were, respectively, *American Trucking Associations v. Michigan Public Service Commission* (2005); *Kelo v. City of New London* (2005); and *Van Orden v. Perry* (2005).
40. Harold J. Spaeth and Jeffrey A. Segal, *Majority Rule or Minority Will: Adherence to Precedent on the U.S. Supreme Court* (New York: Cambridge University Press, 1999).
41. *State Farm Mutual v. Campbell* (2003).
42. See Thomas G. Hansford and James F. Spriggs II, *The Politics of Precedent on the U.S. Supreme Court* (Princeton: Princeton University Press, 2006).
43. Mark J. Richards and Herbert M. Kritzer, "Jurisprudential Regimes in Supreme Court Decision Making," *American Political Science Review* 96 (June 2002): 305–320; Herbert M. Kritzer and Mark J. Richards, "Jurisprudential Regimes and Supreme Court Decisionmaking: The *Lemon* Regime and Establishment Clause Cases," *Law and Society Review* 37 (2003): 827–840.
44. *Roper v. Simmons*, 161 L. Ed. 2d 1, 49, 123–135 (2005); Tony Mauro, "Supreme Court Opening Up to World Opinion," *Legal Times*, July 7, 2003, 1, 8; Tony Mauro, "Ginsburg Discloses Threats on Her Life," *Legal Times*, March 20, 2006, 8.
45. See Joseph L. Thai, "The Law Clerk Who Wrote *Rasul v. Bush:* John Paul Stevens's Influence from World War II to the War on Terror," *Virginia Law Review* 92 (2006): 501–532. The case was *Ahrens v. Clark* (1948).
46. A good example is Segal and Spaeth, *Supreme Court and the Attitudinal Model Revisited.*
47. For two competing positions, see Lee Epstein and Jack Knight, *The Choices Justices Make* (Washington, D.C.: CQ Press, 1998); and Segal and Spaeth *Supreme Court and the Attitudinal Model Revisited.*
48. Jeffrey A. Segal, Lee Epstein, Charles M. Cameron, and Harold J. Spaeth, "Ideological Values and the Votes of Justices Revisited," *Journal of Politics* 57 (August 1995): 812–823.
49. *City of Erie v. Pap's A.M.*, 529 U.S. 277, 316–317 (2000). A case citation is omitted from the opinion excerpt, but Souter was referring to *Barnes v. Glen Theatre, Inc.*, 501 U.S. 560 (1991).

50. David G. Savage, "Stevens, Souter: Supremely Vexing to GOP," *Los Angeles Times,* June 10, 2001, A22.
51. Figures on agreement between Blackmun and his colleagues are taken from the annual statistics on the Supreme Court term in the November issues of *Harvard Law Review,* vols. 85–100 (1972–1987). See also "The Changing Social Vision of Justice Blackmun," *Harvard Law Review* 96 (1983): 717–736.
52. See Linda Greenhouse, *Becoming Justice Blackmun: Harry Blackmun's Supreme Court Journey* (New York: Times Books, 2005).
53. Richard A. Posner, "A Tribute to Justice William J. Brennan, Jr.," *Harvard Law Review* 104 (November 1990): 13.
54. Spaeth and Segal, *Majority Rule or Minority Will,* 290–301.
55. Examples include *United States v. Morrison* (2000) and *Board of Trustees v. Garrett* (2001).
56. Examples include *Legal Services Corp. v. Velasquez* (2001) and *Ashcroft v. Free Speech Coalition* (2002).
57. See Richard Kluger, *Simple Justice: The History of* Brown v. Board of Education *and Black America's Struggle for Equality* (New York: Knopf, 1976), 582–699. The quotation is from William O. Douglas, *The Court Years, 1939–1975: The Autobiography of William O. Douglas* (New York: Random House, 1980), 115.
58. David G. Savage, "The Rescue of Roe vs. Wade," *Los Angeles Times,* December 13, 1992, A1, A28, A29.
59. Howard Gillman, *The Votes That Counted: How the Court Decided the 2000 Presidential Election* (Chicago: University of Chicago Press, 2001); David Margolick, "Bush's Court Advantage," *Vanity Fair,* December 2003, 144–162.
60. Institute of Governmental Studies, "Justice Stephen Breyer Visits IGS for an Informal Talk about the Supreme Court," *Public Affairs Report* 38 (May 1997): 10.
61. William H. Rehnquist, "Chief Justices I Never Knew," *Hastings Constitutional Law Quarterly* 3 (summer 1976): 647.
62. Rehnquist, *Supreme Court,* 222.
63. Sandra Day O'Connor, *The Majesty of the Law: Reflections of a Supreme Court Justice* (New York: Random House, 2003), 119.
64. See Maltzman, Spriggs, and Wahlbeck, *Crafting Law on the Supreme Court.*
65. Sandra L. Wood, "Negotiating on the Burger Court" (paper presented at the annual meeting of the Midwest Political Science Association, Chicago, April 1999), 22–23.
66. Maltzman, Spriggs, and Wahlbeck, *Crafting Law on the Supreme Court,* 116.
67. Forrest Maltzman and Paul J. Wahlbeck, "Strategic Policy Considerations and Voting Fluidity on the Burger Court," *American Political Science Review* 90 (September 1996): 587.
68. Segal and Spaeth, *Supreme Court and the Attitudinal Model Revisited,* 286.
69. O'Connor, *Majesty of the Law,* 195.
70. Douglas, *The Court Years,* 18.
71. Rehnquist, *Supreme Court,* 225–226.
72. James F. Simon, *The Antagonists: Hugo Black, Felix Frankfurter and Civil Liberties in Modern America* (New York: Simon and Schuster, 1989), 249.
73. Charles A. Reich, "Deciding the Fate of *Brown*," *Green Bag* 7 (winter 2004): 138.

74. Ruth Wedgwood, "Constitutional Equity," *Yale Law Journal* 104 (October 1994): 33.
75. Hunter R. Clark, *Justice Brennan: The Great Conciliator* (New York: Birch Lane Press, 1995); Kim Isaac Eisler, *A Justice for All: William J. Brennan, Jr., and the Decisions That Transformed America* (New York: Simon and Schuster, 1993).
76. Alexander Wohl, "What's Left," *American Bar Association Journal* 77 (February 1991): 42.
77. Nina Totenberg, "A Tribute to Justice William J. Brennan, Jr.," *Harvard Law Review* 104 (November 1990): 37.
78. Bernard Schwartz, *A History of the Supreme Court* (New York: Oxford University Press, 1993), 318.
79. Joan Biskupic, "Justice Stevens' Quiet Strength Can Be Persuasive," *USA Today*, June 3, 2004, 11A.
80. Jeffrey Rosen, "The Agonizer," *New Yorker*, November 11, 1996, 87.
81. *In the Matter of Wilkins*, 777 N.E. 2d 714, 720 (Ind. Sup. Ct. 2002).
82. Mark Tushnet, *A Court Divided: The Rehnquist Court and the Future of Constitutional Law* (New York: Norton, 2005), 150.
83. Dahlia Lithwick, "A High Court of One: The Role of the 'Swing Voter' in the 2002 Term," in *A Year at the Supreme Court*, ed. Neal Devins and Davison M. Douglas (Durham, N.C.: Duke University Press, 2004), 21.
84. David S. Broder, "O'Connor's Special Role," *Washington Post*, October 1, 2003, A23.
85. Jonathan Turley, "Unpacking the Court: The Case for the Expansion of the United States Supreme Court in the Twenty-first Century," *Perspectives on Political Science* 33 (summer 2004): 155–162.
86. Joan Biskupic, *Sandra Day O'Connor* (New York: HarperCollins, 2005).
87. Rehnquist, "Chief Justices I Never Knew," 637.
88. Forrest Maltzman and Paul J. Wahlbeck, "A Conditional Model of Opinion Assignment on the Supreme Court," *Political Research Quarterly* 57 (December 2004): 555n6.
89. This discussion of criteria for opinion assignment is based largely on the findings for the 1953–1990 period in Maltzman and Wahlbeck, "Conditional Model of Opinion Assignment," and Forrest Maltzman and Paul J. Wahlbeck, "May It Please the Chief? Opinion Assignments in the Rehnquist Court," *American Journal of Political Science* 40 (May 1996): 421–443.
90. Rehnquist, *Supreme Court*, 260.
91. Ruth Marcus, "Alumni Brennan, Blackmun Greet Harvard Law Freshmen," *Washington Post*, September 6, 1986, 2.
92. Tony Mauro, "The Highs and Lows of the 1992 Court," *Legal Times*, December 28, 1993, 14.
93. Bernard Schwartz, *Behind Bakke: Affirmative Action and the Supreme Court* (New York: New York University Press, 1988), 99.
94. See Timothy R. Johnson, James F. Spriggs, II, and Paul J. Wahlbeck, "Passing and Strategic Voting on the U.S. Supreme Court," *Law and Society Review* 39 (June 2005): 349–377.
95. David J. Garrow, *Liberty and Sexuality: The Right to Privacy and the Making of Roe v. Wade* (New York: Macmillan, 1994), 568.
96. John C. Jeffries Jr., *Justice Lewis F. Powell, Jr.* (New York: Scribner's, 1994), 545.
97. This discussion of Rehnquist is based in part on David G. Savage, "The Rehnquist Court," *Los Angeles Times Magazine*, September 29, 1991, 12–16,

38, 40; David J. Garrow, "The Rehnquist Reins," *New York Times Magazine,* October 6, 1996, 65–71, 82, 85; Sue Davis, "The Chief Justice and Judicial Decision-Making: The Institutional Basis for Leadership on the Supreme Court," in *Supreme Court Decision-Making: New Institutionalist Approaches,* ed. Cornell W. Clayton and Howard Gillman (Chicago: University of Chicago Press, 1999), 141–149; and Jeffrey Rosen, "Rehnquist the Great?" *Atlantic Monthly,* April 2005, 79–90.

98. Rosen, "Rehnquist the Great?" 79–80.
99. Tony Mauro, "Into the Robe and Off to the Races," *Legal Times,* October 10, 2005, 10.
100. Tony Mauro, "Court Singing in Harmony," *Legal Times,* March 13, 2006, 8.
101. Ibid.
102. "This Week with George Stephanopoulos," ABC News, July 6, 2003.
103. O'Connor, *Majesty of the Law,* 6.
104. Lawrence M. Friedman, "The Rehnquist Court: Some More or Less Historical Comments," in *The Rehnquist Court: A Retrospective,* ed. Martin H. Belsky (New York: Oxford University Press, 2002), 146.
105. Biskupic, *Sandra Day O'Connor,* 333–334.
106. Forrest Maltzman, Lee Sigelman, and Paul J. Wahlbeck, "Supreme Court Justices Really Do Follow the Election Returns," *P.S.: Political Science and Politics* 37 (October 2004): 839–842.
107. *Lincoln Property Co. v. Roche,* 163 L. Ed. 2d 415, 421 (2005).
108. Jeffrey Rosen, "The O'Connor Court: America's Most Powerful Jurist," *New York Times Magazine,* June 3, 2001, 35.
109. James L. Gibson, Gregory A. Caldeira, and Lester Kenyatta Spence, "The Supreme Court and the U.S. Presidential Election of 2000: Wounds, Self-Inflicted or Otherwise?" *British Journal of Political Science* 33 (2003): 535–556; Stephen P. Nicholson and Robert M. Howard, "Framing Support for the Supreme Court in the Aftermath of *Bush v. Gore,*" *Journal of Politics* 65 (August 2003): 676–695.
110. *Elk Grove Unified School District v. Newdow* (2004).
111. See Helmut Norpoth and Jeffrey A. Segal, "Popular Impact on Supreme Court Decisions: Comment," *American Political Science Review* 88 (September 1994): 711–716; Roy B. Flemming and B. Dan Wood, "The Public and the Supreme Court: Individual Justice Responsiveness to American Policy Moods," *American Journal of Political Science* 41 (April 1997): 468–498; and Kevin T. McGuire and James A. Stimson, "The Least Dangerous Branch Revisited: New Evidence on Supreme Court Responsiveness to Public Preferences," *Journal of Politics* 66 (November 2004): 1018–1035.
112. Foskett, *Judging Thomas,* 18.
113. Charles Lane, "Kennedy's Assault on Editorial Writers," *Washington Post,* April 3, 2006, A17.
114. Greenhouse, *Becoming Justice Blackmun,* 48.
115. Thomas Sowell, "Blackmun Plays to the Crowd," *St. Louis Post Dispatch,* March 4, 1994, 7B; Michael Barone, "Justices Have Typically Felt Little Compunction about Overturning Laws and Making Public Policy," *Chicago Sun-Times,* July 13, 2005, 55.
116. Paul M. Collins Jr., "Friends of the Court: Examining the Influence of Amicus Curiae Participation in U.S. Supreme Court Litigation," *Law and Society Review* 38 (2004): 807–832.

117. Timothy R. Johnson, Paul J. Wahlbeck, and James F. Spriggs II, "The Influence of Oral Arguments on the U.S. Supreme Court," *American Political Science Review* 100 (February 2006): 99–113.
118. That proportion was calculated from the Court's decisions in cases decided on the merits, those listed in the front section of the *Supreme Court Reports, Lawyers' Edition.*
119. Linda Greenhouse, "Affirmative Reaction: Can the Justices Buck What the Establishment Backs?" *New York Times,* March 30, 2003, sec. 4, p. 4. The cases were *Gratz v. Bollinger* (2003) and *Grutter v. Bollinger* (2003).
120. See Rebecca E. Deen, Joseph Ignagni, and James Meernik, "Individual Justices and the Solicitor General: The Amicus Curiae Cases, 1953–2000," *Judicature* 89 (September–October 2005): 68–77.
121. For contrasting arguments and evidence, see Segal and Spaeth, *Supreme Court and the Attitudinal Model Revisited,* 326–356; and Mario Bergara, Barak Richman, and Pablo T. Spiller, "Modeling Supreme Court Strategic Decision Making: The Congressional Constraint," *Legislative Studies Quarterly* 28 (May 2003): 247–280.
122. David Yalof, "The Presidency and the Judiciary," in *The Presidency and the Political System,* 8th ed., ed. Michael Nelson (Washington, D.C.: CQ Press, 2006), 501–504.
123. These decisions were, respectively, *Clinton v. Jones* (1997); *Morrison v. Olson* (1988); *Clinton v. City of New York* (1998); *Hamdi v. Rumsfeld* (2004); and *Hamdan v. Rumsfeld* (2006).

Chapter 5

Policy Outputs

The last two chapters examined the processes that shape the Supreme Court's policies. In this chapter, I consider the substance of those policies by addressing several questions. What kinds of issues does the Court address? How active is the Court as a policymaker? What is the ideological content of its policies? I conclude the chapter by developing an explanation for historical patterns in the Court's outputs.

Areas of Activity: What the Court Addresses

During any given term, the Supreme Court resolves a broad range of issues in fields as varied as antitrust, environmental protection, and freedom of speech. In this sense the Court's agenda is highly diverse. But the Court generally devotes most of its efforts to a few policy fields. To a considerable degree, then, the Court is a specialist.

The Court's Current Activity

The content of the Court's agenda can be illustrated with the cases that it heard in the 2004 term. It is useful to begin by describing the issues in a fairly representative sample of cases decided during that term.

1. Does a federal statute that makes it illegal for a person convicted of a serious crime "in any court" to possess a firearm apply to convictions in foreign courts (*Small v. United States*, 2005)?

2. Did a lawsuit for defamation become moot with the death of the plaintiff, when an injunction against the defendant had been issued (*Tory v. Cochran*, 2005)?

3. Does the visible shackling of a convicted defendant during the penalty phase of a capital case ordinarily violate the defendant's right to due process of law (*Deck v. Missouri*, 2005)?

4. Does the use of patented drug compounds in preclinical research constitute patent infringement when the research is related to federal drug regulation but the results of the research are not ultimately submitted to the government? (*Merck v. Integra Lifesciences,* 2005)?

5. In a capital case, does a defense lawyer's decision to concede the defendant's guilt without the defendant's express consent automatically violate the constitutional right to effective counsel (*Florida v. Nixon,* 2004)?

6. Does the power of the federal government to regulate interstate commerce include the power to prohibit cultivation and use of marijuana that is allowed by California law (*Gonzales v. Raich,* 2005)?

7. Is someone who distributes a device with the purpose of promoting its use to infringe copyrights legally liable for the infringement that results from use of the device (*Metro-Goldwyn-Mayer Studios v. Grokster,* 2005)?

8. Does an amended petition for habeas corpus "relate back" to the date of the original petition and thus avoid the deadline for filing of the petition when it offers a new ground for overturning the defendant's conviction supported by facts that were not put forward earlier (*Mayle v. Felix,* 2005)?

9. Is generic advertising for beef, managed by the Department of Agriculture, "government speech" and thus exempt from challenge under the First Amendment by those required to contribute money for the advertising (*Johanns v. Lifestock Marketing Association,* 2005)?

10. Does the federal Age Discrimination in Employment Act allow plaintiffs to recover damages for practices that have a "disparate impact" on older employees (*Smith v. City of Jackson,* 2005)?

Table 5-1 provides a more systematic picture of the Court's agenda in the 2004 term by summarizing the characteristics of the eighty decisions with full opinions in that term. The Court's decisions were closely connected with the other branches of government. The federal government or one of its agencies was a party in one-quarter of the cases, a smaller proportion than usual but still a substantial number. State governments were parties in most other cases, so that four in five cases had at least one government party. Moreover, most of the disputes between private parties were based directly on government policy in fields such as environmental protection and civil rights.

Only a large minority of cases were decided on constitutional grounds, although several additional cases had constitutional issues in the background. In the 2004 term, as in other recent terms, the majority of cases involved interpretations of federal statutes. Observers of the Court tend to focus on its interpretations of the Constitution, which often involve

TABLE 5-1
*Characteristics of Decisions by the Supreme Court with Full Opinions,
2004 Term*

Characteristic	Number	Percentage
Number of decisions	80	NA
Cases from lower federal courts	65	81
Cases from state courts	13	16
Original cases	2	3
Federal government party[a]	20	25
State or local government party[a]	44	55
No government party	16	20
Constitutional issue decided[b]	32	40
No constitutional issue decided	48	60
Civil liberties issue present[c]	48	60
No civil liberties issue	32	40
Criminal cases[d]	31	39
Civil cases	49	61

Source: Data based on listings of cases in the front section of *United States Supreme Court Reports, Lawyers' Edition,* vols. 160–162.

Note: NA = not applicable. Consolidated cases decided with one set of opinions were counted once.

a. Cases with both a federal government party and another government party were listed as federal government. Government as party includes agencies and individual government officials.
b. In 14 additional cases, the parties raised constitutional issues or those issues were present in the underlying case.
c. Includes cases in which the Court did not decide the civil liberties issue directly.
d. Includes actions brought by prisoners to challenge the legality of their convictions but excludes cases concerning rights of prisoners.

fundamental issues about the structure and power of government. But the Court devotes much of its collective energy to statutory interpretation, adjudicating disputes about the meaning of federal laws.

In the 2004 term, as has been true for several decades, the Court's primary area of activity was civil liberties. As in earlier discussions, the term "civil liberties" refers here to three general types of rights: procedural rights of people involved in government proceedings; the right of disadvantaged groups to equal treatment; and certain "substantive" rights, the most important of which are freedom of expression and freedom of religion. By that definition, 60 percent of the Court's decisions fell into this area.

Related to the Court's civil liberties emphasis is its work in criminal law and procedure. More than one-third of the 2004 decisions resulted from criminal prosecutions, and some others related to criminal law and procedure. In most terms criminal cases are less prominent on the agenda, but in the current era they always constitute a large minority of the Court's cases. In a large majority of the criminal cases the Court interprets constitutional protections of due process rights.

The list of representative cases from the 2004 term illustrates two other areas in which the Court is active. Outside of civil liberties, the largest number of cases concerns economic issues. Most civil liberties cases are based on constitutional questions, but economic cases generally involve statutory interpretation. Most of these cases arise from government regulation of economic activity, such as labor-management relations, antitrust, and environmental protection.

Another major subject of Court activity is federalism, the division of power between federal and state governments. Federalism overlaps with other categories, and most federalism cases concern economic issues. This concern has been especially prominent in the past decade.

Taken together, civil liberties, economic policy, and federalism cover a large portion of the issues that arise in American government. Still, the Court's emphasis on those issues constitutes something of a specialized focus. Most striking is its concentration on civil liberties. Although civil liberties cases are quite varied, the fact that half or more of the Court's decisions concern this single kind of issue is an indication of the Court's specialization.

Change in the Court's Agenda

The Court's agenda is far from static. Even over a few terms, the Court's attention to specific categories of cases sometimes increases or decreases substantially. The shape of its agenda as a whole changes more slowly, but over long periods it may undergo fundamental change.[1]

Changes in Specific Areas. Sometimes an issue that has occupied a very small place on the Court's agenda, or no place at all, becomes more prominent. More often than not, the source is action by Congress. In the absence of legislation prohibiting discrimination in employment, for instance, people who felt that they had been subjected to discrimination had little basis for bringing cases to court. The series of statutes in this field from 1963 on provided that basis, and the resulting cases created a substantial number of legal questions that the Court chose to resolve. It has now heard more than one hundred cases in this area.

Perhaps more striking are issues concerning employee pension plans. Until 1980 the Court decided few cases involving those issues. Since then the Court has decided more than forty cases in this area. The source of this change is simple: Congress enacted the Employee Retirement Income Security Act of 1974. This regulation of pension plans raised a variety of legal questions that the courts had to address, and the justices have seen a need to resolve many of these questions themselves. As a result, even though few justices have much interest in the complex issues in this area, pensions have become a staple of the Court's work.

The Court itself can open up new areas on its agenda with decisions that create legal rights or add to existing rights. When the Court ruled in *Roe v. Wade* (1973) that the abortion laws of most states violated the constitutional right to privacy, it ensured that it would have to decide a stream of cases involving challenges to new abortion laws. The same was true of the Court's death penalty decisions in 1976, which established that capital punishment was constitutionally acceptable but also held that there were limits on its use.[2] Since then the Court has addressed a wide range of issues involving the death penalty in more than seventy cases.

Just as issues can rise on the Court's agenda, they can also recede. Often, a new statute or Court decision raises a series of issues that the Court resolves. Once they are resolved, the Court need not decide as many cases in this area. In *Benton v. Maryland* (1969), the Court ruled that the constitutional protection against double jeopardy for criminal offenses applied to the states. This decision opened the way for state cases involving claims of double jeopardy to reach the Court, and in the 1970s and 1980s the Court decided more than fifty cases in this field. But with so many issues resolved, the Court has heard only occasional double jeopardy cases since then.

The rise and fall of poverty law illustrates the complexities of the agenda-setting process. President Lyndon Johnson's War on Poverty in the mid-1960s raised national concern with poverty and established programs to benefit people with low incomes. One program, the Legal Services Program (later the Legal Services Corporation), provided lawyers for the poor in civil cases. Some of those lawyers brought cases challenging government practices related to the poor, and the Warren Court and early Burger Court were receptive to those challenges. That encouraged lawyers to bring more cases on behalf of the poor, but an increasingly conservative Burger Court of the late 1970s and early 1980s ruled more frequently against the poor. As a result, lawyers saw less value in bringing poverty cases to the Court, and the justices themselves were less interested in hearing such cases. Further, Congress put significant restrictions on the litigation activity of Legal Services lawyers in 1975. As a result, a field that accounted for five cases per term at its peak dwindled to less than one case a year in the Rehnquist Court.

Changes in the Agenda as a Whole. Beyond such changes in specific areas, the overall pattern of the Court's agenda may change over a period of several decades.[3] The current agenda reflects a fundamental change that occurred between the 1930s and 1960s. In the half century up to the 1930s the largest part of the Court's agenda was devoted to economic issues, issues that arose primarily from government economic policies. Also important but clearly secondary were cases about federalism. Issues of procedural due process constituted a small proportion of the agenda, and other civil liberties issues were barely present.

Over the next three decades the Court evolved from an institution concerned primarily with economic issues to one that gave attention primarily to individual liberties. The proportion of decisions dealing with civil liberties grew from 8 percent of the agenda in the 1933–1937 terms to 59 percent in the 1968–1972 terms.[4] Issues involving the rights of criminal defendants became far more numerous, and other civil liberties issues, such as racial equality, took a substantial share of the agenda. At the same time, some kinds of economic cases declined precipitously. In 1933–1937, one of every three cases involved federal taxation or economic disputes between private parties over such issues as personal injuries. By 1968–1972, the two areas accounted for only 6 percent of the Court's agenda. Federalism also took a reduced share of the agenda, falling from 14 percent in 1933–1937 to 5 percent in 1968–1972.

Many forces contributed to this change, ranging from public opinion to federal legislation. Interest groups that brought civil liberties cases to the Court played an especially important role. But actions by the Court itself had the most direct effect. Perhaps most important, the justices became more interested in protecting civil liberties and thus in hearing challenges to government policies that allegedly infringed on liberties. Because they had to make room on the agenda for civil liberties cases and because they were less interested in scrutinizing economic policies, the justices gave more limited attention to fields other than civil liberties.

The Court's agenda has changed in some respects since then. In particular, federalism has had something of a resurgence. But on the whole, the broad contours of the agenda have remained stable. In particular, as the agenda for the 2004 term illustrates, the Court retains a primary focus on civil liberties. Thus, the Court's work still reflects the changes in its agenda that occurred between the 1930s and the 1960s.

The change in the Court's agenda was massive but not total. Since the 1960s the Court has continued to decide substantial numbers of economic cases, largely because of the need to resolve conflicting interpretations of federal statutes in the lower courts. If the Court in the future reverses the shift from economics to civil liberties, the same need will ensure that the justices do not abandon civil liberties altogether. As Richard Pacelle has pointed out, the Court's agenda at any time is a product of both the justices' interests and their perceptions of their duty to bring greater clarity and consistency to the federal law.[5]

A Broader View of the Agenda

If the Supreme Court's current agenda differs from the agendas of previous Courts, it also differs from those of other policymakers. In turn, those differences provide some perspective on the Court's role.

Comparison with Other Institutions. In some respects, the Supreme Court's agenda is similar to that of other appellate courts, especially state supreme courts and federal courts of appeals. To a considerable extent, all of these courts focus on government parties and government policy. Criminal cases are prominent on the agendas of virtually all appellate courts, and most give substantial attention to economic issues. Except for the rights of criminal defendants, however, civil liberties issues are relatively rare in lower appellate courts. The Supreme Court stands alone in the prominence of issues involving rights to equal treatment and freedom of expression.

Like the Court, the president is something of a specialist. But the president's agenda has its own emphases: foreign policy and maintenance of the nation's economic health. In contrast, the Court makes few decisions about foreign policy, and its decisions on economic policy barely touch the function of managing the economy.

More than the president and the Court, Congress is a generalist, spreading its activity across a large set of issues. One result is that the congressional agenda covers virtually all the types of policy that the Supreme Court deals with. But some of the issues that are central to the Court, especially in civil liberties, receive much less attention from Congress. And Congress gives a high priority to several fields, ranging from foreign policy to agriculture, that are less important to the Court.

The Court's Position. These comparisons of agendas underline the limited range of the Court's work. Its jurisdiction is very broad, but the bulk of its decisions are made in a few policy areas.

The Court's specialization affects its role as a policymaker. By deciding as many civil liberties cases as it does, the Court can do much to shape law and policy in this area. In contrast, the Court's more limited activity in some major policy areas severely narrows its potential impact in those fields. Because of its agenda the Court today can have little impact on government management of the economy and even less impact on foreign policy.[6] Many people consider these the two most important areas of government policy.

These realities should caution against the conclusion that the Supreme Court is the most important policymaker in the United States. The Court should not be regarded as preeminent when the range of its activities is so limited. It could not possibly be dominant as a policymaker except in federalism, civil liberties, and some limited areas of economic policy. For

Secretary of State Condoleezza Rice in Iraq with U.S. soldiers and Massoud Barzani, leader of the Kurdistan Democratic Party, in 2005. Except for the legal rights of suspected terrorists, the Supreme Court has not dealt with issues arising from the war in Iraq.

reasons that are discussed in the rest of this chapter and in Chapter 6, even in those areas the Court is far from dominant.

The Court's Activism

The Court's attention or inattention to various areas of policy helps determine where it is likely to play a significant role. But its impact also depends on what it rules in those policy areas. Of particular importance is how much it uses its decisions to make significant changes in government policy, engaging in what is sometimes labeled judicial activism.

Of the various forms of judicial activism, perhaps the most important is making decisions that conflict with policies of the other branches. This form of activism is often gauged by the Court's use of judicial review, its power to overturn acts of other policymakers on the ground that they violate the Constitution. The Court intervenes in government policy most directly and most clearly through its use of judicial review. And judicial review, unlike some other forms of activism, is easy to measure. For these reasons, it is a good focus for analysis of activism.

Overturning Acts of Congress

The most familiar use of judicial review comes in decisions holding that federal statutes are unconstitutional. Such rulings represent a striking assertion of power by the Court. When the Court overturns a federal law on constitutional grounds, it directly negates a decision by another branch of the federal government.

There is sometimes disagreement about whether the Court actually has struck down a statute. By one count, however, by the end of 2005 the Court had overturned 160 federal laws completely or in part.[7] This number in itself is noteworthy. On the one hand, it indicates that the Court has made fairly frequent use of its review power—on average, more than once every two years. On the other hand, the laws struck down by the Court constitute a minute fraction of the laws that Congress has adopted. A closer look at these decisions provides a better sense of their significance.[8]

One question is the importance of the statutes that the Court has overturned. The Court has struck down some statutes of major significance. Among these were the Missouri Compromise of 1820, concerning slavery in the territories, which the Court declared unconstitutional in the *Dred Scott* case in 1857, and the New Deal economic legislation that was overturned in 1935 and 1936.[9] In contrast, many of the Court's decisions declaring statutes unconstitutional have been unimportant to the policy goals of Congress and the president, either because the statutes were minor or because they were struck down only as they applied to particular circumstances.

A related question is the timing of judicial review. The Court's decisions striking down federal statutes fall into three groups of nearly equal size: those that came no more than four calendar years after a statute's enactment, those that came five to twelve years later, and those that occurred at least thirteen years later. Congress sometimes retains a strong commitment to a statute from an earlier period. But often few members care much if an older law is overturned: the statute becomes less relevant over time, or the collective point of view in Congress becomes less favorable to the provision in question.

For these reasons the Court's frequent use of its power to invalidate congressional acts is somewhat misleading. Any decision that strikes down a federal statute might seem likely to bring about a major conflict between the Court and Congress, but that is not necessarily the case. Conflict is most likely when the Court invalidates an important congressional policy within a few years of its enactment, but most decisions striking down statutes do not meet both those criteria.

Another way to gauge the significance of judicial review is in terms of the historical pattern of its use. As Table 5-2 shows, the Court has not

TABLE 5-2
Number of Federal Statutes Held Unconstitutional
by the Supreme Court, 1790–2005

Period	Number	Period	Number
1790–1799	0	1900–1909	9
1800–1809	1	1910–1919	6
1810–1819	0	1920–1929	15
1820–1829	0	1930–1939	13
1830–1839	0	1940–1949	2
1840–1849	0	1950–1959	5
1850–1859	1	1960–1969	16
1860–1869	4	1970–1979	20
1870–1879	7	1980–1989	16
1880–1889	4	1990–1999	23
1890–1899	5	2000–2005	13
		Total	160

Sources: Congressional Research Service, *The Constitution of the United States of America: Analysis and Interpretation, 2000 Edition* and *2004 Supplement* (Washington, D.C.: Government Printing Office, 2004, 2004); author's analysis of 2005 cases.

overturned federal statutes at a consistent rate. Before 1865 it struck down only two statutes. The Court then began to exercise its judicial review power more actively, overturning thirty-five federal laws between 1865 and 1919. Two more increases, even more dramatic, followed: the Court struck down fifteen federal laws during the 1920s, and twelve from 1934 through 1936. Over the next quarter century, the Court used this power sparingly. But between 1960 and 2005, it overturned eighty-eight statutes, far more than in any previous period of the same length and more than half of the total for the Court's entire history.

The period of greatest conflict between the Court and Congress was 1918 to 1936, when the Court overturned twenty-nine federal laws. Many of these laws were significant. Between 1918 and 1928, the Court struck down two child labor laws and a minimum wage law, along with several less important statutes. Then, between 1933 and 1936, a majority of the Court engaged in a frontal attack on the New Deal program, an attack that ended with the Court's 1937 shift in position.

Among all the statutes that the Court struck down between 1960 and 1994, a few were of major importance. *Buckley v. Valeo* (1976) and several later decisions invalidated major provisions of the Federal Election Campaign Act on First Amendment grounds and thereby made comprehensive regulation of campaign finance impossible. In *Immigration and Naturalization Service v. Chadha* (1983), the Court struck down a relatively minor provision of an immigration law. But its ruling indicated that the legislative veto, a widely used mechanism for congressional control of the executive branch, violated the constitutional separation of powers. These decisions were exceptions. In general, the laws overturned by the Court in the 1960–1994 period were not nearly as significant as the economic legislation that it struck down in the 1930s. Indeed, most of the Court's decisions striking down federal laws received little attention from the mass media or the general public.

Between 1995 and 2002, the Court invalidated thirty-one federal laws, a record number for an eight-year period. During this period, as in prior periods, most of the laws struck down were relatively minor. One exception was *Clinton v. City of New York* (1998), in which the Court ruled that Congress could not give presidents the power to veto individual items within budget bills and thereby ended a major innovation in policymaking.

The Court also handed down ten decisions that limited the power of Congress to regulate state governments. In these decisions the Court gave narrow interpretations to the Commerce Clause and the Fourteenth Amendment as bases for federal power while giving a broad interpretation to the Eleventh Amendment as a limit on lawsuits against states. In *Board of Trustees v. Garrett* (2001), for example, the Court ruled that Congress could not authorize disabled individuals to seek monetary damages from states in lawsuits for discrimination. This set of decisions constitutes a substantial change in the federal-state balance. But it has not been as consequential as the economic decisions of the 1920s and 1930s, because the current Congress is not inclined to assert federal power against the states in the areas where the Court has limited that power.

The pace of overturnings slowed considerably after 2002. In the three years that followed, the Court struck down provisions of only two federal laws. But one of the two was the statute creating the federal sentencing guidelines. In *United States v. Booker* (2005), the Court invalidated the provision that made the guidelines mandatory, thereby overturning the sentencing system that had operated in the federal courts for nearly two decades.

One scholar argued that the Rehnquist Court was "the most activist Supreme Court in history," and another wrote of the "insistent judicial assertiveness" of the Rehnquist Court.[10] The perceptions of activism from these and other observers stem in part from the large number of federal statutes that the Court struck down between 1995 and 2002. More broadly, some observers perceived a lack of judicial deference to the other branches of government. As they saw it, the justices collectively sought to maintain a powerful role in resolving the national issues that came before them.

Overturning State and Local Laws

The Supreme Court's exercise of judicial review over state and local laws has less of an activist element than does its use of that power over federal laws. When the Court strikes down a state law, it does not put itself in conflict with the other branches of the federal government. Indeed, it may be supporting their powers over those of the states. Still, it is invalidating the action of another policymaker. For that reason, this form of judicial review is significant.

From 1790 to 2005, by one count, the Court overturned 1,065 state statutes and local ordinances as unconstitutional. It ruled that another 228 state and local laws were invalid because they were preempted by federal law under the constitutional principle of federal supremacy. The total of nearly thirteen hundred state and local laws struck down is about eight times the number for federal statutes (see Table 5-2). The disparity is even greater than this figure suggests, because many of the Court's decisions overturning particular state and local laws also applied to similar laws in other states.

As shown in Table 5-3, the rate at which the Court invalidates state and local laws has increased tremendously over time. One jump came in the 1860s, another early in the twentieth century. The highest rate of decisions striking down state and local laws occurred from the 1960s through the 1980s. In that period, the Court declared unconstitutional an average of seventeen such laws per year. The rate of invalidations has been much lower since 1990, returning to the level of the 1940s and 1950s. That decline probably reflects the same sympathy for the states that led the Rehnquist Court to limit federal power over the states.

Although the Court struck down relatively few state laws before 1860, its decisions during that period were important because they limited state powers under the Constitution. For example, under John Marshall (1801–1835) the Court weakened the states with such decisions as *McCulloch v. Maryland* (1819), which denied the states power to tax federal agencies, and *Gibbons v. Ogden* (1824), which narrowed state power to regulate commerce.

The state and local laws the Court has overturned in more recent periods have been a mixture of the important and the minor. In the aggregate, the Court's decisions have given it a significant role in shaping state policy. During the late nineteenth century and the first third of the twentieth, the Court struck down a great deal of state economic legislation, including many laws regulating business practices and labor relations. The net effect was to turn back much of a major tide of public policy.

Some of the Court's decisions since the mid-1950s have also impinged on major elements of state policy. A series of rulings helped to break down the legal bases of racial segregation and discrimination in southern states.

TABLE 5-3

Number of State Laws and Local Ordinances Held Unconstitutional by the Supreme Court, Including Those Preempted by Federal Laws, 1790–2005

Period	Number	Period	Number
1790–1799	0	1900–1909	40
1800–1809	1	1910–1919	119
1810–1819	7	1920–1929	139
1820–1829	8	1930–1939	92
1830–1839	3	1940–1949	61
1840–1849	10	1950–1959	66
1850–1859	7	1960–1969	151
1860–1869	24	1970–1979	195
1870–1879	36	1980–1989	164
1880–1889	46	1990–1999	62
1890–1899	36	2000–2005	26
		Total	1,293

Sources: Congressional Research Service, *The Constitution of the United States of America: Analysis and Interpretation, 2000 Edition* and *2004 Supplement* (Washington, D.C.: Government Printing Office, 2004, 2004); author's analysis of 2005 cases.

Totals for some decades prior to 2000 differ from those in the 8th edition of this book because of changes in the Congressional Research Service publication.

In 1973 the Court overturned the broad prohibitions of abortion that existed in most states, thereby requiring a general legalization of abortion; it has struck down several new laws regulating abortion since then, and its rulings have indirectly invalidated many other abortion laws. And through a long series of decisions, the Court limited state power to regulate the economy in areas that Congress has preempted under its constitutional supremacy. In doing so, the Court shifted power further toward the federal government and away from the states. The current Court is reversing this shift to a degree, but it is not yet clear how far the reversal will extend.

Other Targets of Judicial Review

The Supreme Court can declare unconstitutional any government policy or practice, not just laws enacted by legislative bodies. The number of non-statutory policies and practices that the Court has struck down is probably much larger than the 1,450 laws it has overturned. One example is a county executive's decision to place a display of the Ten Commandments in the county courthouse, declared unconstitutional in *McCreary County v. American Civil Liberties Union* (2005). On constitutional grounds the Court has also overruled actions taken by federal cabinet departments, local school boards, and state courts, among others.

The Court is especially active in overseeing criminal procedure under the Constitution, and it frequently holds that actions by police officers or trial judges violate the rights of defendants. During the 2004 term, for instance, the Court declared unconstitutional a trial judge's instruction to a jury, another trial judge's reversal of her own initial ruling in favor of a criminal defendant, and the shackling of a defendant during the penalty phase of a death penalty trial.[11] And there has been a long series of decisions holding that police searches and questioning of suspects violated constitutional protections.

Of particular interest is the Court's review of presidential orders and policies. Decisions of presidents or officials acting on their behalf can be challenged on the grounds that they are unauthorized by the Constitution or that they violate a constitutional rule. It is difficult to say how frequently the Court strikes down presidential actions as unconstitutional, because it is often unclear whether an action by the executive branch should be considered "presidential." But such decisions by the Court seem to be relatively rare.[12]

The Court has invalidated a few major actions by presidents, however. In *Ex parte Milligan* (1866), it held that President Abraham Lincoln had lacked the power to suspend the writ of habeas corpus for military prisoners during the Civil War. And in *Youngstown Sheet and Tube Co. v. Sawyer* (1952), it declared that President Harry Truman had acted illegally during the Korean War when he ordered the federal government to seize and operate major steel mills because their workers were preparing to go on strike. Decisions of another type, which limited presidents' power to withhold information from courts and their immunity from lawsuits, led to President Nixon's resignation and President Clinton's impeachment.[13]

In 2004 the Court ruled that U.S. citizens are entitled to a hearing to contest their designation as enemy combatants. In 2006 the Court held that the military commissions set up at Guantanamo Bay to try suspected terrorists were not authorized by law. Those decisions did not declare unconstitutional any decisions by President George W. Bush, but they overruled aspects of the president's policies relating to terrorism.[14]

Judicial Review: The General Picture

The Supreme Court's record of judicial review is complex. The Court has been more activist in some eras than others. On the whole, the level of activism has increased over time, in part because of the growth in the volume of government activity that can be challenged. The Court has struck down far more state and local policies than federal policies, and it has done more to limit state and local action than federal action.

The Court's overall record is ambiguous. The justices have made considerable use of the power of judicial review, thereby making the Court a major participant in the policymaking process. Yet the justices also have been quite selective in using their power to strike down laws. Partly as a result, the great majority of public policies at all levels of government have continued without Court interference. Thus, important as judicial review has been, it has not given the Court anything like a dominant position in the national government.

Statutory Interpretation

Historically, only a minority of the Supreme Court's decisions have determined whether some government practice is unconstitutional. Instead, most have interpreted federal statutes. Statutory interpretation may seem routine, but it can involve activism in at least two senses.

For one thing, the Court's statutory decisions often determine whether an administrative agency has interpreted a statute correctly in the process of implementing it. If the Court concludes that an agency has erred, it strikes down the agency's action as contrary to the statute. More broadly, the Court often puts its own stamp on a statute through its interpretations of that statute over the years. It has done so with its decisions on antitrust, labor relations, and environmental protection. In this way the Court affects national policy in the fields covered by those statutes.

This process is exemplified by Title VII of the Civil Rights Act of 1964, the most important of the federal statutes that prohibit employment discrimination. As with many other statutes, Congress laid out the broad outlines of the law and left it to the other branches to fill in the gaps. Over the years the Court has resolved many major issues. For example, it has established and revised the guidelines that courts use to determine whether an employer has engaged in discrimination.[15] It ruled that a company's policies could violate Title VII on the basis of their impact, even if the employer did not intend to discriminate.[16] It held that sexual harassment may constitute sex discrimination under Title VII and set up rules to determine when an employer is legally responsible for harassment.[17] Through these and other rulings the Court has affected the use and impact of this statute and thus has shaped federal policy concerning employment discrimination.

The Content of Policy

In the preceding sections of this chapter I have examined the areas in which the Supreme Court concentrates its efforts and the extent of its activism. A third aspect of the Court's role as a policymaker is the substance or content of its policies. This content can best be understood in terms of its ideological direction and its beneficiaries. Dividing the Court's history into eras is arbitrary, but it is useful to think of the period since the late nineteenth century as containing three eras.

The 1890s to the 1930s

During any period of several decades, the Supreme Court is certain to shift its position on some broad issues. That was true of the four-decade period that began near the end of the nineteenth century. But in ideological terms, the Court of that era was predominantly conservative. Most of its activism was on behalf of advantaged interests, such as business corporations. In contrast, it did little to protect such disadvantaged groups as racial minorities.

Scrutinizing Economic Regulation. In 1915 the Supreme Court decided *South Covington & Cincinnati Street Railway Co. v. City of Covington.* The company, which ran streetcars between Covington, Kentucky, and Cincinnati, Ohio, challenged several provisions of a Covington ordinance regulating its operations. The Court struck down some provisions on the ground that they constituted a burden on interstate commerce between Ohio and Kentucky. The Court also declared invalid a regulation stipulating that the temperature in the cars never be permitted to go below fifty degrees Fahrenheit: "We therefore think ... this feature of the ordinance is unreasonable and cannot be sustained"—apparently on the ground that the regulation violated the Fourteenth Amendment by depriving the company of its property without due process of law.

The *South Covington* case illustrates some important characteristics of the Court's decisions during the period from the 1890s to the late 1930s. In that period, as discussed earlier, the Court dealt primarily with economic issues. Most important, it ruled on challenges to growing government regulation of business practices.

In these cases, the Court frequently decided in favor of government, rejecting most challenges to federal and state policies and giving broad interpretations to some government powers.[18] But the Court limited government regulatory powers in important respects, and over time its limits on regulation became tighter. This development is reflected in the number of laws involving economic policy that the Court struck down each decade: 43 from 1900 to 1909, 114 from 1910 to 1919, and 133 from 1920 to 1929.[19] The Court's attacks on government regulation peaked in the mid-1930s, when it struck down most of the major statutes in President Franklin Roosevelt's New Deal program to deal with the Great Depression.

The theme of limiting government regulatory powers was reflected in the Court's constitutional doctrines. At the national level, the Court gave narrow interpretations to congressional powers over taxation and interstate commerce. In contrast, the Court read the general limitation on federal power in the Tenth Amendment broadly as a bar to certain federal action on the ground that it interfered with state prerogatives. At the state level, the Court ruled in 1886 that corporations were "persons" with rights protected by the Fourteenth Amendment.[20] Further, it interpreted the Fourteenth Amendment requirement that state governments provide "due process of law" as an absolute prohibition of regulations that interfered unduly with the liberty and property rights of businesses. The Court's ruling against the streetcar temperature regulation was one of many such decisions.

The Court's Beneficiaries. The business community benefited from the Court's policies during this period, and major corporations benefited the most. Of the regulatory legislation that the Court overturned or limited, much was aimed at the activities of large businesses. The railroads were the most prominent example. Although the Court allowed a good deal of government control over railroads, it also struck down a large body of railroad regulation.[21] In the decade from 1910 to 1919, the Court overturned forty-one state laws in cases brought by railroad companies. Major corporations such as railroads might be considered the clientele of the Court from the 1890s to the 1930s.

Large corporations did not simply benefit from the Court's policies; they helped to bring them about.[22] Beginning in the late nineteenth century, the corporate community employed much of the best legal talent in the United States to challenge the validity of regulatory statutes, and the effective advocacy of these attorneys laid some of the groundwork for the Court's policies favoring business.

Corporate interests came to the judiciary because of their defeats elsewhere in government. On the whole, Congress and the state legislatures were friendly to business interests, but they did enact a good many regulations of private enterprise. In scrutinizing these regulations closely, the Court served as a court of last resort for corporations in a political sense as well as the legal sense.

Civil Liberties: A Limited Concern. Although the Court decided relatively few civil liberties cases in this era, it gave enough attention to that field to establish a record.[23] Overall, the justices gave much less protection to individual liberties than to the economic rights of businesses. The Court's limited support for racial equality was exemplified by *Plessy v. Ferguson* (1896), in which it promoted racial segregation by ruling that state governments could mandate "separate but equal" facilities for different racial groups. In 1908 the Court held that only a small subset of the procedural rights for criminal defendants in the Bill of Rights was "incorporated" into the Due Process Clause of the Fourteenth Amendment and thus applicable to proceedings in state courts.[24] Late in that era, the Court ruled that the Due Process Clause protected freedom of speech and freedom of the press from state violations. But in a series of decisions it held that the federal government could prosecute people whose expressions allegedly endangered military recruitment and other national security interests.[25]

A Long-Standing Position. The Court's conservatism during this period was not new; the dominant themes of the Court's work in earlier periods were also conservative. The Court provided considerable support for the rights of property holders and much less support for such values as civil liberties.

Because of this history, observers of the Supreme Court in the New Deal period had reason to conclude that the Court was a fundamentally conservative body. Indeed, this was the position of two distinguished observers in the early 1940s. Henry Steele Commager argued in 1943 that, with one possible exception, the Court had never intervened on behalf of the underprivileged; in fact, it frequently had blocked efforts by Congress to protect the underprivileged.[26] Two years earlier, Attorney General Robert Jackson, a future Supreme Court justice, reached this stark conclusion: "Never in its entire history can the Supreme Court be said to have for a single hour been representative of anything except the relatively conservative forces of its day."[27] Jackson may have exaggerated for effect, but he captured an important theme in the Court's history.

1937 to 1969

Even before Commager and Jackson described this record of conservatism, however, the Court was beginning a shift in its direction that one historian has called "the Constitutional Revolution of 1937." That revolution, he said,

altered fundamentally the character of the Court's business, the nature of its decisions, and the alignment of its friends and foes. From the Marshall Court to the Hughes Court, the judiciary had been largely concerned with questions of property rights. After 1937, the most significant matters on the docket were civil liberties and other personal rights.... While from 1800 to 1937 the principal critics of the Supreme Court were social reformers and the main supporters people of means who were the principal beneficiaries of the Court's decisions, after 1937 roles were reversed, with liberals commending and conservatives censuring the Court.[28]

Acceptance of Government Economic Policy. In the first stage of the revolution, the Court abandoned its opposition to government intervention in economic matters. That step came quickly. In a series of decisions beginning in 1937, majorities accepted the constitutional power of government—

especially the federal government—to regulate and manage the economy. This shift culminated in *Wickard v. Filburn* (1942), in which the Court held that federal power to regulate interstate commerce extended so far that it applied to a farmer who grew wheat for his own livestock.

This collective change of heart proved to be of long duration. The Court consistently upheld major economic legislation against constitutional challenge, striking down only one minor provision of federal law regulating business in the period from the 1940s through the 1960s.[29] Supporting federal supremacy in economic matters, the Court struck down many state laws on the ground that they impinged on the constitutional powers of the federal government or that they were preempted by federal statutes. But in other respects it gave state governments more freedom to make economic policy.

The Court continued to address economic issues involving interpretations of federal statutes. In some instances it overrode decisions of regulatory agencies, such as the Interstate Commerce Commission and the National Labor Relations Board, holding that those decisions misinterpreted statutes. Some of these interventions were significant, but the Court did not challenge the basic economic programs of the federal government.

Support for Civil Liberties.   In a 1938 decision, *United States v. Carolene Products Co.,* the Court signaled that there might be a second stage of the revolution. The case was one of many in which the Court upheld federal economic policies. But in what would become known as "footnote 4," Justice Harlan Stone's opinion for the Court argued that the Court was justified in taking a tolerant view of government economic policies while it gave "more exacting judicial scrutiny" to policies that infringed on civil liberties.

This second stage took a long time to develop. In the 1940s and 1950s, the Court gave more support to civil liberties than it had in earlier eras, but it did not make a strong and consistent commitment to the expansion of individual liberties. This stage of the revolution finally came to full fruition in the 1960s. Civil liberties issues dominated the Court's agenda for the first time. The Court's decisions expanded liberties in many areas, from civil rights of racial minority groups to procedural rights of criminal defendants to freedom of expression.

As in the preceding era, the Court's policy position was reflected in the constitutional doctrines it adopted. Departing from its earlier view, the Court of the 1960s ruled that nearly all the rights of criminal defendants in the Bill of Rights were incorporated in the Fourteenth Amendment and therefore applied to state proceedings. In interpreting the Equal Protection Clause of the Fourteenth Amendment, the Court held that some government policies challenged as discriminatory would be given "strict scrutiny," if the groups that the law disfavored were especially vulnerable or if the rights involved were especially important.

The Court's sympathies for civil liberties were symbolized by *Griswold v. Connecticut* (1965), which established a new constitutional right to privacy. A majority of the justices discovered that right in provisions of the Bill of Rights nearly two centuries after those provisions were written.

The Court's direction after 1937 is illustrated by the pattern of decisions declaring laws unconstitutional. Figure 5-1 shows the number of economic statutes and statutes limiting civil liberties that the Court overturned in each decade of the twentieth century. The number of economic laws the Court struck down declined precipitously between the 1920s and the 1940s and remained relatively low in the 1950s and 1960s. In contrast, the number of statutes struck down on civil liberties grounds became significant in the 1940s and 1950s and rose sharply in the 1960s, reflecting the Court's growing liberalism. The reversal of these trends in the 1980s is also noteworthy; I discuss its implications later in this section.

The Court's Beneficiaries. The groups that the Court's policies benefited most were those that gained from expansions of legal protections for civil liberties. Among them were socially and economically disadvantaged groups, criminal defendants, and people who took unpopular political stands. In 1967, during the Court's most liberal period, an unsympathetic editorial cartoonist depicted the Court as a Santa Claus whose list of gift recipients included communists, pornographers, extremists, drug pushers, criminals, and perverts.[30] Whatever one may think of this characterization, it underlines the change in the Court.

The segment of the population that the Court supported most strongly was black citizens, particularly in the fields of education and voting rights. The Court also made great efforts to protect the civil rights movement when southern states attacked the movement in the late 1950s and 1960s. Like the Court's policies favoring corporations in an earlier era, this support reflected effective litigation efforts, chiefly those of the NAACP Legal Defense Fund.

The Court was generally more favorable to liberties than were the other branches of government. Congress did not adopt a strong civil rights bill attacking racial discrimination until 1964, ten years after *Brown v. Board of Education*. The Court's support for some other liberties diverged even more from the positions of the other branches. The procedural rights of criminal defendants had few advocates in the executive and legislative branches. Congress did much to attack leftist political groups, such as the Communist Party. As it had done when it favored business interests, the Court provided relief for groups that fared less well elsewhere in government.

FIGURE 5-1
Number of Economic and Civil Liberties Laws (Federal, State, and Local) Overturned by the Supreme Court by Decade, 1900–2005

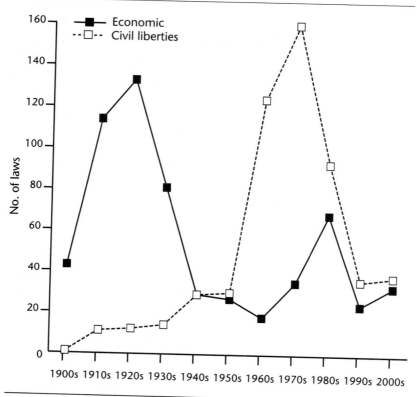

Sources: Congressional Research Service, *The Constitution of the United States of America: Analysis and Interpretation, 2000 edition* and *2004 Supplement* (Washington, D.C.: Government Printing Office, 2004, 2004); author's analysis of 2005 cases.

Note: Civil liberties category does not include laws supportive of civil liberties. Figure for 2000s is the number for the full decade if the rate for 2000–2005 continues.

1969 to 2005: The Burger and Rehnquist Courts

It is always more difficult to characterize the Supreme Court's policies in the recent past than in more distant eras. That certainly is true of the Burger and Rehnquist Courts. The Court's policies became more conservative from the 1970s on, but there is considerable disagreement about the extent of the Court's ideological shift. Complaints from political liberals that the Court moved too far to the right have been matched by complaints from conservatives that it did not move far enough.

Uneven Support for Civil Liberties. On the whole, especially under Chief Justice Rehnquist, the Court narrowed legal protections for individual liberties. The Court's shift is reflected in the rate of success for parties bringing civil liberties claims, shown in Table 4-4. The Burger and Rehnquist Courts ruled in favor of those claims at a considerably lower rate than had the Warren Court. As shown in Figure 5-1, the number of laws struck down on the ground that they violated constitutional protections of civil liberties increased in the 1970s but declined dramatically after that.

The reduction in support for civil liberties came most quickly on defendants' rights. From the early 1970s on, the Court narrowed the *Miranda* rules for police questioning of suspects and the *Mapp* rule disallowing the use of evidence obtained through illegal searches, although it reaffirmed *Miranda* itself in *Dickerson v. United States* (2000). The Court's policies on capital punishment took a series of twists: the Court struck down existing death penalty laws in *Furman v. Georgia* (1972), upheld a new set of laws in *Gregg v. Georgia* (1976), set some limits on the death sentence while rejecting others, and then ruled that capital punishment could not be imposed for offenses committed by juveniles or the retarded.[31] In conjunction with Congress, the Court limited the use of habeas corpus petitions as a means for criminal defendants to challenge their convictions after their original appeals ran out.

On issues of equality, the Court moved in a conservative direction more slowly and unevenly. The Burger Court was the first to strike down laws under the Equal Protection Clause on the ground that they discriminated against women. It also held that northern-style school segregation, in which schools were not explicitly segregated by law, could be unconstitutional. It generally gave broad interpretations to federal laws against discrimination but limited constitutional challenges to discrimination by private institutions that are connected to government. The Rehnquist Court interpreted antidiscrimination laws more narrowly than its predecessor across a wide range of issues. It approved the termination of court orders that maintained racial integration of public schools and limited the power of the federal government to enforce antidiscrimination laws against states. However, the Court continued to strengthen legal protections against sex discrimination in some important respects.

Freedom of expression is the only field in which the Court has directly overruled major Warren Court decisions favoring civil liberties — specifically, on the definition of obscenity.[32] The Burger and Rehnquist Courts narrowed some other First Amendment protections as well. But this is the field in which the Burger and Rehnquist Courts gave the greatest support to civil liberties. One example is their protections for commercial speech, such as advertising. The Court struck down much of the congressional scheme for regulation of campaign finance on First Amendment grounds in *Buckley v. Valeo* (1976), but it upheld the bulk of a more limited scheme in *McConnell v. Federal Election Commission* (2003).

Conservatism on Economic Issues. In interpreting federal statutes that regulate economic practices, the Burger and Rehnquist Courts took more conservative positions than the Warren Court. The Court narrowed the application of antitrust laws to business practices. It gave more support to employers in labor law, and for the most part it interpreted environmental laws narrowly.

The Burger Court maintained the Court's broad interpretation of government powers under the Constitution to regulate economic activity. In contrast, the Rehnquist Court took some steps to limit those powers. In the economic arena, as in civil liberties, the Rehnquist Court limited federal power over state governments. However, the Court ruled that several state regulations of business practices were preempted by federal laws that allowed those practices. It expanded the right of property owners to monetary compensation when government regulates the use of their property, but in *Kelo v. City of New London* (2005) it rejected the argument that the "public use" for which property could be taken should be defined narrowly.

The Court's Beneficiaries. State governments benefited in some respects from policies of the Burger and Rehnquist Courts. The Court limited federal power over state governments, and the Rehnquist Court struck down relatively few state laws. But as the preemption decisions illustrate, the Court's support for the power and autonomy of state governments varied with the issues and interests that were implicated by cases.

The business community received more consistent support from the Court in this period, and that community can be considered the chief beneficiary of the Burger and Rehnquist Courts. Those Courts generally favored business interests across a wide range of fields, from labor law to freedom of speech. The Burger and Rehnquist Courts were not uniformly favorable to business interests. As in other eras, the Court's recent policies are too mixed in theme to allow easy generalizations. Still, both the Court's major beneficiaries and its dominant ideological direction differed from those of the period from the late 1930s to the late 1960s.

Explaining the Court's Policies

In the preceding sections, I described changes over time in the Supreme Court's agenda, the extent of its activism, and the content of its policies. All these changes are summarized in Table 5-4.

The magnitude of these changes underlines the need for explanation. What forces can account for the various elements of the Court's policies?

TABLE 5-4
Summary of the Supreme Court's Policies during Three Historical Periods

Period	Predominant area on agenda	Extent of activism	Content of policy
1890s to 1930s	Economic regulation	Variable, becoming more inclined to strike down legislation	Mixed, primarily conservative
1937 to 1969	Economic regulation, then civil liberties	Initially low, becoming higher and then very high in 1960s	Generally liberal, very liberal in 1960s
1969 to 2005	Civil liberties	High, declining in some respects after the 1970s	Moderate in 1970s, then more conservative

Note: Characterizations of each period are approximate and subject to disagreement. Extent of activism is gauged primarily by striking down of government policies.

These forces were discussed in earlier chapters, but in this section I pull them together and apply them to the broad patterns described in this chapter.

The Court's Environment

Freedom from External Pressures. The life terms of Supreme Court justices give them considerable freedom from the rest of government and from the general public. This freedom is reinforced by the usual reluctance of Congress and the president to use their powers over the Court as an institution. The Court's relative freedom from external pressures distinguishes it from the other branches of government.

The Court's freedom is reflected in some of the positions that it takes in individual decisions. Political realities would not allow Congress or a state legislature to support the right to burn the American flag as a form of political protest, nor could it prohibit student-led prayers at football games. But the Court could and did make such decisions.

More important, the Court has adopted some broad lines of policy that run counter to the majority view in the general public and elsewhere in government. To a considerable degree, it resisted the widespread support for regulation of business in the early twentieth century. Even more striking was the Court's expansion of the procedural rights of criminal defendants in the 1960s. No elected body, even a court, could have adopted so many rules that favored so unpopular a segment of society.

Influence from the Other Branches. The Court is not entirely free from external pressure. Congress and the president do hold substantial powers over the Court. Although these powers are seldom used, their use is often threatened. The other branches can legislate to raise the justices' salaries or leave them as they are, allow the Court's interpretations of statutes to stand or override them, and control its jurisdiction. They also can shape the implementation of the Court's decisions. Because such threats and criticisms are unpleasant in themselves, and because they might affect the Court's public standing, the justices have an incentive to minimize direct conflicts with Congress.

It is difficult to ascertain the effect of this incentive on the Court's policies. It may be that the other branches of government have little impact on the justices. In at least a few instances, however, the justices seemed to avoid or minimize conflict with the other branches. Examples include the Court's retreat from some of its expansions of civil liberties in the late 1950s and its refusal to decide whether American participation in the Vietnam War was unconstitutional. More broadly, the Court has limited its use of judicial review to strike down significant national policies. It is noteworthy that the Court has struck down far more state laws than federal laws. The activism of the Warren Court in civil liberties was directed primarily at the states, and on the whole that Court was sympathetic to the federal government.[33] The Rehnquist Court's limitations on federal power provoked little conflict with the other branches because members of Congress were largely sympathetic to those limitations.[34]

Societal Influence. The justices are also influenced by developments in society as a whole. Those developments can affect the justices' attitudes toward such issues as women's rights and terrorism. They can exert an influence on their own as well.

One form of influence concerns what might be called a requirement of minimum support: the justices are unlikely to take a sustained policy position that lacks significant support outside the Court, especially from the segments of society whose judgment is most important to them. Justices may see such positions as potentially damaging the Court's institutional position; more fundamentally, the justices may see positions with little support as unreasonable in themselves. Another form of influence derives from the litigation process. The Court acts on the cases that come to it: the Court cannot reshape its agenda without action by litigants and, more generally, without interest groups that support litigation and the broad social movements from which groups develop.

These influences are reflected in the two most distinctive patterns in the Court's policies during the twentieth century. The Court's resistance to government regulation of the economy before 1937 may have had only minority support in society, but most of the business community and much of the legal community strongly approved that position. Corporations and their representatives engaged in a concerted litigation campaign, bringing to the Court a steady flow of litigation and strong legal arguments against government economic policies.

The Court's expansions of civil liberties from the 1940s to the 1970s also benefited from social support. If these expansions were not always popular, they were favored by significant portions of society as a whole, including political elites and the legal community.[35] The development of organizations such as the NAACP and the ACLU and other social changes allowed civil liberties to take a more prominent place on the Court's agenda and allowed the Court to broaden its interpretations of constitutional rights.[36]

To a degree, the Court's increased conservatism since the 1970s reflects changing attitudes in the general public and a growth in litigation by conservative groups. By the same token, there is probably too little support for the Court to reverse fully its earlier expansions of government regulatory power and of protections for civil liberties. The Court has considerable freedom from societal opinion and social trends, but its freedom is not total.[37]

Policy Preferences and the Appointment Power

The freedom the justices do have generally allows them to make their own judgments about the issues they face. Those judgments are based in part on their assessments of cases in legal terms. But because the questions before the Court seldom have clear legal answers, justices' policy preferences are the chief basis for the positions they take.

The importance of policy preferences suggests that a great deal about the Court's policies can be explained simply and directly: during any given period in the Court's history, its policies have reflected the collective preferences of its members. Most of the justices who served from the 1890s to the 1930s were political conservatives who generally accepted government restrictions on civil liberties but questioned government regulation of business enterprises. In contrast, the justices who came to the Court from the late 1930s to the late 1960s were predominantly liberals who supported government management of the economy and, in most instances, broader protections of civil liberties. On the whole, the justices who joined the Court from the 1970s to the 1990s were more conservative on civil liberties and economic issues than the justices of the preceding period.

This explanation is not entirely satisfying, because it does not show why certain preferences predominated on the Court during particular periods. One reason is that some national values were dominant during the periods in which justices were developing their attitudes. Another is that the justices came from backgrounds that instilled particular values in them. Most important, the higher-status backgrounds that predominated during most of the Court's history fostered sympathy for the views and interests of higher-status segments of society. Further, the prevailing ideology in elite segments of the legal profession shapes the views of its members, including future Supreme Court justices. The most direct source of the Court's collective preferences, however, is the decisions that presidents make in appointing justices.

Indeed, the predominant pattern of Supreme Court policy at any given time tends to reflect patterns of presidential appointments. If a series of appointments is made by conservative presidents, the Court is likely to become a conservative body. And because vacancies occur on the Court with some frequency—on average, once every two years—most presidents can significantly affect the Court's direction.

Robert Dahl argued that for this reason "The policy views dominant on the Court are never for long out of line with the policy views dominant among the lawmaking majorities of the United States."[38] In Dahl's judgment, the president's power to make appointments has limited the frequency with which the Court overturns major federal statutes: justices generally take the same view of policy as members of Congress and the president, so they seldom upset the policies of these branches. I think there is much to Dahl's argument. But because of several complicating factors, the appointment power produces only imperfect control by "lawmaking majorities."

One factor is time lag. Most justices serve for many years, so the Court usually reflects the views of past presidents and Senates more than those of the current president and Senate. That is why Fred Rodell suggested that the aphorism "the Supreme Court follows the election returns" be amended to refer to the returns "of ten or twelve years before."[39]

The lag varies in length, chiefly because presidents have differing opportunities to make appointments. Richard Nixon could select four justices during his first term in office, but Franklin Roosevelt and Jimmy Carter chose none in the four years after they took office. Had Roosevelt been able to replace two conservative justices early in his first term, the Court probably would not have blocked much of his New Deal program. Carter's luck was even worse; the absence of vacancies during his term, combined with his failed reelection bid in 1980, made him the first president to serve at least four years without appointing any justices. Bill Clinton chose two justices in his first two years in office, but the absence of vacancies in the next six years limited his effect on the Court's direction. George W. Bush had to wait until his second term to make his first appointments. A president's influence on the Court depends on its ideological configuration and on which members leave it as well as the simple number of appointments.

Another complicating factor is the deviation of justices from presidential expectations. Presidents usually get most of what they want from their appointees, but this is not a certainty. The unprecedented liberalism of the Court in the 1960s resulted largely from Dwight Eisenhower's miscalculations in nominating Earl Warren and William Brennan. The Rehnquist Court would have been more conservative if Sandra Day O'Connor, Anthony Kennedy, and especially David Souter had not diverged from the expectations of the Republican presidents who chose them.

The role of chance in shaping the Court's general direction also deserves emphasis. Chance plays a part in the timing of Court vacancies and in the performance of justices relative to their appointers' expectations. For that matter, the identity of the president who fills vacancies on the Court sometimes reflects chance. The close electoral victories of John Kennedy in 1960 and Richard Nixon in 1968 were hardly inevitable. The election of George W. Bush in 2000 was even narrower than Kennedy's or Nixon's. Kennedy and Nixon had a major impact on the Court's policies with their appointments, and Bush may achieve a similar impact.

The policy orientations of the Supreme Court between the 1890s and the 1960s reflected the existence of strong lawmaking majorities during two periods: the conservative Republican governments that dominated much of the period from the Civil War to the Great Depression, and the twelve-year tenure of Franklin Roosevelt accompanied by heavily Democratic Senates. These orientations also reflected patterns of resignations and deaths, unexpected behavior on the part of justices, and other factors that were a good deal less systematic. By the same token, if these factors had operated differently since 1969, the current Court might be less conservative—or even more so—than the one that actually exists. The forces that shape the Court's policy positions, like so much about the Court, are highly complex.

Conclusion

In this chapter, I have examined several issues relating to the Supreme Court's policy outputs. A few conclusions merit emphasis.

First, in some periods the Court's policymaking has had fairly clear themes. During the first part of the twentieth century, the dominant theme was scrutiny of government economic policies. Later, the primary theme was scrutiny of policies and practices that impinged on individual civil liberties. In each instance, the theme was evident in both the Court's agenda and the content of its decisions.

Second, these themes and the Court's work as a whole reflect both the justices' policy preferences and the influence of the Court's environment. In large part the Court's policies are what its members would like them to be. But the Court is subject to environmental influences that limit the divergence between Supreme Court decisions and the policies adopted by the other branches of government. In a different way, the president's appointment power creates a link between the justices' policy preferences and their political environment.

Finally, the Court's role as a policymaker—although clearly significant— is a limited one. The Court gives considerable attention to some areas of policy but scarcely touches others. Some critical matters, such as foreign policy, are left almost entirely to the other two branches. Even in the areas that the Court gives the most attention, it seldom disturbs the basic features of national policy.

The significance of the Supreme Court as a policymaker ultimately depends on the impact of its decisions, the subject of Chapter 6. After examining the effect of the Court's decisions, I make a broader assessment of the Supreme Court's role in the policymaking process.

NOTES

1. This discussion of agenda change is drawn in part from Richard L. Pacelle Jr., *The Transformation of the Supreme Court's Agenda from the New Deal to the Reagan Administration* (Boulder, Colo.: Westview Press, 1991); and Richard L. Pacelle Jr., "The Dynamics and Determinants of Agenda Change in the Rehnquist Court," in *Contemplating Courts,* ed. Lee Epstein (Washington, D.C.: CQ Press, 1995), 251–274. Numbers of cases involving particular issues were calculated from data in the U.S. Supreme Court Database created by Harold Spaeth, at www.as.uky.edu/polisci/ulmerproject/sctdata.htm.
2. The primary case was *Gregg v. Georgia* (1976).
3. This discussion is based on analysis of data in the U.S. Supreme Court Database; data collected and presented by Pacelle in *Transformation of the Supreme Court's Agenda* and "Dynamics and Determinants of Agenda Change"; and Drew Noble Lanier, *Of Time and Judicial Behavior: United States Supreme Court Agenda-Setting and Decision-Making, 1888–1997* (Selinsgrove, Pa.: Susquehanna University Press, 2003), chap. 3.
4. These and other data in this paragraph are taken from Pacelle, *Transformation of the Supreme Court's Agenda,* 56–57. The civil liberties category includes cases classified by Pacelle as due process, substantive rights, and equality.
5. Ibid., 28.
6. On the Court and foreign policy, see Thomas M. Franck, *Political Questions/ Judicial Answers: Does the Rule of Law Apply to Foreign Affairs?* (Princeton: Princeton University Press, 1992).
7. Because of ambiguities, different people have obtained different numbers of federal and state laws that the Supreme Court struck down. The numbers presented in this chapter are based on data in Congressional Research Service, *The Constitution of the United States of America: Analysis and Interpretation, 2000 Edition* and *2004 Supplement* (Washington, D.C.: Government Printing Office, 2004, 2004); and my analysis of cases decided in 2005. In the Congressional Research Service data, although the count is of statutes, the overturning of different sections of the same statute in different situations is

sometimes counted as two overturnings. There are some other respects in which the rules for counting of statutes have not been fully consistent over time, but any inconsistencies would not affect the broad patterns shown in Tables 5-2 and 5-3.

8. The distinctions made in the paragraphs that follow are drawn chiefly from Robert A. Dahl, "Decision-Making in a Democracy: The Supreme Court as a National Policy-Maker," *Journal of Public Law* 6 (fall 1957): 279–295.

9. *Scott v. Sandford* (1857); *Hammer v. Dagenhart* (1918); *Bailey v. Drexel Furniture Co.* (1922). Decisions overturning New Deal economic legislation include *United States v. Butler* (1936) and *Schechter Poultry Corp. v. United States* (1935).

10. Thomas M. Keck, *The Most Activist Supreme Court in History: The Road to Modern Judicial Conservatism* (Chicago: University of Chicago Press, 2004); David J. Garrow, "A Revolutionary Year: Judicial Assertiveness and Gay Rights," in *A Year at the Supreme Court*, ed. Neal Devins and Davison M. Douglas (Durham, N.C.: Duke University Press, 2004), 59.

11. The cases were, respectively, *Smith v. Texas* (2004); *Smith v. Massachusetts* (2005); and *Deck v. Missouri* (2005).

12. Robert Scigliano, "The Presidency and the Judiciary," in *The Presidency and the Political System*, 3d ed., ed. Michael Nelson (Washington, D.C.: CQ Press, 1990), 471–499. See David A. Yalof, "The Presidency and the Judiciary," in *The Presidency and the Political System*, 8th ed., ed. Michael Nelson (Washington, D.C.: CQ Press, 2006), 501–504.

13. The decisions were *United States v. Nixon* (1974) and *Clinton v. Jones* (1997).

14. The decisions were *Hamdi v. Rumsfeld* (2004) and *Hamdan v. Rumsfeld* (2006).

15. See, for example, *Desert Palace, Inc. v. Costa* (2003).

16. *Griggs v. Duke Power Co.* (1971).

17. *Meritor Savings Bank v. Vinson* (1986); *Burlington Industries v. Ellerth* (1998).

18. Sandra L. Wood, Linda Camp Keith, Drew Noble Lanier, and Ayo Ogundele, "The Supreme Court, 1888–1940: An Empirical Overview," *Social Science History* 22 (summer 1998): 215–216; William G. Ross, *A Muted Fury: Populists, Progressives, and Labor Unions Confront the Courts, 1890–1937* (Princeton: Princeton University Press, 1994).

19. To obtain these figures and others to be presented later in the chapter, I categorized decisions that struck down laws according to whether they pertained to economics, civil liberties, or other subjects. The criteria that I used were necessarily arbitrary; other criteria would have resulted in slightly different totals. The figures differ slightly from those in the 8th edition of the book because of changes in the source used for declarations of unconstitutionality (see Table 5-3) and a new classification of cases by subject matter.

20. *Santa Clara County v. Southern Pacific Railroad Co.* (1886).

21. James W. Ely Jr., *Railroads and American Law* (Lawrence: University Press of Kansas, 2001); Richard C. Cortner, *The Iron Horse and the Constitution: The Railroads and the Transformation of the Fourteenth Amendment* (Westport, Conn.: Greenwood Press, 1993).

22. Benjamin Twiss, *Lawyers and the Constitution* (Princeton: Princeton University Press, 1942).

23. This discussion draws from John Braeman, *Before the Civil Rights Revolution: The Old Court and Individual Rights* (Westport, Conn.: Greenwood Press, 1988).

24. *Twining v. New Jersey* (1908).

25. See, for example, *Schenck v. United States* (1917). See also David Rabban, *Free Speech in Its Forgotten Years* (New York: Cambridge University Press, 1997).
26. Henry Steele Commager, "Judicial Review and Democracy," *Virginia Quarterly Review* 19 (summer 1943): 428. The possible exception was *Wing v. United States* (1896).
27. Robert H. Jackson, *The Struggle for Judicial Supremacy* (New York: Knopf, 1941), 187.
28. William E. Leuchtenburg, *The Supreme Court Reborn: The Constitutional Revolution in the Age of Roosevelt* (New York: Oxford University Press, 1995), 235.
29. *United States v. Cardiff* (1952).
30. Ken Alexander, *San Francisco Examiner,* December 14, 1967, 42.
31. The decisions were, respectively, *Roper v. Simmons* (2005) and *Atkins v. Virginia* (2002).
32. *Miller v. California* (1973).
33. Lucas A. Powe Jr., *The Warren Court and American Politics* (Cambridge: Harvard University Press, 2000).
34. See Keith E. Whittington, "Taking What They Give Us: Explaining the Court's Federalism Offensive," *Duke Law Journal* 51 (2001): 477–520.
35. See Powe, *Warren Court and American Politics,* 485–501.
36. Charles R. Epp, *The Rights Revolution: Lawyers, Activists, and Supreme Courts in Comparative Perspective* (Chicago: University of Chicago Press, 1998), chaps. 3 and 4.
37. See John R. Howard, *The Shifting Wind: The Supreme Court and Civil Rights from Reconstruction to Brown* (Albany: State University of New York Press, 1999).
38. Dahl, "Decision-Making in a Democracy," 285.
39. Fred Rodell, *Nine Men* (New York: Random House, 1955), 9. The original aphorism was coined by Finley Peter Dunne and put in the mouth of his character Mr. Dooley in 1901. See Finley Peter Dunne, *Mr. Dooley on Ivrything and Ivrybody,* selected by Robert Hutchinson (New York: Dover Publications, 1963), 160.

Chapter 6

The Court's Impact

In June 2005, the Supreme Court decided *Kelo v. City of New London*. By a 5–4 vote, the Court rejected a challenge to a Connecticut city's use of its power of eminent domain to take some homes with compensation for a development project. The Fifth Amendment indicates that governments can take property only for a "public use." In *Kelo* the Court gave a broad interpretation to "public use" as it related to economic development. Its decision was a defeat for the Institute for Justice, the group that had sponsored the effort to limit the use of eminent domain.

But the Supreme Court did not have the last word. *Kelo* aroused a strong negative reaction, and opponents mobilized to negate the effects of the Court's decision. Among the state legislatures that were still in session when the Court issued its decision, several passed bills to narrow the conditions under which governments could take property. By April 2006, more than three hundred bills with this purpose had been introduced in forty-seven state legislatures, and bills had already been enacted in several additional states. Five months after the Court's decision, Congress prohibited the use of federal urban development funds to support the use of eminent domain for "economic development that primarily benefits private entities." As it turned out, the victory in the Supreme Court for proponents of broad eminent domain powers was far less valuable in practice than the Court's opinion had indicated. For their part, the sponsors of the legal challenge to the city's action had reason to hope that the negative response to the *Kelo* decision would end up doing even more to advance their cause than a favorable Supreme Court decision would have done.[1]

What happened after *Kelo* underlines an important reality. The Supreme Court is the highest interpreter of federal law, and people often think of it as the final arbiter of the issues it addresses. Occasionally, the Court *is* the final arbiter: its decision in *Bush v. Gore* resolved the presidential election of 2000. But that is unusual. Most of the time the Court is one of many institutions that shape law and policy on an issue.

Often the Court decides only one aspect of an issue or offers general guidelines that other policymakers have to fill in. Even when the Court fully decides an issue, other institutions may limit the impact of that ruling or negate it altogether. Congress and the president can write a new statute to override the Court's interpretation of an old one. Congress and the states can amend the Constitution to overcome a constitutional decision. Judges and administrators can carry out a Supreme Court policy as they see fit. And the Court's ultimate impact on society depends on the actions of people in and out of government. The Court affects the structure of industries and the status of women, but so do many other forces—including some that have far greater impact than the Court.

This chapter explores the impact of Supreme Court decisions. I begin by looking at what happens to the litigants themselves. In the remainder of the chapter I examine the broader effects of the Court's policies: their implementation, responses to them by legislatures and chief executives, and their effects on society as a whole.

Outcomes for the Parties

Whatever else it does, a Supreme Court decision affects the parties in the case. But the Court's ruling does not always determine the final outcome for the two sides. Indeed, a great deal can happen to the parties after the Court rules in their case.

If the Court affirms a lower-court decision, that decision usually becomes final. If the Court reverses, modifies, or vacates a decision, it almost always remands (sends back) the case to the lower court for "further proceedings consistent with this opinion," or the like. When it remands a case, the Court sometimes gives the lower court little leeway about what to do. More often, the lower court has wide discretion about how to apply the Court's ruling, and the party who wins in the Court may end up the ultimate loser.

Cases in which the Court overturns a criminal conviction on procedural grounds are good examples. The defendant is often retried, and the retrial may produce a second conviction. After the Court reversed Wilbert Rideau's 1961 conviction for murder because of pretrial publicity, Rideau was convicted again in 1964 and 1970. Those convictions were reversed by lower courts on other grounds. In 2005 Rideau was tried a fourth time and found guilty of manslaughter rather than murder; he was then released on the basis of time served.[2]

Nor does a successful challenge to a sentence necessarily benefit the defendant. The Court threw out Freddie Booker's 30-year sentence for drug dealing when it ruled that the federal sentencing guidelines were unconstitutional in 2005, but Booker received the same sentence four months later.[3] The Court ruled that mentally retarded defendants could not receive the death penalty in *Atkins v. Virginia* (2002), but in 2005 a jury found that Daryl Atkins was not retarded and sentenced him to death. (A year later, the state supreme court reversed that finding and ordered that the case be reconsidered.)[4]

Most such outcomes are quite consistent with the Supreme Court rulings that preceded them, although lower-court judges occasionally respond to remands in ways that conflict with the Court's intent. In either situation, a litigant who won in the Court but then lost in a lower court can ask the Court to hear the case once again. In *Miller-El v. Cockrell* (2003), the Court held that the federal Court of Appeals for the Fifth Circuit should have fully considered a claim of racial discrimination in jury selection. On remand the court of appeals provided that full consideration but rejected the claim. The defendant asked the Court to hear the case a second time; the Court did, and it ruled in 2005 that the claim of discrimination was valid. In response, the court of appeals followed the Court's lead and ordered that the defendant be given a new trial.[5]

The ultimate outcome for the parties is often determined outside of court. Sometimes the parties settle the case, with the Court's decision providing leverage for the party that it favored. In *Hamdi v. Rumsfeld* (2004), the Court ruled that a U.S. citizen who was held in the United States as an enemy combatant must "be given a meaningful opportunity to contest the factual basis for that detention before a neutral decisionmaker." Three months later, the Justice Department and Hamdi's lawyers reached an agreement under which Hamdi would be freed and returned to Saudi Arabia, where he had lived for most of his life.[6]

Occasionally, the other branches of government become involved after the Supreme Court rules in a case. In *Board of Education v. Grumet* (1994), the Court struck down a New York statute that had created a school district for a religious enclave, allowing children from the enclave to receive publicly funded special education services while remaining separate from students outside the group. In response the governor and legislature enacted three successive statutes, each designed to meet the Court's objections to the original statute while maintaining the same separate district. New York's highest court ruled that the first two of these statutes were also unconstitutional. A lower court upheld the third statute in 2001, and its opponents decided not to appeal, so the religious enclave ultimately won.[7]

The lives of Supreme Court litigants can undergo all kinds of twists after their cases conclude. In *Runyon v. McCrary* (1976), the parents of three-year-old Michael McCrary challenged the whites-only admissions policy of a Virginia private school. The Court ruled in their favor, holding that this policy violated federal law. Justice Byron White, nicknamed "Whizzer" White when he was a football star, wrote a strong dissent, arguing that the Court should have ruled against the McCrarys. Michael McCrary grew up to become a football player himself, and he ultimately played for the Baltimore Ravens of the National Football League. In 2001 he was honored by the NFL Players Association for his good works off the field. The honor he received was the Byron "Whizzer" White Award.[8]

Implementation of Supreme Court Policies

More important than the outcome of a case for the litigants are the broader effects of the legal rules that the Court lays down in its opinions. Like statutes or presidential orders, these rules have to be implemented by administrators and judges. Judges are obliged to apply the Court's interpretations of law whenever they are relevant to a case. Similarly, administrators such as cabinet officers and police officers are expected to follow Court-created rules that are relevant to their work.

The responses of judges and administrators to the Court's rules of law can be examined in terms of their compliance or noncompliance with these rules. But the Court's decisions may evoke responses ranging from complete rejection to enthusiastic acceptance and extension, and the concept of compliance does not capture all the possible variations.

The Effectiveness of Implementation

In 1997 federal district judge Loretta Preska ruled that a school board's refusal to rent space in a public school to a church for Sunday morning meetings did not violate the First Amendment rights of the church. Four years later the Supreme Court's ruling in another case changed the law in favor of the church's position. The church renewed its request to meet at the school. In response, Judge Preska issued a preliminary injunction allowing the church to meet. In 2005 she reached a final decision in favor of the church, pointing to the Supreme Court's decision as the reason for her change in position.[9]

What Judge Preska did fits the image that most people have about the implementation of Supreme Court decisions. Having ruled one way on a legal issue, she changed her stance in order to follow a subsequent Court ruling. Because judges and administrators are subordinate to the Supreme Court as interpreters of the law, it is expected that they will follow the Court's lead and carry out its decisions fully.

Indeed, this is what happens a great deal of the time. Yet implementation of the Court's policies is often highly imperfect. In this respect the Court is in the same position as Congress. For the Court, as for Congress, the record of implementation is mixed. Some Court rulings are carried out more effectively than others, and specific decisions often are implemented better in some places or situations than in others.

Implementation of the Court's decisions is most successful in lower courts, especially appellate courts. When the Court announces a new rule of law, judges generally do their best to follow its lead. And when a series of decisions indicates that the Court has changed its position in a policy field, lower courts tend to follow the new trend.

But even appellate judges sometimes diverge from the Court's rulings. Seldom do they explicitly refuse to follow the Court's decisions. More common is what might be called implicit noncompliance, in which a court purports to follow the Supreme Court's lead but actually evades the implications of the Court's ruling. To take one example, the federal Court of Appeals for the Eleventh Circuit in Atlanta has given a narrow interpretation of a Supreme Court decision limiting the immunity of law enforcement officers from lawsuits, and one legal scholar charged that "the circuit essentially has thumbed its nose" at the Court.[10] In a 2006 decision, five judges on the federal Court of Appeals for the Sixth Circuit charged that a decision by their court had failed to follow a Supreme Court ruling on display of the Ten Commandments in public places.[11]

The Court enjoys considerable success in gaining compliance from administrative bodies, especially at the federal level.[12] Yet implementation problems seem more common among administrators than among judges. For example, some evidence exists that the Immigration and Naturalization Service has evaded the Court's 2001 decision limiting the time that non-citizens can be imprisoned pending deportation.[13]

State trial courts resemble administrative agencies in some respects. Some of the Court's decisions about criminal procedure have suffered from evasion by prosecutors and judges. One observer in a Chicago court found substantial deviations from the Court's decisions on judicial oversight of jailing after arrest, the prosecutor's obligation to turn evidence over to the defense, and discrimination in jury selection.[14] The Court's efforts to prevent discriminatory challenges to prospective jurors have suffered from widespread noncompliance by prosecutors and defense attorneys, as Justice Breyer noted in a 2005 opinion, and trial judges are often less than vigilant about reining in that noncompliance.[15]

Two Case Studies of Implementation

A detailed picture of the implementation process can be obtained by examining two case studies. School desegregation and police investigations highlight the difficulties of implementation and variation in its success.

School Desegregation. Before the Supreme Court's 1954 decision in *Brown v. Board of Education,* separate schools for black and white students existed throughout the Deep South and in most districts of border states such as Oklahoma and Maryland. The Court's decision required that these

A defense attorney questions a prospective juror in a 2006 Michigan case. Supreme Court decisions that prohibit racial discrimination in challenges to prospective jurors have not ended that discrimination.

dual school systems be eliminated. Full desegregation in the border states took time, but considerable compliance with the Court's ruling came within a few years. In contrast, policies in the Deep South changed very slowly. As late as 1964–1965, there was no Deep South state in which even 10 percent of the black students went to school with any white students—a minimal definition of desegregation.[16] This resistance requires a closer look.

Judges and school officials in the Deep South responded to the *Brown* decision in an atmosphere hostile to desegregation. Visible opinion among white citizens was strongly opposed to desegregation; the opinion of black citizens was far less important, because a large proportion of them were prevented from voting. Throughout the South, public officials encouraged resistance to the Supreme Court. Governor Orval Faubus of Arkansas, for example, intervened to block desegregation in Little Rock in 1957.

In this atmosphere, school officials generally sought to maintain the status quo. Most administrators personally favored segregation and did everything possible to preserve it. Those administrators who wanted to comply with the Court's ruling were deterred from doing so by pressure from state officials and local citizens.

In places where the schools did not comply on their own, parents could file suits in the federal district courts to challenge the continuation of segregated systems. In many districts no suits ever were brought; one reason was fear of retaliation.

TABLE 6-1
Percentage of Black Elementary and Secondary Students Going to School with Any Whites, in Eleven Southern States, 1954–1973

School year	Percentage	School year	Percentage
1954–1955	0.001	1964–1965	2.25
1956–1957	0.14	1966–1967	15.9
1958–1959	0.13	1968–1969	32.0
1960–1961	0.16	1970–1971	85.6
1962–1963	0.45	1972–1973	91.3

Sources: For 1954–1967, Southern Education Reporting Service, *A Statistical Summary, State by State, of School Segregation-Desegregation in the Southern and Border Area from 1954 to the Present* (Nashville: Southern Education Reporting Service, 1967); for 1968–1973, U.S. Bureau of the Census, *Statistical Abstract of the United States* (Washington, D.C.: Government Printing Office, 1971 and 1975).

Note: The states are Alabama, Arkansas, Florida, Georgia, Louisiana, Mississippi, North Carolina, South Carolina, Tennessee, Texas, and Virginia.

Even where suits were brought, their success was hardly guaranteed. In its second decision in *Brown* in 1955, the Supreme Court gave federal district judges substantial freedom to determine the appropriate schedule for desegregation in a school district. Many judges themselves disagreed with the *Brown* decision, and all felt local pressure to proceed slowly, if at all. As a result, few demanded speedy desegregation of the schools, and many supported school officials in resisting change. Some judges did support the Court wholeheartedly, but they found it difficult to overcome delaying tactics by school administrators and elected officials.

After a long period of resistance, officials in the southern states began to comply. In the second decade after *Brown,* most dual school systems in the South were finally dismantled. Although school segregation was not eliminated altogether, the proportion of black students attending school with whites increased tremendously, as shown in Table 6-1.

The major impetus for this change came from Congress. The Civil Rights Act of 1964 allowed federal funds to be withheld from institutions that practiced racial discrimination. In carrying out that provision, the Department of Health, Education, and Welfare required that schools make a "good-faith start" toward desegregation to receive federal aid. Faced with a threat to important financial interests, school officials felt some compulsion to go along. The 1964 act also allowed the Justice Department to bring desegregation suits where local residents were unable to do so, and this provision greatly increased the potential for litigation against school districts that refused to change their policies. The Court reinforced the congressional action with decisions in 1968 and 1969 that demanded effective desegregation without further delay.[17]

In the 1970s the Court turned its attention to the North. In many northern cities, a combination of housing patterns and school board policies had created a situation in which white and nonwhite students generally went to different schools. In a Denver case, *Keyes v. School District No. 1* (1973), the Court held that segregation caused by government in such cities violated the Fourteenth Amendment and required a remedy. In a line of decisions over the next decade, the Court spelled out rules by which to identify segregation that violated the Constitution and to devise remedies for such segregation.

On the whole, federal district judges in the North supported the Court more than had their southern counterparts. Many were willing to order sweeping remedies for segregation in the face of strong local opposition to those remedies, especially busing. One judge ordered the imposition of higher property taxes to pay for school improvements that might facilitate desegregation in Kansas City. Another held a city in New York State and some of its council members in contempt for failing to approve new public housing for a similar purpose.[18] Ironically, the Court found some of these remedies *too* sweeping.

Few northern school districts took significant steps to eliminate segregation until they were faced with a court order or pressure from federal administrators. For the most part, however, northern districts complied with desegregation orders rather than resisting them. Compliance was increased by the willingness of some district judges to supervise school desegregation directly and closely. Congress and some presidents took steps to limit northern desegregation, but their actions were mostly symbolic and had little impact.

Once desegregation plans were put in place, the question arose as to whether and when such plans could be terminated. In a pair of decisions in 1991 and 1992, the Court indicated that these plans need not remain permanent even if ending them would produce high levels of racial segregation within a school district.[19] With support for desegregation declining, many administrators have accepted this invitation and returned to systems in which students are assigned to schools based on where they reside. Not surprisingly, school officials have been most willing to follow the Court's lead when the Court's rulings are consistent with what they want to do.

Police Investigation. The Warren Court imposed substantial procedural requirements on the police in two areas of criminal investigation, issuing a landmark decision in each. In search and seizure, *Mapp v. Ohio* (1961) extended to the states the "exclusionary rule," under which evidence illegally seized by the police cannot be used against a defendant in court. The *Mapp* decision provided an incentive for police to follow rules for legal searches that the Court established in other decisions. In the area of interrogation, *Miranda v. Arizona* (1966) required that suspects be given a series of warnings before police questioned them if their statements were to be used as evidence.

Lower-court responses to *Mapp* and *Miranda* have been mixed. Some state supreme courts criticized the decisions and interpreted them narrowly. At the trial level, many judges who sympathize with the police are reluctant to exclude evidence from trials on the basis of Supreme Court rules. But some lower-court judges have applied the Court's rulings vigorously.

Although the basic rules of *Mapp* and *Miranda* remain standing, the Burger and Rehnquist Courts narrowed their protections of suspects in some respects. Many lower courts have followed this new direction enthusiastically. But some state supreme courts that support the rulings of the 1960s have found a legitimate means to establish broader protections of procedural rights by declaring that rights denied by the Court under the U.S. Constitution are protected independently by state constitutions. The most important example concerns the Court's ruling in *United States v. Leon* (1984). In *Leon* the Court held that evidence seized on the basis of a search warrant that was improperly issued could be used in court if the officers engaging in the search had a "good faith" belief that the warrant was justified. Fifteen state supreme courts have held that their states' constitutions or statutes rule out a good faith exception to the exclusionary rule.[20]

Inevitably, *Mapp* and *Miranda* have been unpopular in the law enforcement community. Most police officers want maximum freedom for their investigative activities and resent court decisions that impose constraints on them. But they also want their evidence to stand up in court. The result has been a complex pattern of police behavior.

In the case of police questioning, it appears that reading the *Miranda* warnings to suspects gradually has become standard practice in most places.[21] One reason is that providing these warnings has had less impact than expected on the ability of police officers to obtain confessions and incriminating information from suspects.[22] The great majority of suspects waive their *Miranda* rights and answer questions, in part because officers structure the situation to encourage waivers.

Even if suspects invoke their right to remain silent or to wait for a lawyer, officers sometimes can get them to change their minds. Some of the means that officers use to do so are of questionable legality. In some California police departments, for example, officers have told suspects who invoke their *Miranda* rights that they want to ask questions off the record, and nothing the suspect says can be used in court. What most suspects do not know is that under *Harris v. New York* (1971), statements obtained by officers who do not comply with *Miranda* can be used to discredit a defendant's testimony in court. The California Supreme Court acknowledged and condemned this practice in a 2003 decision, and a year later Justice Souter noted the existence of this and other mechanisms to evade the dictates of *Miranda*.[23]

To a considerable degree, then, police officers have learned to live with *Miranda,* complying partially with its requirements and continuing to get the information they seek from most suspects. Indeed, *Miranda* serves them well in one important respect: when suspects sign a form in which they waive their rights, it is difficult for them to contest the use of their statements in court. Yet most officers still perceive *Miranda* as a constraint on their ability to obtain evidence.

Before the *Mapp* decision, as one scholar put it, state and local law enforcement officers "*systematically* ignored the requirements of the Fourth Amendment because there was no reason to pay attention to it."[24] *Mapp* was intended to achieve greater compliance with search rules by providing a reason for compliance—potential exclusion of evidence from cases in court. To a degree, it has achieved this goal.[25] Faced with potential loss of evidence, many police departments changed their practices substantially. Most important, some made much greater use of search warrants.[26]

But the available evidence indicates that compliance is far from perfect. One example is a study based on a sample of searches by a metropolitan police department in the early 1990s. The authors of the study concluded that at least 30 percent of the searches violated constitutional rules.[27]

Some noncompliance is inadvertent, reflecting the complexity and ambiguity of the body of rules that police are asked to follow in searches and seizures. Other noncompliance is intentional, resulting most fundamentally from the conflict that police officers often perceive: if they follow the applicable legal rules, they cannot obtain evidence they see as critical. Because violations of the rules for searches often do not result in the exclusion of evidence, officers may resolve this conflict by violating those rules. Indeed, one scholar concluded that "for many police officers," the exclusionary rule "is not a significant influence when contemplating a search or seizure."[28]

Explaining the Implementation Process

It should be clear by now that the effectiveness with which Supreme Court policies are implemented varies a great deal. That effectiveness depends on several conditions: communication of policies to relevant officials, the motivations of those officials to follow or resist the Court's policies, the Court's authority, and the sanctions it can use to deter noncompliance.

Communication. Judges and administrators can carry out Supreme Court decisions well only if they know what the Court wants them to do. The communication process begins with the Court's opinions. Ideally, an opinion would state the Court's legal rules with sufficient precision and specificity that an official who reads the opinion would know how to apply those rules to any other case or situation. Frequently, however, opinions fall far short of that ideal: the Court's messages contain considerable ambiguity.

Much of this ambiguity is unavoidable. The Court's opinions proclaim general legal principles in the context of specific cases. As the example of police searches indicates, the application of those principles to other cases or situations often is uncertain. In part for this reason, judges frequently disagree about what a Court ruling requires of them, as the members of a federal court of appeals did in a 2004 immigration case.[29]

Officials who are uncertain about what the Court wants may not carry out the Court's intent properly even if they would like to do so. When officials do *not* want to carry out the Court's intent, ambiguity gives them leeway to interpret decisions as they see fit. For example, the Court's vague timetable for school desegregation gave southern judges and school administrators an excuse to delay desegregation.

Whether the Court's position on an issue is clear or ambiguous, its decisions must be transmitted to relevant judges and administrators. Sometimes communication is quick and effective: after the Supreme Court struck down the federal sentencing guidelines in 2005, a federal district judge in Utah issued an opinion the next day that applied the Court's decision to a case before him.[30] But the communication of decisions is not usually so automatic. Even judges seldom monitor the Supreme Court's output systematically to identify relevant decisions. Instead, decisions come to the attention of officials through other channels.

One channel is the mass media. A few Supreme Court decisions are sufficiently interesting that they receive heavy publicity in newspapers and on television. But most decisions garner little or no coverage in the mass media, and what the media report is sometimes misleading.[31] And even the best-publicized decisions may not get through to everyone. Few of the Court's rulings have received as much attention as the 1989 decision striking down state laws against flag desecration. Yet in recent years prosecutors in Illinois and Utah have charged individuals under those laws. After the Illinois prosecution, an ACLU official asked in some surprise, "Have they not heard of *Texas v. Johnson* down there?"[32]

Attorneys communicate decisions to some officials. Through their arguments in court proceedings and administrative hearings, lawyers bring favorable precedents to the attention of judges and administrators. Staff lawyers in administrative agencies often inform agency personnel of relevant decisions. But such administrators as teachers and public welfare workers lack that source of information.

Another channel of information is professional hierarchies. State trial judges often become aware of the Court's decisions when they are cited by state appellate courts. Police officers learn of decisions from department superiors. Here, too, there is considerable potential for misinformation, especially when the communicator disagrees with a decision. Many state supreme courts and most police officials conveyed negative views of liberal criminal justice decisions by the Warren Court when they informed their subordinates of those decisions.

Effective communication of decisions depends on the receivers as well as the channels of transmission. Legally trained officials are the most capable of understanding decisions and their implications. Police officers and other nonlawyers who work regularly with the law also have some advantage in interpreting decisions. On the whole, administrators who work outside the legal system have the greatest difficulty in interpreting what they learn about Supreme Court rulings.

Where transmission problems exist, they have an obvious impact. Policymakers who do not know of a decision cannot implement it, and those who misunderstand the Court's requirements will not follow them as intended. Police officers who do not fully understand the complex body of rules for searches cannot fully comply with those rules. In sum, effective transmission of the Court's policies, like clarity in the policies themselves, is needed for their effective implementation.

Motivations for Resistance. If policymakers know of a Supreme Court policy that is relevant to a choice they face, they must decide what to do with that policy. As one would expect, officials are likely to carry out a policy faithfully if they think it is a good policy and that they will benefit from doing so. But if that policy conflicts with their policy preferences or their self-interest, they may resist the Court's lead.

When appellate judges fail to implement Supreme Court decisions fully, the most common reason is a conflict between those decisions and their policy preferences. After the Court adopts a new policy, lower-court judges may conclude that it has made a serious mistake. Those judges sometimes rebel against the Court's policy, although their rebellion is usually quiet.

Disagreement about judicial policy tends to follow ideological lines. For many years the federal Court of Appeals for the Ninth Circuit on the West Coast has been the most liberal court of appeals, distinctly more liberal than the Supreme Court. As a result, it is relatively common for three-judge panels of the Ninth Circuit to take positions that diverge from those of the Supreme Court. Similarly, the conservative Fifth Circuit in the Deep South has given narrow interpretations to Court decisions that favor criminal defendants, especially on the death penalty. The stances of both courts have been reflected in reversals by the Supreme Court, sometimes accompanied by rebukes for deviating from the Court's positions. In one 2004 decision, Justice O'Connor's opinion for the Court said that the Fifth Circuit was "paying lipservice" to the relevant legal rules and that the legal test it used "has no foundation in the decisions of this Court."[33]

Trial judges and administrators may also disagree with Supreme Court decisions. Beginning with a pair of decisions in 1962 and 1963, the Court prohibited organized religious observances, such as classroom prayer and Bible reading exercises, in public schools.[34] A great many teachers and school administrators disapprove of those decisions, and some disapprove strongly. As a result, many schools have maintained the prohibited practices or modified them only marginally.[35]

Supreme Court policies may conflict with officials' self-interest if they threaten existing practices that serve important purposes. Trial judges who handle criminal cases may feel considerable time pressure because of their heavy caseloads. As a result, they often fail to follow decisions where compliance would slow down their disposition of cases.

Elected officials sometimes have good reason not to carry out highly unpopular decisions. Rulings in favor of criminal defendants may provide an issue to opponents of elected judges, and some judges have lost their positions as a result. The Texas Court of Criminal Appeals, the state's highest court for criminal cases, has deviated from some Supreme Court decisions expanding defendants' rights. One reason appears to be the electoral advantage of taking pro-prosecution positions.[36]

Because their positions are secure, federal judges might seem to be immune from these political concerns. But they too may wish to avoid incurring public wrath. Full adherence to *Brown v. Board of Education* would have made the lives of district judges less pleasant because of the reactions of their friends and neighbors.[37] A federal judge in Florida said that he had "lost more friends in the last four years following the Constitution of the United States than I made in the first forty."[38]

A few federal judges in the South were willing to accept the costs of supporting the Supreme Court, and many northern federal judges ordered school desegregation despite the prospect of severe public criticism. But they were exceptions. If officials expect to suffer serious consequences for carrying out a decision fully, few will do so.

Differences in the implementation of Supreme Court policies result chiefly from differences in the policy preferences and self-interest of implementers. Police departments tend to resist decisions that limit their powers but follow with alacrity those that expand them. The Deep South and the border states responded differently to the *Brown* decision because attitudes toward race and segregation were not the same in the two regions.

The Court's Authority. In 2003 the Supreme Court upheld California's "three-strikes" law, which required long sentences for people convicted of a felony after two prior convictions for serious or violent felonies. Two months later the federal Court of Appeals for the Ninth Circuit reviewed a long sentence under the law. In a concurring opinion, Judge Stephen Reinhardt protested that this sentence was "unconscionable and unconstitutional," but he voted to uphold it "under compulsion of the Supreme Court's decision."[39] Judge Reinhardt was accepting both the Supreme Court's authority to make conclusive judgments about the law and his own obligation to comply with the Court's decisions. This acceptance, broadly shared among judges and administrators, does much to enhance the implementation of Supreme Court decisions.

The Court's authority is strongest for judges, who have been socialized to accept the leadership of higher courts and who also benefit from acceptance of judicial authority. Rarely does a judge deny the Court's authority, as an Alabama Supreme Court justice did in 2006 when he rebuked his colleagues "because they chose to passively accommodate—rather than actively resist—the unconstitutional opinion of five liberal justices on the U.S. Supreme Court."[40] But judges may give narrow interpretations to Court decisions with which they strongly disagree, thereby limiting the impact of those decisions while acknowledging the Court's authority. And general acceptance of the Court's authority does not prevent some judges from taking positions that are difficult to reconcile with the Court's rulings.

The Court's authority extends to administrators. Some school officials eliminate religious observances that they would prefer to maintain because they accept their duty to follow Supreme Court rulings.[41] On the whole, however, the Court's authority is weaker for administrators than it is for judges. Administrative agencies are somewhat removed from the judicial system and its norm of obedience to higher courts, and relatively few administrators have had the law school training that supports this norm. As a result, administrative officials find it somewhat easier to justify deviation from Supreme Court policies than judges do.

The Court's authority tends to decline as organizational distance from the Court increases. Officials at the grassroots level may not feel obliged to adjust their policies to the Court's decisions. State trial judges typically orient themselves more closely to appellate courts in their state than to the Supreme Court, several steps away from them in the judicial hierarchy.

The Court's authority is an important reason for acceptance of its policies. Especially within the judiciary, the authority attached to Supreme Court decisions increases compliance with those decisions. But the Court's authority has limits: it does not always outweigh the motivations that move some officials toward noncompliance.

Sanctions for Disobedience. In 1906 the Supreme Court ordered a stay of execution for a Tennessee prisoner. The local sheriff responded by allowing the prisoner to be lynched. In response, the Court held the sheriff in contempt of court and ordered him to jail.[42]

This episode was the only time the Court has held an official in contempt for failure to comply with its decisions, but it illustrates the Court's power to punish noncompliance through sanctions. Such sanctions can give judges and administrators an incentive to follow the Court's lead, an incentive more concrete than the Court's authority.

For judges, the most common sanction is reversal. If a judge does not follow an applicable Supreme Court policy, the losing litigant may appeal the case and secure a reversal of the judge's decision. This sanction is significant, chiefly because it suggests that a judge erred. Indeed, lawyers and judges sometimes evaluate judicial performance by the frequency of reversals. The Court can give an extra sting to its reversals by rebuking the lower court.

The threat of reversal helps the Supreme Court to draw lower courts toward its policies. When she was inducted into the National Cowgirl Hall of Fame in 2002, Justice O'Connor spoke of her childhood ambition to become a cattle rancher. "And I now find myself riding herd on lower court judges."[43]

But reversal has its limits as a sanction. Judges who feel strongly about an issue may be willing to accept reversals on that issue as the price of following their personal convictions. For that matter, failure to follow the Supreme Court's lead does not always lead to reversal. The losing litigant may not appeal. Moreover, the great majority of judges are reviewed by a court other than the Supreme Court, and the reviewing court may share their opposition to the Court's policies.

For administrators, the most common sanction is a court order that directs compliance with a decision. If a public welfare agency fails to follow an applicable Supreme Court policy, someone who is injured by its failure may bring a lawsuit to compel compliance with the Court's decision. Any suit hurts the agency because of the trouble and expense it entails. A successful suit is even worse, because an order to comply with a Supreme Court rule puts an agency under judicial scrutiny and may embarrass agency officials. The agency may also be required to pay monetary damages to the person who brought the lawsuit. An Arkansas school district and its officials were ordered to pay damages and later were held in contempt by a federal court for maintaining religious observances that the Supreme Court had prohibited.[44]

But this sanction has weaknesses. Most important, it can occur only if people bring lawsuits against agencies, and agency noncompliance often goes unchallenged. If a lawsuit is threatened or actually brought, agencies can usually change their practices in time to avoid serious costs. And in situations in which compliance is difficult to ascertain, sanctions lose some of their efficacy.

Still, to follow a policy that conflicts with a Supreme Court ruling carries risks that officials usually prefer to avoid. This attitude helps to account for the frequency with which administrative organizations on their own initiative eliminate practices prohibited by the Court. Administrators whose actions require court enforcement, such as officials in some regulatory agencies, have even more reason to avoid noncompliance that may cost them judicial support.

Police practices in searches and seizures illustrate both the strength and limitations of this sanction. Under *Mapp*, noncompliance with rules for searches prevents the use of evidence in court. Largely for this reason, officers frequently comply with rules that they would prefer to ignore. Officers, however, seldom receive any personal sanctions for noncompliant practices that cause evidence to be thrown out. Moreover, illegal searches may not prevent convictions. Most defendants plead guilty, and by doing so they generally waive their right to challenge the legality of searches. Trial judges often give the benefit of the doubt to police officers on border-line evidentiary questions. And evidence that is ruled illegal may not be needed for a conviction. Thus, police officers have an incentive to avoid illegal searches, but not so strong an incentive that they always try to follow the applicable rules.

This discussion points to two conditions that affect the implementation process. First, interest groups can play an important part in enforcement of Supreme Court decisions. The ACLU frequently challenges religious observances in public schools, and by doing so it has enhanced compliance with the Court's rules. Second, the Court's decisions are easiest to enforce when the affected policymakers are few in number and highly visible. It is relatively simple for the Court to oversee the fifty state governments that must carry out its decisions on the drawing of legislative districts. It is far more difficult for the Court to oversee the day-to-day activities of all the police officers who investigate crimes.

In general, the sanctions available to the Court are fairly weak, so help from Congress and the president can make a great deal of difference when the Court faces widespread noncompliance. In enforcing school desegregation, that help was a necessity.

Summary. The Supreme Court's policies are implemented more effectively in some settings than in others. Judges generally carry out the Court's policies more fully than administrators for several reasons: communication of decisions to judges is relatively good; most judges accord the Court considerable authority; and their self-interest is less likely to conflict with the implementation of decisions. For similar reasons, federal judges and administrators are probably better implementers of decisions than are their state counterparts. The Court's decisions are communicated to them more effectively, and its authority and sanctions affect them more directly.

On the whole, the Court's policies are implemented fairly well. But there is often a substantial gap between the rules of law that the Court establishes and the actions taken by judges and administrators. To a degree, this gap reflects the Court's limited power, in that it can exert little control over the implementation process. Most important, the sanctions that the Court can apply to disobedient officials are relatively weak compared with those available to Congress and the president. But more striking than this difference is the similarity in the basic positions of Court, Congress, and president: each proclaims policies that have uncertain and often unhappy fates in the implementation process.

Responses by Legislatures and Chief Executives

Congress, the president, and their state counterparts also respond regularly to Supreme Court decisions. Their responses shape the impact of the Court's decisions and affect the Court itself.

Congress

Congressional responses to the Court's rulings take several forms. Within some limits, Congress can modify or override the Court's decisions. It also shapes the implementation of decisions, and it can act against individual justices or the Court as a whole.

Statutory Interpretation. The federal sentencing guidelines that Congress enacted in 1984 allowed district judges to depart from the sentences recommended by the guidelines under certain conditions. In *Koon v. United States* (1996), the Supreme Court faced the question of how the courts of appeals should review such departures from the guidelines when the prosecution or defense appealed. The Court ruled that the proper standard was whether the district court had "abused its discretion," a standard that gave considerable deference to the district judge's decision. By 2003 many members of Congress had become unhappy with what they regarded as too many departures from the sentencing guidelines toward more lenient sentences. Because of this unhappiness Congress enacted a statute with a provision requiring that courts of appeals review departures from the guidelines under a "de novo" standard, a standard that gave no deference to the district judge. In doing so, Congress overturned the *Koon* decision.

This action was completely legitimate because Congress is supreme in statutory law: it can override the Supreme Court's interpretation of a statute simply by adopting a new statute with different language. Congress can also ratify or extend the Court's interpretation of a statute, but overrides of statutory decisions are especially significant.

A high proportion of statutory decisions receive some congressional scrutiny, and proposals to override decisions are common. Most of these proposals fail, for the same reasons that most bills of any type fail: legislation must survive several decision points, at each of which it can be killed, and there is usually a presumption in favor of the status quo. Still, overrides are far from rare. Over a recent period of three decades, an average of more than ten statutory decisions were overturned in part or altogether in each two-year Congress. Of the statutory decisions in the Court's 1978–1989 terms, Congress had overridden more than 5 percent by 1996.[45]

Sometimes Congress takes a long time to override a decision. One 1998 statute removed part of the exemption of major league baseball from the antitrust laws, an exemption that the Court first established in a 1922 decision.[46] But most overrides come within a few years of a decision. *Zadvydas v. Davis* (2001), a decision limiting the detention of noncitizens under certain conditions, was overturned in part by Congress within four months. Occasionally, Congress acts even more quickly. In *Commissioner v. Banks* (2005), the Court ruled that a successful litigant was required to pay federal tax on the portion of the money recovered that was paid to the litigant's attorney as a contingent fee. But a few months earlier, while the case was awaiting argument in the Court, Congress enacted a statute that provided a tax exemption for such attorney fees in discrimination and employment cases.

In most respects, the politics of congressional response to the Court's statutory decisions resembles congressional politics generally.[47] The initiative for bills to overturn decisions often comes from interest groups. Just as groups that fail to achieve their goals in Congress frequently turn to the courts for relief, groups whose interests suffer in the Supreme Court frequently turn to Congress.

The success of efforts to overturn statutory decisions depends on the same broad array of factors that influences the fates of other bills in Congress. The political strength of the groups that favor or oppose overrides is important. Not surprisingly, the federal executive branch enjoys considerable success in getting Congress to overturn unfavorable decisions; in contrast, nearly all decisions that work to the detriment of criminal defendants are left standing.[48] When a significant group favors action and organized opposition does not exist, Congress may override a decision quickly and easily. Many successful overrides are enacted not as separate bills but as provisions of broader bills, such as appropriations. The partial override of *Zadvydas,* the 2001 decision on the detention of aliens, was part of the long and complex Patriot Act that most members of Congress had limited time to study. Members who vote for those bills sometimes are unaware that they are overriding a Supreme Court decision.

Congress does not necessarily have the last word when it overrides a statute, because the new statute is subject to judicial interpretation. In *Westfall v. Erwin* (1988), the Court held that federal officials could be sued for personal injuries under some circumstances. A few months later Congress overrode *Westfall* by allowing the attorney general to certify that an employee who had been sued was acting as a federal official and thereby substituting the federal government for the employee as a defendant. But in *Gutierrez de Martinez v. Lamagno* (1995), the Court weakened the override by holding that the attorney general's certification could be challenged in court.

Constitutional Interpretation. When the Supreme Court strikes down a statute as unconstitutional, Congress can choose from a wide range of responses, including no response at all. A study of decisions in which the Court struck down federal statutes between 1954 and 1997 found that about half the time, Congress acted to restore at least a portion of the policy that the Court had invalidated.[49] In all but one instance, its action involved adoption of a new statute aimed at avoiding the constitutional problems the Court had found in its predecessor.

For example, in *United States v. Lopez* (1995), the Court struck down a federal law that prohibited possession of a gun near a school. The law had been based on congressional power to regulate interstate commerce, and the Court held that the commerce power did not reach far enough to justify this law. In response, a year later Congress passed a new statute that prohibited people from carrying guns near schools if the gun was one "that has moved in or that otherwise affects interstate or foreign commerce."[50] Its collective hope was that the Court would see this narrower prohibition as fitting within the commerce power.

The Court often does rule on whether statutes enacted after its decisions avoid the constitutional problems they were designed to overcome. One example concerns congressional efforts to limit children's exposure to sexually oriented material on the Internet. In *Reno v. American Civil Liberties Union* (1997), the Court held that a 1996 statute with this aim violated the First Amendment. In 1998 Congress enacted a new statute, aimed at achieving the same goal without running into the First Amendment problems that the Court had cited in *Reno*. In *Ashcroft v. American Civil Liberties Union* (2004), the Court upheld a district court injunction against enforcement of the statute based on First Amendment problems, and it sent the case back to the lower courts to consider whether this law too should be struck down.

When the Court holds that a right is not protected by the Constitution, Congress can protect that right by enacting a statute, so long as it is acting within its constitutional powers and does not violate other constitutional

TABLE 6-2
Resolutions Introduced in Congress in 2005–2006 for
Constitutional Amendments to Overturn Supreme Court Decisions

Purpose	Decisions that would be overturned
Limiting the number of consecutive terms that members of Congress can serve	*U.S. Term Limits v. Thornton* (1995)
Giving Congress power to limit campaign spending	*Buckley v. Valeo* (1976), later decisions
Allowing organized prayer in public schools	*Engel v. Vitale* (1962), later decisions
Giving federal and state governments power to prohibit flag desecration	*Texas v. Johnson* (1989) *United States v. Eichman* (1990)

rights. The Supreme Court may hold that such a statute is unconstitutional. In 1993 Congress enacted the Religious Freedom Restoration Act (RFRA) to overcome a 1990 decision that had made it easier for government to justify neutral rules that put a burden on particular religious practices. The Court held in 1997 that RFRA was unconstitutional as applied to state and local governments because it went beyond congressional power to enforce the Fourteenth Amendment. Congress tried a second time in 2000 with a narrower version of RFRA based on two other constitutional provisions. In 2005 the Court rejected one constitutional argument against a section of this second law but did not address a second argument that it might consider later.[51]

In situations where constitutional decisions cannot be negated by statute, members of Congress may introduce resolutions to overturn them with constitutional amendments. Such resolutions are regularly submitted on a wide range of issues, as illustrated by the set of recent resolutions in Table 6-2. Not surprisingly, these efforts seldom achieve success. Only five times has Congress proposed an amendment that was aimed directly at Supreme Court decisions. One of these, proposed in 1924 to give Congress the power to regulate child labor, was not ratified by the states. (A few amendments have indirectly negated Supreme Court decisions.) Since the child labor proposal, the only amendment that Congress has proposed in order to overturn a decision was the Twenty-sixth Amendment, adopted in 1971. In *Oregon v. Mitchell* (1970), the Court had ruled that Congress could not regulate the voting age in elections to state office; Congress acted quickly to propose an amendment overturning the decision, and the states quickly ratified it.

A first-year college student at Southwest Missouri State University votes in the 2004 election. After the Supreme Court ruled in 1970 that Congress could not lower the voting age to eighteen for state elections, a constitutional amendment negated the Court's decision by setting the minimum voting age at eighteen.

In contrast with the Twenty-sixth Amendment, the most prominent failed campaigns for amendments in recent years have been aimed at decisions that expanded legal protections for civil liberties. Even highly unpopular decisions, such as prohibitions of school prayer, stood up against efforts to overturn them. In these instances, the general reluctance to amend the Constitution was compounded by a special reluctance to limit the protections of rights in the Bill of Rights.

That reluctance is illustrated by the effort to propose an anti–flag desecration amendment. In 1989 and 1990, the Supreme Court struck down state and federal statutes prohibiting flag burning on the ground that they punished people for political expression. Shortly after the 1989 decision, some members of Congress began working for a constitutional amendment to allow prohibition of flag desecration. Its passage might seem inevitable, because most members of Congress share an abhorrence of flag burning and because a member's vote against the amendment could provide an election opponent with a powerful issue. But both houses defeated a flag-desecration amendment in 1990. Similar amendments have won approval in the House in each two-year Congress since 1995, but as of 2006 none of the proposals had made it through the Senate. In 2006 the Senate came within one vote of sending a flag-desecration amendment to the states, and such an amendment may well get through

Congress in the future. Even so, the absence of success for these proposals so far is striking.

Affecting the Implementation of Decisions. By passing legislation, Congress can influence the implementation of Supreme Court decisions by other institutions. Its most important tool is money. Congress can provide or fail to provide funds to carry out a decision. It can also affect responses to decisions by state and local governments through its control over federal grants to them. Congressional use of this latter power was critical to school desegregation in the Deep South.

In a 2001 education statute, Congress employed the same power in two different ways. The first was related to *Boy Scouts of America v. Dale* (2000), in which the Court held that the First Amendment allows the Boy Scouts to prohibit membership to gay men and boys. In response, some schools ended their ties with the Scouts. One provision of the 2001 law required that no federal funds be provided to schools that "deny equal access" to or "discriminate against" the Scouts. Another provision required that schools receiving federal money allow "constitutionally protected prayer." By enacting this provision, Congress gave school districts an incentive to interpret the Court's limitations on school religious observances narrowly.[52]

Occasionally, a Supreme Court decision requires implementation by Congress itself. In these situations Congress generally has accepted its obligation with little resistance. The legislative veto is an exception. In *Immigration and Naturalization Service v. Chadha* (1983), the Court indicated that any statutes allowing Congress as a whole, one house, or a committee to "veto" proposed executive branch actions are invalid. After the decision, Congress eliminated legislative veto provisions from several statutes. But it maintained others and adopted more than four hundred new legislative veto provisions by 2004—most requiring that specific congressional committees approve action by administrative agencies. To maintain good relations with congressional committees and to avoid even more stringent congressional controls, agency officials are willing to accept these provisions rather than challenge their legality. Thus, political realities have allowed noncompliance with *Chadha* to continue.[53]

Attacks on Justices and the Court. When members of Congress are unhappy with the Supreme Court's policies, they can attack the Court or the justices directly. The easiest way to do so is verbally, and members of Congress sometimes denounce the Court publicly. Such denunciations have become more common in recent years, as conservative Republicans have criticized what they see as inappropriate activism by the Court and by the federal courts in general. In 2005, for instance, the House majority leader, Tom DeLay, referred to decisions on abortion and school prayer as examples "of a judiciary run amok."[54]

More concretely, Congress can take several types of formal action against the Court or its members. One type is reduction of the Court's jurisdiction.[55] The Constitution allows Congress to alter the Court's appellate jurisdiction and the jurisdiction of other federal courts through legislation, although some scholars argue that there are limits to congressional power over the Court's jurisdiction. Such limits aside, if members of Congress are unhappy with the Court's decisions in a field of policy, they can eliminate the Court's appellate jurisdiction in that field. Since the 1960s Congress has considered many bills that would have limited the Court's jurisdiction on issues such as abortion and school busing. Bills on legislative districting in 1964 and school prayer in 1979 passed one house but were not enacted. In 2004 the House passed bills to eliminate the jurisdiction of all federal courts over issues involving the Pledge of Allegiance or the Defense of Marriage Act, the 1996 federal statute intended to limit legal recognition of single-sex marriages. Neither passed the Senate.

In 1869 Congress acted to limit the Court's jurisdiction even before the Court had ruled on the issue in question. It withdrew the Court's right to hear appeals in habeas corpus actions to prevent it from deciding a pending challenge to the post–Civil War Reconstruction legislation. In *Ex parte McCardle* (1869), the Court ruled that Congress had acted properly.

In 2005 Congress limited the federal courts' jurisdiction and simultaneously overrode one of the Court's statutory decisions. In *Rasul v. Bush* (2004), the Court held that federal courts had jurisdiction to hear habeas corpus cases brought by prisoners at Guantanamo Bay who challenged their detention as suspected terrorists. Congress then outlawed such lawsuits, allowing only limited judicial review of administrative decisions about the status of detainees. The Court's rationale in *Rasul* still might apply to other situations, but the decision no longer had any impact at Guantanamo Bay.

Congress controls the Court budget, limited only by the constitutional prohibition against reducing the justices' salaries. In 1964 Congress singled out the justices by increasing their salaries by $3,000 less than those of other federal judges. A year later the House defeated a proposal to restore the $3,000, after a debate in which several members attacked the Court and Robert Dole of Kansas suggested that this pay increase be contingent on the Court's reversing a legislative districting decision that he disliked.[56] Dissatisfaction with the Court's decisions can affect congressional responses to its budget requests, and in 2005 a Republican member of the House introduced an amendment to reduce the Court's budget by $1.5 million to express his unhappiness with its *Kelo* decision on eminent domain.[57]

The most extreme action that Congress can take against individual justices is to remove them through impeachment. Members of Congress sometimes talk of impeachment when they dislike a justice's policy positions. In 2005 the chief of staff for Senator Tom Coburn, an Oklahoma Republican, suggested "mass impeachment" of many federal judges, including Justices Breyer, Ginsburg, Kennedy, and Souter.[58]

In light of the range of congressional powers over the Court and the frequency with which they are threatened, it is striking how little Congress has actually used its powers over the past century. Of the many actions that members of Congress contemplated using against the conservative Court in the early part of the twentieth century, culminating in Franklin Roosevelt's Court-packing plan, none was carried out.[59] All the attacks on the liberal Court in the second half of the century resulted in nothing more serious than the salary "punishment" of 1964 and 1965. Why has Congress been so hesitant to use its powers, even at times when most members are unhappy about the Court's direction?

Several factors help to explain this hesitancy. First, there are always some members of Congress who agree with the Court's policies and lead its defense. Second, serious forms of attack against the Court, such as impeachment and reducing its jurisdiction, seem illegitimate to many people. Finally, when threatened with serious attack, the Court occasionally retreats to reduce the impetus for congressional action. For these reasons, the congressional bark at the Supreme Court has been a good deal worse than its bite. And at least so far, the relatively ferocious congressional attacks on the Court in recent years have not been translated into much concrete action.

The President

Presidents affect the use of congressional power over the Court, and they may also act on their own to shape the outcomes of decisions.

Influencing Congressional Response. The president can influence congressional responses to the Supreme Court by taking a position on proposals for action. Sometimes it is the president who first proposes anti-Court action. The most dramatic example in the last century was Franklin Roosevelt's Court-packing plan.

Since the 1960s conservative presidents have encouraged efforts in Congress to limit or overturn some of the Court's liberal rulings on civil liberties. For example, George H. W. Bush led the effort to overturn the Court's flag-burning decisions in 1989 and 1990, and George W. Bush has supported a constitutional amendment to prohibit flag desecration. For his part, Bill Clinton supported legislation in response to conservative decisions on regulation of tobacco and prohibition of guns in and around schools. In 2006 President Bush proposed that Congress give the president the power to veto portions of budget laws. In *Clinton v. City of New York*

(1998), the Court had struck down a statute establishing a line-item veto. But the president's proposal took a somewhat different form, one that might meet the Court's objections to the earlier statute.

Using Executive Power. As chief executive, the president has means to shape the implementation of Supreme Court decisions. For one thing, presidents can decide whether to support the Court with the power of the federal government when its decisions encounter open resistance from officials with the responsibility to carry them out.

The most coercive form of federal power is deployment of the military. In 1957, when a combination of state interference and mob action prevented court-ordered desegregation of the schools in Little Rock, Arkansas, Dwight Eisenhower abandoned his earlier position against the use of federal troops to enforce *Brown v. Board of Education.* In 1962 President John Kennedy used federal troops to enforce desegregation at the University of Mississippi.

Presidents can also employ litigation and their control over federal funds, and the Johnson administration used both mechanisms vigorously to break down segregated school systems in the Deep South. More recently, federal funds have been the subject of a battle that began with *Communications Workers of America v. Beck* (1988). This decision held that nonunion members are not required to pay the portion of union dues that is used for purposes (such as political activities) other than collective bargaining. In 1992 President George H.W. Bush ordered companies with federal contracts to notify their nonunion workers of the right to obtain refunds for part of their dues. President Clinton rescinded the order shortly after taking office in 1993. Shortly after *he* took office in 2001, President George W. Bush issued a new order similar to his father's. Two years later a federal court of appeals upheld his authority to do so.[60]

Presidents can shape the impact of Supreme Court decisions through their interpretations of the law. In 2005 President Bush gave a broad reading to the congressional override of *Rasul v. Bush* (2004). When he signed that override into law, the president announced his view that the law's prohibition of habeas corpus challenges to the detention of suspected terrorists at Guantanamo Bay applied to pending lawsuits as well as future ones. Using that interpretation, the solicitor general argued that the Supreme Court should dismiss *Hamdan v. Rumsfeld* (2006), a case in which a detainee challenged the president's authority to have prisoners tried before military commissions. However, in *Hamdan* the Court rejected that interpretation of the override.

Presidential Compliance. Occasionally, a Supreme Court decision requires compliance by the president, either as a party in the case or—more often— as head of the executive branch. Some presidents and commentators have argued that the president need not obey an order of the Supreme Court, which is a coequal body rather than a legal superior. In any case, presidents would seem sufficiently powerful to disobey the Court with impunity.

In reality their position is not that strong. The president's political power is based largely on the ability to obtain support from other policymakers. This ability, in turn, depends in part on perceptions of the president's legitimacy. Because disobedience of the Court would threaten this legitimacy, presidents feel some pressure to comply with the Court's decisions.

That conclusion is supported by presidential responses to two highly visible Court orders. In *Youngstown Sheet and Tube Co. v. Sawyer* (1952), the Court ruled that President Harry Truman had acted illegally during the Korean War when he seized steel mills to keep them operating if a threatened strike took place. The Court ordered an end to the seizure, and Truman immediately complied.

Even more striking is *United States v. Nixon* (1974). During the investigation of the Watergate scandal, President Richard Nixon withheld recordings of certain conversations in his offices that were sought by special prosecutor Leon Jaworski. In July 1974 the Supreme Court ruled unanimously that Nixon must yield the tapes.

In oral argument before the Court, the president's lawyer had indicated that Nixon might not comply with an adverse decision. But he did comply. At the least, this compliance speeded Nixon's departure from office. The content of the tapes provided strong evidence of presidential misdeeds, and opposition to impeachment evaporated. Fifteen days after the Court's ruling, Nixon announced his resignation.

In light of that result, why did Nixon comply with the Court order? He apparently did not realize how damaging the evidence in the tapes actually was. Perhaps more important, noncompliance would have fatally damaged his remaining legitimacy. For many members of Congress, noncompliance in itself would have constituted an impeachable offense, one for which there would be no dispute about the evidence. Under the circumstances, compliance may have been the better of two unattractive choices.

State Legislatures and Governors

State governments have no direct power over the Supreme Court as an institution. But state legislatures and governors, like Congress and the president, can influence the impact of the Court's decisions in a variety of ways.

Any legislature can rewrite a statute to try to meet the Court's constitutional objections to it. After the Court struck down existing death penalty laws in *Furman v. Georgia* (1972), thirty-five state legislatures soon wrote new laws that were designed to avoid arbitrary use of capital punishment and thus meet the objections raised by the pivotal justices in *Furman*. In a series of decisions over the past three decades, the Court has upheld some of the new statutes and overturned others. States whose laws were rejected by the Court have then adopted the forms that the Court had found acceptable.

Like Congress, state legislatures sometimes leave a statute on the books even though a Supreme Court decision makes it clear that the statute is unconstitutional. That situation creates a problem only if the statute is actually enforced. Legislatures occasionally act directly against the Court by enacting a new statute that seems clearly to violate the Court's decisions. In the decade after *Brown v. Board of Education,* southern states passed a large number of statutes to prevent school desegregation. Some states have enacted laws to restore public school religious observances that the Court invalidated. When challenged, most noncomplying statutes are overturned quickly by the federal courts. Adopting such laws might seem futile, but they allow legislators to gain personal satisfaction and political credit by expressing opposition to the Court's rulings.

Occasionally, state legislatures act to protect rights that the Supreme Court has held to be unprotected by the Constitution. Recent state laws to limit the use of eminent domain, discussed at the beginning of this chapter, fall into that category. The Court ruled in *City of Boerne v. Flores* (1997) that Congress lacked the power to give religious practices greater protection from state regulation. Since then, several legislatures have enacted similar laws to provide expanded protection in their own states.

Like presidents, governors can influence both legislative responses to the Court's decisions and their implementation. Southern governors helped to block school desegregation in the 1950s and 1960s through their efforts to stir up resistance. Some governors have played a similar role in opposition to the Court's limitations on religious observances in public schools. In 2002 Texas governor Rick Perry appeared at a required public school assembly in which a minister led students in a prayer, contrary to the Court's long-standing rules.[61]

Legislatures, governors, and their local counterparts must act to put some Supreme Court decisions into effect. *Gideon v. Wainwright* (1963) and later decisions required that indigent criminal defendants be provided with legal counsel. The Court's decisions spurred state and local governments to increase their commitment to defense for the indigent. That commitment has been reflected in much higher levels of funding, and low-income defendants are in a far better position than they were prior to 1963.

But funding of counsel has never been adequate throughout the country, and it has become less so with growth in the number of criminal cases and declining support for assistance to criminal defendants. Studies of the quality of indigent defense in states and local areas regularly report serious deficiencies.[62] Although the Court has achieved considerable change in state and local practices, they still fall short of what many people saw as the promise of the *Gideon* decision.

State legislatures and governors engage in direct defiance of the Court's decisions more often than do Congress and the president. This difference may result chiefly from the sheer number of states rather than from differences in the behavior of state and federal officials. Still, it underlines the difficulties that confront the Court when it seeks to bring about fundamental changes in state policies. Yet resistance to the Court by state governments should not be exaggerated. Undoubtedly, their most frequent response to the Court's decisions is compliance. And much of what governors and legislatures do to limit the Court's impact, such as their reinstatement of the death penalty, is an effort to maintain the policies they want within the constraints of the Court's rulings.

Two Policy Areas

Patterns of response to the Court's decisions by the other two branches of government can be examined more closely by looking at two areas in which the Court and other policymakers interact.

Civil Rights Statutes. Over the past half century, Congress has adopted a series of statutes that prohibit discrimination by race and other characteristics of individuals. The Supreme Court has issued many major and minor decisions interpreting these provisions.

Democrats controlled the House from 1957 through 1994, and they enjoyed a Senate majority for all but six of those years.[63] Through the mid-1980s, the Court generally gave broad interpretations to the civil rights laws, a stance that was consistent with the majority view in Congress. But Congress did override some decisions that narrowed the reach of the laws. The Pregnancy Discrimination Act of 1978 overturned a 1976 decision that exclusion of pregnancy from programs providing pay to disabled workers did not violate the Civil Rights Act of 1964.[64] Congress in 1988 reversed *Grove City College v. Bell* (1984), which had limited the reach of several statutes prohibiting discrimination by recipients of federal funds. And even with a Republican Senate in 1982, Congress reversed a 1980 decision that established a heavy burden of proof for people trying to prove racial discrimination in election rules.[65] In comparison with its predecessors, the Rehnquist Court gave narrower interpretations to civil rights laws. This stance aroused opposition from Congress in the early 1990s. The Civil Rights Act of 1991 overrode eight different Rehnquist Court decisions, most of them on employment discrimination.

The Republican administrations of the 1980s and early 1990s were less favorable than Congress to a broad interpretation of the civil rights laws, and this stance shaped legislative response to the Court's decisions. President

Reagan's opposition delayed the reversal of *Grove City,* and ultimately it was enacted by an override of his veto. The Civil Rights Act of 1991 became law only after President George H. W. Bush had vetoed an earlier version. Congress would have done even more to reverse conservative decisions under a Democratic president.

With the exception of the Senate in 2001–2002, both houses have had Republican majorities since 1995. As a result, the Court's interpretations of civil rights laws have been compatible with congressional views. The Court has ruled that parts of several civil rights laws were unconstitutional because they went beyond congressional power under the Constitution, and those decisions might seem likely to spur a major confrontation between the branches. But with a conservative Congress, nearly all of these decisions have been uncontroversial.

Abortion. The Supreme Court's decision in *Roe v. Wade* (1973) marked the beginning of an interplay between the courts and the other branches of government. Legislatures and chief executives have adopted measures to limit abortion, those measures are usually challenged in court, and the other branches respond to favorable or unfavorable court decisions with new measures.

State legislatures have been the most active in responding to *Roe.* Across the country, legislators have enacted a variety of laws intended to reduce the number of abortions. These laws deal with such matters as the facilities in which abortions can be performed, waiting periods for women seeking abortions, and requirements for the consent of parents or husbands for abortions.

In the first fifteen years after *Roe,* the Supreme Court and lower federal courts generally struck down laws that substantially limited access to abortion, although it upheld prohibitions of state funding for abortion. The Court's decisions in 1989 and 1992 seemed to give states more room to restrict abortion, and they helped to spur additional state legislation.[66] However, federal courts have continued to strike down much of this legislation. During the 1990s, a majority of states enacted a new type of regulation, one prohibiting an abortion method that opponents label "partial-birth abortion." The Court struck down these laws in *Stenberg v. Carhart* (2000). Following a well-established pattern in this field, legislators immediately began to draft new laws that might meet the Court's objections to the existing ones. Lower courts have struck down some of these new laws on the basis of *Stenberg.* In 2006 South Dakota enacted a bill to prohibit all abortions except those necessary to save the pregnant woman's life. This legislation came shortly after the appointment of Justice Alito to succeed Justice O'Connor, a shift that some people thought would change the Court's collective views on abortion. If South

Dakota voters do not repeal the law, a challenge to the law is likely to reach the Court.

At the federal level, many bills to overturn *Roe* with a constitutional amendment and to limit the Supreme Court's jurisdiction over abortion cases have been introduced but not adopted. Congress has enacted some restrictions on abortion, including annual provisions limiting the use of federal Medicaid funds for abortion (upheld by the Supreme Court) and a 2003 law aimed at partial-birth abortion (struck down by several lower courts).

Chief executives have played an active role in this field. Governors in some states have encouraged restrictions on abortion, and other governors have prevented their enactment. The Reagan and George H. W. Bush administrations established restrictions on the availability of abortion in some areas of federal activity, such as the military. In the early 1990s, Congress took steps to overturn some of the restrictions, but President Bush used the veto power to block these initiatives.

Two days after he became president, Bill Clinton eliminated several of the Reagan and Bush restrictions on abortion. When the Court ruled in 1993 that abortion clinics could not use a civil rights law to sue people who engaged in protests obstructing access to the clinics, the Clinton administration encouraged Congress to pass a statute aimed at curbing those protests.[67] Congress did so in 1994, allowing criminal prosecutions and civil lawsuits against those engaged in activities such as blockading abortion clinics. After Congress came under Republican control in 1995, Clinton used veto threats and actual vetoes to block antiabortion legislation.

Shortly after taking office, President George W. Bush prohibited U.S. foreign aid to groups that use their own money to promote abortion, reestablishing a policy that President Reagan had initiated and President Clinton had repealed. His election and reelection also eliminated the threat that bills to limit abortion would be vetoed. As of 2006, however, Congress and the president had done relatively little to change federal policy on abortion. But the states remained active in this field, continuing their interplay with the courts over the shape of abortion policy.

Impact on Society

People who are unhappy with the Supreme Court's policies often portray the Court as a source of great harm to the country. One commentator has argued that the Court's decisions are largely responsible for disorder and other problems in public schools.[68] When the Court ruled in 2004 that some people held by the United States as suspected terrorists or enemy combatants could challenge their detention in legal proceedings, one commentator accused the Court of doing great damage to national security.

"Imagine if our troops had to deal with such legal intrusions in World War II. We'd be a bilingual country today, speaking German *and* Japanese." According to another commentator, Justice Anthony Kennedy—whose unexpected moderation has helped to limit the Court's conservatism—is "the most dangerous man in America."[69] Observers who approve of the Court's policies sometimes speak of the Court as a powerful force for good on matters such as racial equality. The belief that the Court shapes society is reflected in the attention that it gets from interest groups, the mass media, and political leaders. But just how strong is the Court's impact? This may be the most important question about the Court.

A General View

Important though this question is, it is very difficult to answer. Whatever effects the Supreme Court may have on public schools or national security, those effects operate alongside the impact of other policymakers and social forces. As a result, it is often difficult to ascertain the Court's own impact. The Court's interpretations of the federal Employee Retirement Income Security Act (ERISA) have helped to shape the health care industry, and the Court's decisions on campaign funding and other election issues have helped determine who gets elected to office and thus what government does. But in neither case can we make confident judgments about the Court's effect.

Even with this uncertainty, however, there is reason to be skeptical about assertions that the Court has sweeping effects on American society. In reality, the effects of Supreme Court policies on society are limited considerably by the context in which those policies operate.

Much of that context is governmental. The Supreme Court seldom issues directives to people or institutions outside government. Rather, its decisions establish legal rules to govern decisions within government. This means that the Court's impact on society is mediated by other public policymakers.

One consequence of this mediation process is that the impact of decisions can be reduced. Some opponents of the Court's limits on religious exercises in public schools have argued that eliminating such exercises did considerable harm to schools and their students. But we know that compliance with the Court's decisions on school religion was far from complete, and that reality reduced any good or bad effects of those decisions.

More broadly, the Court is seldom the only government agency that deals with a particular set of issues. Rather, in most areas the Court is one policymaker among many that make decisions and undertake initiatives. In environmental policy, for instance, Congress sets the basic legal rules, administrative agencies elaborate on these rules and apply them to specific cases, and lower courts resolve most disagreements over agency decisions.

The Court's participation is limited to resolving a few of the legal questions that arise in the lower courts. Under these conditions, the Court can hardly determine the character of environmental policy by itself.

The Court's policies also operate within a context of nongovernmental action. The direct impact of most decisions depends largely on the responses of people outside government. Especially important are the actions of institutions and people to whom the Court gives greater freedom. These beneficiaries of the Court's policies may not take full advantage of the freedom that the Court provides them. One reason is that they may not be aware of favorable decisions. But even those who know about such decisions do not always act on them. For example, welfare recipients may not insist on their procedural rights because they do not want to alienate officials who hold power over them.

Forces outside of government also limit the broad impact of Supreme Court decisions on society. The crime rate and the quality of education are affected by family socialization, the mass media, and the economy. Those forces are likely to exert a much stronger impact on the propensity to commit crimes or the performance of students than does a Supreme Court policy. This limitation is common to all public policies, no matter which branch issues them. But the Supreme Court is in an especially weak position, because it has little control over the behavior of the private sector and because it seldom makes comprehensive policy in a particular area.

Despite all these limitations, Supreme Court decisions can and do have significant effects on society. By helping to allocate legal rights, the Court shapes the balance between competing values and segments of society. One example is a 1938 decision allowing companies to hire new employees as permanent replacements for workers who are on strike.[70] Gradually, employers took advantage of the Court's ruling. It appears that the use of replacement workers grew considerably in the 1980s, a growth symbolized by President Reagan's hiring of replacements for striking air traffic controllers. This trend helped to weaken the power of organized labor.

Some Areas of Court Activity

We can gain a better sense of the Court's impact on society and the forces that determine that impact by looking at a few areas of the Court's activity. These examples demonstrate that the Court's impact is complex, highly variable, and sometimes quite difficult to measure.

Abortion.   Prior to the Court's 1973 decisions in *Roe v. Wade* and *Doe v. Bolton*, two-thirds of the states allowed abortion only under quite limited circumstances, and in only four states was abortion generally legal. With its decisions the Court disallowed nearly all significant legal restrictions on abortion. In every year since 1976, more than one million legal abortions

Air traffic controllers at Newark International Airport. A 1938 Supreme Court decision said that employers could hire permanent replacements for striking workers, and President Reagan did so after controllers went on strike in 1981. Employers' growing use of replacement workers helped to weaken labor unions in the United States.

have been performed. In light of the sequence of events, it seems reasonable to conclude that the Court is responsible for the large number of legal abortions. But the reality is more complicated, and it is impossible to assess the Court's impact with any precision.[71]

As shown in Figure 6-1, the number of legal abortions increased by about 150 percent between 1972 and 1979. This massive change suggests that the Court made a great deal of difference. But the rate of increase was actually greater between 1969 and 1972. That increase reflected changes in state laws before and during that period, as some states relaxed their general prohibitions of abortion and a few eliminated most restrictions. If the Court had never handed down *Roe v. Wade,* the number of legal abortions probably would have continued to rise because of more changes in state laws and because of an increasing abortion rate in the states that allowed abortion. But it is impossible to know how state laws would have evolved and how the abortion rate would have changed if the Court had not intervened.

After the Court decided *Roe v. Wade,* policies by the other branches of government shaped its impact. Decisions by the federal government and most states to fund abortions through Medicaid only under limited

FIGURE 6-1

Estimated Numbers of Legal Abortions and Related Government Policy Actions, 1966–2002

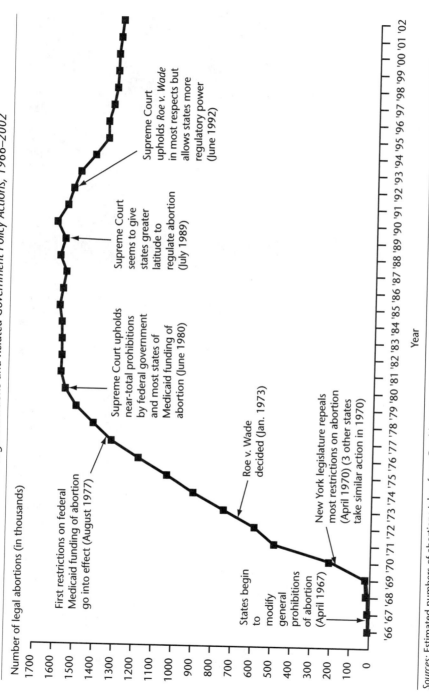

Sources: Estimated numbers of abortions taken from Gerald N. Rosenberg, *The Hollow Hope: Can Courts Bring About Social Change?* (Chicago: University of Chicago Press, 1991), 180 (for 1968–1985), and Lawrence B. Finer and Stanley K. Henshaw, "Estimates of Abortion Incidence in 2001 and 2002," Alan Guttmacher Institute (www.agi-usa.org/sections/abortion.php?pub=stats), 7 (for 1986–2002).

circumstances affect the rate of abortion among low-income women. Decisions not to perform abortions in government-run medical facilities also affect the abortion rate. Other relevant policies range from rules for medical clinics that receive federal money to state-mandated waiting periods before abortions can be performed. The Court influences these policies through its rulings on what kinds of restrictions on abortion are allowable, but that influence falls far short of full control.

Conditions other than government policy also affect the abortion rate.[72] First, the number of abortions largely depends on the number of unintended pregnancies and on women's choices to seek abortions. A second condition is the ability of women who want abortions to obtain them. Only a small minority of privately owned hospitals perform abortions. Urban areas generally have clinics that perform abortions, but many rural areas lack such clinics. The number of facilities that perform abortions has declined substantially in the past two decades. These patterns reflect the personal beliefs of medical personnel as well as restrictive laws and pressures against providing abortions, ranging from disapproval in the local community to threatened and actual violence. The decline in facilities that perform abortions helps to explain the lower numbers of abortions in recent years.

Roe v. Wade had major political effects, effects that the justices could not have foreseen. The Court helped to make abortion a major issue in national politics, one that affects both political activity and government policy on a variety of issues. *Roe* strengthened and energized the groups that opposed the legalization of abortion by creating a perceived need for action and a target to attack. More broadly, reaction against *Roe v. Wade* played a part in the development of the religious right as a major political force, one that has strengthened the conservative movement and the Republican Party.

Political Dissent. In its First Amendment cases, the Supreme Court often reviews government policies aimed at people who take unpopular political positions. The Court has a mixed record in these cases, but over the past half century it has made many decisions limiting censorship and punishment of political dissenters. In the 1960s it struck down government policies that penalized people for association with groups on the far left. During the Vietnam War it issued decisions protecting opponents of official U.S. policy from punishment for their activities. In an era without such direct confrontations between government and political dissenters, the Rehnquist Court established some additional protections. For example, it struck down criminal penalties for burning the flag as a political statement and limited economic retaliation against public employees and business owners who criticize government policy.

The impact of these decisions is difficult to measure, but in all likelihood they have restrained government action against dissent and thereby encouraged dissenters. For example, the Court's protection of opponents of the war in Vietnam probably encouraged the open expression of opposition.

Yet the Court has not brought about a massive increase in the level of political dissent in the United States. One reason is that the Court's support for political dissent has not gone as far as it could have. But more important are forces that limit the impact of the Court's support for free speech.

For one thing, government officials do not always comply with the letter of the Court's decisions, and noncompliance with their spirit is quite common. Thus public school administrators sometimes punish students for expressing their political beliefs in ways that the Court has protected. Local governments occasionally establish limits on political demonstrations that clearly run counter to the Court's decisions.

But perhaps most important are conditions in the private sector. First Amendment rights protect people only against actions by government. As a result, people may suffer serious consequences for political dissent. A factory worker can be fired for having a John Kerry bumper sticker on her car.[73] Homeowners' associations can punish people for putting political signs on their property, and the father-in-law of Justice Thomas was told by his retirement community to take down an American flag until publicity forced the community to relent.[74] People may refrain from saying what they think because they fear that neighbors will ostracize them or people in the community will attack them. Threats and violence have been directed against environmentalists who oppose economic activities that are important in their area and at opponents of government-sponsored religious activities. When one father opposed mandatory student drug tests in a rural Texas school, he received threats and faced what a reporter called "life as a pariah."[75]

Incentives to avoid unpopular speech become especially strong in times of perceived danger to national security. Concern about terrorism and the war in Iraq have produced pressures against dissent from national policy.[76] In the best-publicized case, members of the Dixie Chicks music group were subjected to boycotts, vandalism, and death threats after one member said that the group's members were "ashamed" to share the home state of President George W. Bush. More quietly, other dissenters against the war have also suffered for their views.

It is not surprising, then, that people often choose to remain silent rather than express controversial views. This result underlines the limits on the Supreme Court's ability to change social realities.

Racial Equality

In debates over the Supreme Court's impact, no issue receives as much attention as racial equality. The Warren Court of the 1950s and 1960s did a great deal to combat racial discrimination. It ruled against discrimination in education and voting, it upheld federal laws prohibiting discrimination, and it sought to protect the civil rights movement from legal attacks. To a degree, that line of policy extended back to the Court of the 1940s and forward to the Court of the 1970s. Implicitly, the Court was making a commitment to improve the status of black Americans. To what extent have the Court's policies achieved that goal?

Change in Status. The first question to ask is how much the status of black Americans has changed. This is the subject of considerable disagreement, in part because progress has varied so much among different areas of life.

In politics, racial barriers to black voting in the South were overcome. This change contributed to growth in the number of black elected officials in the country, from about three hundred in 1965 to more than nine thousand in 2001.[77] And white officials, especially in the South, have become considerably more willing to respond to black concerns.

The social segregation of American life has broken down unevenly. Segregation of hotels and restaurants went from a standard practice to an anomaly. Legally segregated school systems have disappeared from the Deep South and the border states, but the level of actual segregation among schools remains high and by some measures has increased somewhat since the 1980s.[78] This school segregation reflects the high level of housing segregation, which has not declined substantially.[79]

In the economic arena, discrimination in employment has not disappeared, but its frequency has declined a good deal. This decline and substantial growth in education levels have helped to bring about a major improvement in economic status for black Americans, but there remains a significant difference in income between the races. Indeed, the average income of blacks has remained at about 60 percent of the average for whites since 1970, both for individuals and for families. The proportion of black people who live in poverty is about three times the proportion for whites.[80]

The Court's Impact. The extent of progress toward racial equality sets an outer limit on the possible impact of the Supreme Court. Within that outer limit, how much of an impact has the Court had? Clearly, the Court is not the only potential source of change. Other relevant forces include the other branches of government, the mass media, and the civil rights movement. In some respects these sources are considerably more powerful than the Court.

The Court's relative weakness is clear in education and voting, the areas in which it was most active. The Court's rulings against dual school systems and devices to limit black voting in the South had only limited effects in themselves. In the Deep South it was the enactment of the Civil Rights Act of 1964 and the Voting Rights Act of 1965 and their vigorous enforcement by the Johnson administration that broke down official school segregation and made the right to vote effective.

Because constitutional protections against discrimination do not apply directly to the private sector, the initiative in attacking housing and employment discrimination had to come from the other branches. Congress enacted statutes in the 1960s that mandated equal treatment in housing and employment, and the executive branch is responsible for enforcing them. In the 1970s and early 1980s, the Court generally gave broad interpretations to the laws against employment discrimination, interpretations that strengthened them. Some evidence indicates that these laws have affected the economic status of black citizens significantly. The Court's decisions may have played a part in producing that effect, although certainly no more than a minor part.

Perhaps the Court played a crucial indirect role. As some observers see it, its early civil rights decisions—especially *Brown v. Board of Education*—helped to spur passage of federal legislation and served as a catalyst for the civil rights movement. The development of a mass civil rights movement in the South was probably inevitable, and the Supreme Court was hardly the major force contributing to its development. But the Court may have speeded the movement's growth. Its decisions in education and other areas created hope for change and established rights to be vindicated by political action.

The series of civil rights laws adopted from 1957 on also may owe something to the Court. In education and voting, the Court initiated government action against discrimination and helped to create expectations that Congress and the executive branch were pressed to fulfill. It is true that congressional action was most directly responsible for bringing about school desegregation in the Deep South. But if the Court had not issued the *Brown* decision, Congress might have had less impetus to act against segregation at all.

An Assessment. The issue of racial equality illustrates both the strengths and limitations of government in achieving societal change. Public policy has helped to bring about significant reductions in the disadvantages of black Americans. But these disadvantages have hardly disappeared, and even a stronger government commitment to equality could not have eliminated them altogether.

For the Supreme Court specifically, the assessment is also mixed. The Court has had little direct impact on discrimination in the private sector. Even in the public sector, it has been weak in the enforcement of rights.

In part for these reasons, some assessments of the Court's impact half a century after *Brown* were gloomy.[81]

But the Court helped to initiate and support processes of change, and its members probably can take some credit for progress toward racial equality. If the Court's impact has been more limited than many people had hoped, the Court *has* contributed to significant social change.[82]

Conclusion: The Court, Public Policy, and Society

It is now possible to reach some tentative conclusions about the role of the Supreme Court as a public policymaker. As suggested in Chapter 5 and this chapter, that role is fundamentally limited in some respects but still quite important.

The most obvious limitation on the Court's role is that it decides relatively few issues. One effect is that the Court can be only a minor participant in fields such as foreign policy, in which it does not address most major issues. Even in its areas of specialization, the Court intervenes only in limited ways. It makes decisions on a small sample of the issues that affect the rights of criminal defendants or freedom of expression.

The justices are not always shy about intervening on major issues of public policy, and the Court often reaches decisions that depart sharply from existing policy. The impact of such decisions is mediated and regularly reduced by the actions of other institutions and individuals. A ruling that public schools must eliminate organized prayers does not guarantee that those observances will disappear. Efforts to broaden freedom of expression may be stymied by conditions in society that the Court cannot influence.

These limitations must be balanced against the Court's strengths. Certainly, a great many Supreme Court decisions have significant direct effects. School desegregation decisions determine which schools students attend. Interpretations of the Voting Rights Act and the Constitution shape politics and policy at all levels of government. The Court's decisions influence business practices and the outcome of conflicts between different economic groups. The effects of capital punishment decisions are literally matters of life and death for some people.

The Court also helps to shape political and social change. Its partial opposition to government regulation of private business was ultimately overcome, but the Court slowed a fundamental change in the role of government. If *Roe v. Wade* was not as consequential as most people think, it *has* been the focus of a major national debate and struggle for more than a quarter century. The Court's decisions have not brought about racial equality, even in conjunction with other forces, but they have helped to spur changes in race relations.

As the examples of abortion and civil rights suggest, the Court is perhaps most important in creating conditions for action by others. Its decisions help to put issues on the national agenda so that other policymakers and the general public consider them. The Court is not highly effective in enforcing rights, but it often legitimates efforts to achieve rights. By doing so, it provides an impetus for people to take legal and political action. Its decisions affect the positions of interest groups and social movements, strengthening some and weakening others.

The Supreme Court, then, is neither all-powerful nor inconsequential. Rather, it is one of many institutions that shape American society in significant ways. That is a more limited role than some have claimed for the Court. But the role that the Court does play is an extraordinary one for a single small body that possesses little tangible power. In this sense, perhaps more than any other, the Supreme Court is a remarkable institution.

NOTES

1. This discussion of *Kelo* is based primarily on newspaper accounts. Especially useful were Terry Pristin, "Developers Can't Imagine a World without Eminent Domain," *New York Times,* January 18, 2006, C5; William Yardley, "After Eminent Domain Victory, Disputed Project Goes Nowhere," *New York Times,* November 21, 2005, A1, A22; and Dennis Cauchon, "States Eye Land Seizure Limits," *USA Today,* February 20, 2006, A1. The figures on bills in state legislatures are from Elizabeth Mehren, "States Acting to Protect Private Property," *Los Angeles Times,* April 16, 2006, A1, A16. The congressional legislation was Public Law 109-115, 109th Cong., 1st sess. (2005), sec. 726.
2. Scott Gold, "After 44 Years, Louisiana Man Is Freed," *Los Angeles Times,* January 17, 2005, A8. The Supreme Court case was *Rideau v. Louisiana* (1963).
3. Ed Treleven, "No Benefit from His Landmark Case," *Wisconsin State Journal,* May 4, 2005. The decision was *United States v. Booker* (2005).
4. "Verdict: Atkins Not Mentally Retarded," *Daily Press* (Hampton Roads, Va.), August 5, 2005. The state supreme court decision was *Atkins v. Commonwealth* (Va. 2006).
5. The second Supreme Court decision was *Miller-El v. Dretke* (2005). The final court of appeals action came in *Miller-El v. Dretke* (5th Cir. 2005).
6. Eric Lichtblau, "U.S. to Free 'Enemy Combatant,' Bowing to Supreme Court Ruling," *New York Times,* September 23, 2004, A1, A19.
7. Tamar Lewin, "Controversy Over, Enclave Joins School Board Group," *New York Times,* April 20, 2002, B4. See Michael A. Bamberger, *Reckless Legislation: How Lawmakers Ignore the Constitution* (New Brunswick, N.J.: Rutgers University Press, 2000), 113–124.
8. "Sharper Remains a Raven with New $22 Million Deal," *Washington Post,* April 24, 2001, D3; post from Michael R. Masinter on the "CONLAWPROF" listserv, May 22, 2001.
9. The Supreme Court's decision was *Good News Club v. Milford Central School* (2001). The final district court decision was *Bronx Household of Faith v. Board of Education* (S.D.N.Y. 2005).

10. Karen M. Blum, "11th Circuit Is Out of Step," *National Law Journal,* April 21, 2003, A13; see Jonathan Ringel, "Divided 11th Circuit Panel Backs Immunity for Cops," *National Law Journal,* December 8, 2003, 7. The Supreme Court decision was *Hope v. Pelzer* (2002).

11. *American Civil Liberties Union v. Mercer County* (2006). The Supreme Court decision was *McCreary County v. American Civil Liberties Union* (2005).

12. James F. Spriggs II, "Explaining Federal Bureaucratic Compliance with Supreme Court Opinions," *Political Research Quarterly* 50 (September 1997): 577–578.

13. Elizabeth Amon, "INS Flouts Court on Prisoners, Critics Say," *National Law Journal,* August 12, 2002, A1, A12; *Seretse-Khama v. Ashcroft* (D.D.C. 2002). The decision was *Zadvydas v. Davis* (2001).

14. Steve Bogira, *Courtroom 302: A Year behind the Scenes in an American Criminal Courthouse* (New York: Knopf, 2005), 16–17, 67, 157–158, 261. The decisions were, respectively, *Gerstein v. Pugh* (1975), *Brady v. Maryland* (1963), and *Batson v. Kentucky* (1986).

15. *Miller-El v. Dretke,* 162 L. Ed. 2d 196, 230–232 (2005). See Leonard Post, "A Loaded Box of Stereotypes," *National Law Journal,* April 25, 2005, 1, 18; and Holly Becka, Steve McGonigle, Tim Wyatt, and Jennifer LaFleur, "Judges Rarely Detect Jury Selection Bias," *Dallas Morning News,* August 23, 2005, 1A, 10A, 11A.

16. Harrell R. Rodgers Jr. and Charles S. Bullock III, *Law and Social Change: Civil Rights Laws and Their Consequences* (New York: McGraw-Hill, 1972), 75.

17. *Green v. School Board* (1968); *Alexander v. Holmes County Board of Education* (1969).

18. *Missouri v. Jenkins* (1990); *Spallone v. United States* (1989). On *Spallone,* see Lisa Belkin, *Show Me a Hero: A Tale of Murder, Suicide, Race, and Redemption* (Boston: Little, Brown, 1999).

19. *Board of Education v. Dowell* (1991); *Freeman v. Pitts* (1992).

20. Wayne R. LaFave, *Search and Seizure: A Treatise on the Fourth Amendment,* 4th ed. (St. Paul, Minn.: Thomson/West, 2004), 1:68n45.

21. Richard A. Leo, "The Impact of *Miranda* Revisited," *Journal of Criminal Law and Criminology* 86 (spring 1996): 652–653; Paul G. Cassell and Bret S. Hayman, "Police Interrogation in the 1990s: An Empirical Study of the Effects of *Miranda, UCLA Law Review* 43 (February 1996): 887–892.

22. This discussion is based in part on Welsh S. White, *Miranda's Waning Protections: Police Interrogation Practices after Dickerson* (Ann Arbor: University of Michigan Press, 2001); and George C. Thomas III and Richard A. Leo, "The Effects of *Miranda v. Arizona:* 'Embedded' in Our National Culture?" *Crime and Justice* (2002): 203–271.

23. *People v. Neal* (Calif. 2003); *Missouri v. Seibert,* 542 U.S. 600, 609–611 (2004).

24. Jerome H. Skolnick, *Justice without Trial: Law Enforcement in Democratic Society,* 3d ed. (New York: Macmillan, 1994), 277 (emphasis in original).

25. Evidence on the impact of *Mapp* is discussed in L. Timothy Perrin, H. Mitchell Caldwell, Carol A. Chase, and Ronald W. Fagan, "If It's Broken, Fix It: Moving beyond the Exclusionary Rule," *Iowa Law Review* 83 (May 1998): 678–711.

26. Bradley C. Canon, "Is the Exclusionary Rule in Failing Health? Some New Data and a Plea against a Precipitous Conclusion," *Kentucky Law Journal* 62 (1974): 702–725; Myron W. Orfield Jr., "The Exclusionary Rule and Deterrence: An Empirical Study of Chicago Narcotics Officers," *University*

of Chicago Law Review 54 (summer 1987): 1024–1049; and Craig D. Uchida and Timothy S. Bynum, "Search Warrants, Motions to Suppress and 'Lost Cases': The Effects of the Exclusionary Rule in Seven Jurisdictions," *Journal of Criminal Law and Criminology* 81 (winter 1991): 1034–1066.

27. Jon B. Gould and Stephen D. Mastrofski, "Suspect Searches: Assessing Police Behavior under the U.S. Constitution," *Criminology and Public Policy* 3 (2004): 901–948.

28. Christopher Slobogin, "Why Liberals Should Chuck the Exclusionary Rule," *University of Illinois Law Review* (1999): 369.

29. *Li v. Ashcroft* (9th Cir. 2004).

30. *United States v. Wilson* (D. Utah 2005). The Supreme Court decision was *United States v. Booker* (2005).

31. Elliot E. Slotnick and Jennifer A. Segal, *Television News and the Supreme Court: All the News That's Fit to Air?* (New York: Cambridge University Press, 1998).

32. Caleb Hale, "Man Pleads Guilty to Desecrating U.S. Flag," *Southern Illinoisian*, December 3, 2003. The Utah case is described in *Winsness v. Yocom* (10th Cir. 2006).

33. *Tennard v. Dretke*, 542 U.S. 274, 283–284 (2004).

34. *Engel v. Vitale* (1962); *Abington School District v. Schempp* (1963).

35. See Kevin T. McGuire, "Schools, Religious Establishments, and the U.S. Supreme Court: An Examination of Policy Compliance" (paper presented at the annual meeting of the Midwest Political Science Association, Chicago, April 2005).

36. Cragg Hines, "Supremes to Texas Appeals Court: You Still Don't Get It," *Houston Chronicle*, November 21, 2004, 3; Michael Hall, "And Justice for Some," *Texas Monthly*, November 2004, 154–157, 259–263.

37. J. W. Peltason, *Fifty-Eight Lonely Men: Southern Federal Judges and School Desegregation* (Urbana: University of Illinois Press, 1971), 9.

38. Robert Carp and Russell Wheeler, "Sink or Swim: The Socialization of a Federal District Judge," *Journal of Public Law* 21 (1972): 373.

39. *Wallace v. Castro*, 65 Fed. Appx. 618, 619 (9th Cir. 2003). The Supreme Court decision was *Lockyer v. Andrade* (2003).

40. Tom Parker, "Alabama Justices Surrender to Judicial Activism," *Birmingham News*, January 1, 2006, 4B. The case was *Adams v. State* (Ala. 2005).

41. William K. Muir Jr., *Prayer in the Public Schools: Law and Attitude Change* (Chicago: University of Chicago Press, 1967); Richard Johnson, *The Dynamics of Compliance* (Evanston, Ill.: Northwestern University Press, 1967).

42. *United States v. Shipp* (1909). See Mark Curriden and Leroy Phillips Jr., *Contempt of Court* (New York: Faber and Faber, 1999).

43. Gracie Bonds Staples, "A Roundup of Cowgirl Memories," *Atlanta Journal and Constitution*, July 21, 2002, 1K.

44. *Warnock v. Archer* (8th Cir. 2004, 2006).

45. William N. Eskridge Jr., "Overriding Supreme Court Statutory Interpretation Decisions," *Yale Law Journal* 101 (November 1991): 338; updating through 1996 is from Lori Hausegger and Lawrence Baum, "Behind the Scenes: The Supreme Court and Congress in Statutory Interpretation," in *Great Theatre: The American Congress in Action,* ed. Herbert F. Weisberg and Samuel C. Patterson (New York: Cambridge University Press, 1998), 228.

46. *Federal Baseball Club, Inc. v. National League of Professional Baseball Clubs* (1922).

47. Michael E. Solimine and James L. Walker, "The Next Word: Congressional Response to Supreme Court Statutory Decisions," *Temple Law Review* 65

(1992): 425–458; Virginia A. Hettinger and Christopher Zorn, "Explaining the Incidence and Timing of Congressional Responses to the U.S. Supreme Court," *Legislative Studies Quarterly* 30 (February 2005): 5–28.

48. Eskridge, "Overriding Supreme Court Statutory Interpretation Decisions," 348, 351, 359–367.

49. J. Mitchell Pickerill, *Constitutional Deliberation in Congress: The Impact of Judicial Review in a Separated System* (Durham, N.C.: Duke University Press, 2004), 42. This discussion draws from the Pickerill book.

50. This language is at *U.S. Code*, Title 18, sec. 922 (q)(2)(A).

51. The Court's decisions were *Employment Division v. Smith* (1990), *City of Boerne v. Flores* (1997), and *Cutter v. Wilkinson* (2005).

52. The provision on school religion is at *U.S. Code*, Title 20, sec. 7904; the provision on the Boy Scouts is at *U.S. Code*, Title 20, sec. 7905.

53. Louis Fisher and Neal Devins, *The Democratic Constitution* (New York: Oxford University Press, 2004), 94–97.

54. Carl Hulse and David D. Kirkpatrick, "DeLay Says Federal Judiciary Has 'Run Amok,' Adding Congress Is Partly to Blame," *New York Times*, April 8, 2005, A21.

55. This discussion draws from Brett W. Curry, "The Courts, Congress, and the Politics of Federal Jurisdiction" (Ph.D. diss., Ohio State University, 2005), chaps. 6–7; and Lauren C. Bell and Kevin M. Scott, "Policy Statements or Symbolic Politics? Explaining Congressional Court-Limiting Attempts," *Judicature* 89 (January–February 2006), 196–201.

56. *Congressional Record,* 89th Cong., 1st sess., 1965, 111, pt. 4: 5275. See John R. Schmidhauser and Larry L. Berg, *The Supreme Court and Congress: Conflict and Interaction, 1945–1968* (New York: Free Press, 1972), 8–12.

57. Sheryl Gay Stolberg, "Republican Lawmakers Fire Back at Judiciary," *New York Times*, July 1, 2005, A10.

58. Ruth Marcus, "Booting the Bench," *Washington Post*, April 11, 2005, A19.

59. William G. Ross, *A Muted Fury: Populists, Progressives, and Labor Unions Confront the Courts, 1890–1937* (Princeton: Princeton University Press, 1994).

60. *UAW–Labor Employment and Training Corporation v. Chao* (D.C. Cir. 2003).

61. Jay Root, "Falwell Backs Perry Prayer Push," *Fort Worth Star-Telegram*, November 1, 2001, 5B.

62. One example is the series of news articles on Washington State by Ken Armstrong, Florangela Davila, and Justin Mayo, published in the *Seattle Times* on April 4–6, 2004.

63. On Congress-Court interaction in civil rights, see William N. Eskridge Jr., "Reneging on History? Playing the Court/Congress/President Civil Rights Game," *California Law Review* 79 (May 1991): 613–684.

64. *General Electric Co. v. Gilbert* (1976).

65. *City of Mobile v. Bolden* (1980).

66. The decisions were *Webster v. Reproductive Health Services* (1989) and *Planned Parenthood v. Casey* (1992).

67. The decision was *Bray v. Alexandria Women's Health Clinic* (1993).

68. Stuart Taylor Jr., "Lawless in Class," *Legal Times*, November 17, 2003, 58–59. See Richard Arum, *Judging School Discipline: The Crisis of Moral Authority* (Cambridge: Harvard University Press, 2003).

69. Daniel J. Popeo, "A Pause for Foresight" (advertisement), *New York Times*, July 26, 2004, A19; Jason DeParle, "In Battle to Pick Next Justice, Right Says Avoid a Kennedy," *New York Times*, June 27, 2005, A12.

70. *National Labor Relations Board v. Mackay Radio & Telegraph Company* (1938).
71. This discussion of abortion is based in part on Gerald N. Rosenberg, *The Hollow Hope: Can Courts Bring about Social Change?* (Chicago: University of Chicago Press, 1991), 175–201; and Matthew E. Wetstein, "The Abortion Rate Paradox: The Impact of National Policy Change on Abortion Rates," *Social Science Quarterly* 76 (September 1995): 607–618.
72. This paragraph draws from Lawrence B. Finer and Stanley K. Henshaw, "Abortion Incidence and Services in the United States in 2000," *Perspectives on Sexual and Reproductive Health* 35 (January/February 2003): 6–15; and Stanley K. Henshaw and Lawrence B. Finer, "The Accessibility of Abortion Services in the United States, 2001," *Perspectives on Sexual and Reproductive Health* 35 (January/February 2003): 16–24.
73. Timothy Noah, "Bumper Sticker Insubordination," *Slate,* September 14, 2004, at www.slate.com.
74. Tony Mauro, "An Unwelcome Mat for Free Speech," *USA Today,* August 18, 2004, 13A.
75. Jim Yardley, "Family in Texas Challenges Mandatory School Drug Test," *New York Times,* April 17, 2000, A1, A16.
76. See Julia Keller, "Speak Your Piece," *Chicago Tribune Magazine,* June 29, 2003, 14–20, 27–29.
77. Gerald David Jaynes and Robin M. Williams Jr., *A Common Destiny: Blacks and American Society* (Washington, D.C.: National Academy Press, 1989), 238; David A. Bositis, *Black Elected Officials: A Statistical Summary 2001* (Washington, D.C.: Joint Center for Political and Economic Studies, n.d.), 13.
78. Charles T. Clotfelter, *After Brown: The Rise and Retreat of School Desegregation* (Princeton: Princeton University Press, 2004); Gary Orfield and Chungmei Lee, *Racial Transformation and the Changing Nature of Segregation* (Cambridge: Civil Rights Project, Harvard University, 2006). A different view is presented in John Logan, "Resegregation in American Public Schools? Not in the 1990s," State University of New York at Albany, 2004, available at http://mumford.albany.edu/census/report.html.
79. John R. Logan, Brian J. Stults, and Reynolds Farley, "Segregation of Minorities in the Metropolis: Two Decades of Change," *Demography* 41 (February 2004): 1–22.
80. Carmen DeNavas-Walt, Bernadette D. Proctor, and Cheryl Hill Lee, *Income, Poverty, and Health Insurance Coverage in the United States: 2004* (Washington, D.C.: U.S. Department of Commerce, 2005). In the comparisons in the text, "whites" refers to non-Hispanic whites.
81. Charles J. Ogletree Jr., *All Deliberate Speed: Reflections on the First Half Century of* Brown v. Board of Education (New York: Norton, 2003); Derrick Bell, *Silent Covenants: Brown v. Board of Education and the Unfulfilled Hopes for Racial Reform* (New York: Oxford University Press, 2004).
82. See Michael J. Klarman, *From Jim Crow to Civil Rights: The Supreme Court and the Struggle for Racial Equality* (New York: Oxford University Press, 2004), 443–468.

Glossary of Legal Terms

Affirm. In an appellate court, to reach a decision that agrees with the result reached in the case by the lower court.

Amicus curiae. "Friend of the court." A person, private group or institution, or government agency, not a party to a case, that participates in the case (usually through submission of a brief) at the invitation of the court or on its own initiative.

Appeal. In general, a case brought to a higher court for review. In the Supreme Court, a small number of cases are designated as appeals under federal law; formally, these must be heard by the Court.

Appellant. The party that appeals a lower court decision to a higher court.

Appellee. A party to an appeal who wishes to have the lower court decision upheld and who responds when the case is appealed.

Brief. A document submitted by counsel to a court, setting out the facts of the case and the legal arguments in support of the party represented by the counsel.

Certiorari, Writ of. A writ issued by the Supreme Court, at its discretion, to order a lower court to send a case to the Supreme Court for review. Most cases come to the Court as petitions for writs of certiorari.

Civil cases. All legal cases other than criminal cases.

Class action. A lawsuit brought by one person or group on behalf of all persons in similar situations.

Concurring opinion. An opinion by a member of a court that agrees with the result reached by the court in the case but offers its own rationale for the decision.

Dicta. *See* Obiter dictum.

Discretionary jurisdiction. Jurisdiction that a court may accept or reject in particular cases. The Supreme Court has discretionary jurisdiction over most cases that come to it.

Dissenting opinion. An opinion by a member of a court that disagrees with the result reached by the court in the case.

Habeas corpus. "You have the body." A writ issued by a court to inquire whether a person is lawfully imprisoned or detained. The writ demands that the persons holding the prisoner justify the detention or release the prisoner.

Holding. In a majority opinion, the rule of law necessary to decide the case. That rule is binding in future cases.

In forma pauperis. "In the manner of a pauper." In the Supreme Court, cases brought in forma pauperis by indigent persons are exempt from the Court's usual fees and from some formal requirements.

Judicial review. Review of legislation or other government action to determine its consistency with the federal or state constitution; includes the power to strike down policies that are inconsistent with a constitutional provision. The Supreme Court reviews government action only under the federal Constitution, not state constitutions.

Jurisdiction. The power of a court to hear a case in question.

Litigants. The parties to a court case.

Majority opinion. An opinion in a case that is subscribed to by a majority of the judges who participated in the decision. Also known as the opinion of the court.

Mandamus. "We command." An order issued by a court that directs a lower court or other authority to perform a particular act.

Mandatory jurisdiction. Jurisdiction that a court must accept. Cases falling under a court's mandatory jurisdiction must be decided officially on their merits, though a court may avoid giving them full consideration.

Modify. In an appellate court, to reach a decision that disagrees in part with the result reached in the case by the lower court.

Moot. A moot case is one that has become hypothetical, so that a court need not decide it.

Obiter dictum. (Also called *dictum* [sing.] or *dicta* [pl.].) A statement in a court opinion that is not necessary to resolve the case before the court. Dicta are not binding in future cases.

Original jurisdiction. Jurisdiction as a trial court.

Per curiam. "By the court." An unsigned opinion of the court, often quite brief.

Petitioner. One who files a petition with a court seeking action or relief, such as a writ of certiorari.

Remand. To send back. When a case is remanded, it is sent back by a higher court to the court from which it came, for further action.

Respondent. The party in opposition to a petitioner or appellant, who answers the claims of that party.

Reverse. In an appellate court, to reach a decision that disagrees with the result reached in the case by the lower court.

Standing. A requirement that the party who files a lawsuit have a legal stake in the outcome.

Stare decisis. "Let the decision stand." The doctrine that principles of law established in earlier judicial decisions should be accepted as authoritative in similar subsequent cases.

Statute. A written law enacted by a legislature.

Stay. To halt or suspend further judicial proceedings. The Supreme Court sometimes issues a stay to suspend action in a lower court while the Supreme Court considers the case.

Vacate. To make void or annul. The Supreme Court sometimes vacates a lower court decision, requiring the lower court to reconsider the case.

Writ. A written court order commanding the designated recipient to perform or not perform acts specified in the order.

Selected Bibliography

General References

Epstein, Lee, Jeffrey A. Segal, Harold J. Spaeth, and Thomas G. Walker. *The Supreme Court Compendium: Data, Decisions, and Developments.* 3d ed. Washington, D.C.: CQ Press, 2003.

Hall, Kermit L., James W. Ely Jr., and Joel B. Grossman, eds. *The Oxford Companion to the Supreme Court of the United States.* 2d ed. New York: Oxford University Press, 2005.

Savage, David G. *Guide to the U.S. Supreme Court.* 4th ed. Washington, D.C.: CQ Press, 2004.

Chapter 1

Hoekstra, Valerie J. *Public Reaction to Supreme Court Decisions.* New York: Cambridge University Press, 2003.

Peppers, Todd C. *Courtiers of the Marble Palace: The Rise and Influence of the Supreme Court Law Clerk.* Stanford, Calif.: Stanford University Press, 2006.

Perry, Barbara A. *The Priestly Tribe: The Supreme Court's Image in the American Mind.* Westport, Conn.: Praeger, 1999.

Rehnquist, William H. *The Supreme Court.* New ed. New York: Knopf, 2001.

Slotnick, Elliot E., and Jennifer A. Segal. *Television News and the Supreme Court: All the News That's Fit to Air?* New York: Cambridge University Press, 1998.

Ward, Artemus, and David L. Weiden. *Sorcerers' Apprentices: 100 Years of Law Clerks at the United States Supreme Court.* New York: New York University Press, 2006.

Chapter 2

Abraham, Henry J. *Justices, Presidents, and Senators: A History of the U.S. Supreme Court Appointments from Washington to Clinton.* Rev. ed. Lanham, Md.: Rowman and Littlefield, 1999.

Atkinson, David N. *Leaving the Bench: Supreme Court Justices at the End.* Lawrence: University Press of Kansas, 1999.

Dean, John W. *The Rehnquist Choice.* New York: Free Press, 2001.

Maltese, John Anthony. *The Selling of Supreme Court Nominees.* Baltimore: Johns Hopkins University Press, 1995.

Ward, Artemus. *Deciding to Leave: The Politics of Retirement from the United States Supreme Court.* Albany: State University of New York Press, 2003.

Watson, George L., and John A. Stookey. *Shaping America: The Politics of Supreme Court Appointments.* New York: HarperCollins, 1995.

Yalof, David Alistair. *Pursuit of Justices: Presidential Politics and the Selection of Supreme Court Nominees.* Chicago: University of Chicago Press, 1999.

Chapter 3

Kluger, Richard. *Simple Justice: The History of Brown v. Board of Education and Black America's Struggle for Equality.* New York: Knopf, 1976.

Lawrence, Susan E. *The Poor in Court: The Legal Services Program and Supreme Court Decision Making.* Princeton: Princeton University Press, 1990.

McGuire, Kevin T. *The Supreme Court Bar: Legal Elites in the Washington Community.* Charlottesville: University Press of Virginia, 1993.

Pacelle, Richard L., Jr. *Between Law and Politics: The Solicitor General and the Structuring of Civil Rights, Gender, and Reproductive Rights Litigation.* College Station: Texas A&M Press, 2003.

Sorauf, Frank J. *The Wall of Separation: The Constitutional Politics of Church and State.* Princeton: Princeton University Press, 1976.

Walker, Samuel. *In Defense of American Liberties: A History of the ACLU.* 2d ed. Carbondale: Southern Illinois University Press, 1999.

Chapter 4

Biskupic, Joan. *Sandra Day O'Connor: How the First Woman on the Supreme Court Became Its Most Influential Justice.* New York: HarperCollins, 2005.

Devins, Neal, and Davison M. Douglas, eds. *A Year at the Supreme Court.* Durham, N.C.: Duke University Press, 2004.

Epstein, Lee, and Jack Knight. *The Choices Justices Make.* Washington, D.C.: CQ Press, 1998.

Greenhouse, Linda. *Becoming Justice Blackmun: Harry Blackmun's Supreme Court Journey.* New York: Times Books, 2005.

Hansford, Thomas G., and James F. Spriggs II. *The Politics of Precedent on the U.S. Supreme Court.* Princeton: Princeton University Press, 2006.

Johnson, Timothy R. *Oral Arguments and Decision Making on the United States Supreme Court.* Albany: State University of New York Press, 2004.

Maltzman, Forrest, James F. Spriggs II, and Paul J. Wahlbeck. *Crafting Law on the Supreme Court: The Collegial Game.* New York: Cambridge University Press, 2000.

Segal, Jeffrey A., and Harold J. Spaeth. *The Supreme Court and the Attitudinal Model Revisited.* New York: Cambridge University Press, 2002.

Spaeth, Harold J., and Jeffrey A. Segal. *Majority Rule or Minority Will: Adherence to Precedent on the U.S. Supreme Court.* New York: Cambridge University Press, 1999.

Chapter 5

Belsky, Martin H., ed. *The Rehnquist Court: A Retrospective.* New York: Oxford University Press, 2002.

Epp, Charles R. *The Rights Revolution: Lawyers, Activists, and Supreme Courts in Comparative Perspective.* Chicago: University of Chicago Press, 1998.

Kahn, Ronald, and Ken I. Kersch, eds. *The Supreme Court and American Political Development.* Lawrence: University Press of Kansas, 2006.

236 *Selected Bibliography*

McCloskey, Robert G. *The American Supreme Court,* 4th ed., rev. Sanford Levinson. Chicago: University of Chicago Press, 2005.
Pacelle, Richard L., Jr. *The Transformation of the Supreme Court's Agenda: From the New Deal to the Reagan Administration.* Boulder, Colo.: Westview Press, 1991.
Tushnet, Mark. *A Court Divided: The Rehnquist Court and the Future of Constitutional Law.* New York: Norton, 2005.
Wolfe, Christopher. *Judicial Activism: Bulwark of Freedom or Precarious Security?* Rev. ed. Lanham, Md.: Rowman and Littlefield, 1997.

Chapter 6

Bell, Derrick. *Silent Covenants: Brown v. Board of Education and the Unfulfilled Hopes for Racial Reform.* New York: Oxford University Press, 2004.
Canon, Bradley C., and Charles A. Johnson. *Judicial Policies: Implementation and Impact.* 2d ed. Washington, D.C.: CQ Press, 1999.
Klarman, Michael J. *From Jim Crow to Civil Rights: The Supreme Court and the Struggle for Racial Equality.* New York: Oxford University Press, 2004.
Leo, Richard A., and George C. Thomas III, eds. *The Miranda Debate: Law, Justice, and Policing.* Boston: Northeastern University Press, 1998.
Rosenberg, Gerald N. *The Hollow Hope: Can Courts Bring about Social Change?* Chicago: University of Chicago Press, 1991.
Stone, Geoffrey R. *Perilous Times: Free Speech in Wartime from the Sedition Act of 1798 to the War on Terrorism.* New York: Norton, 2004.
White, Welsh S. *Miranda's Waning Protections: Police Interrogation Practices after Dickerson.* Ann Arbor: University of Michigan Press, 2001.

Sources on the Web

There are many sources on the Supreme Court on the World Wide Web. Some of the most useful ones are listed here; several of these Web sites have links to other useful sites. Access to each of these Web sites is available without charge.

Many colleges and universities subscribe to the LexisNexis Academic database, which provides access to all published court decisions as well as articles in newspapers, law reviews, and legal newspapers. The database includes the text of briefs submitted to the Supreme Court in cases with oral arguments.

As is true of Web sites in general, the content of these sites can change over time, and Web sites sometimes disappear altogether. However, each of the sites listed below has been maintained for several years.

Supreme Court of the United States (www.supremecourtus.gov/). This is the Court's official Web site. The site includes the Court's rules and the calendar for oral arguments in the current term. The Web site also includes the docket sheets in each case that comes to the Court, sheets that list all the briefs filed and the actions taken by the Court. The site provides transcripts of oral arguments and briefs submitted by the parties in cases accepted for argument.

FindLaw (www.findlaw.com/casecode/supreme.html/). This Web site includes a database of Supreme Court decisions since 1893 and separate files of decisions by year since 1999. Under "Supreme Court resources" the site has links to a wide range of other sites, including several media organizations. Some of the links provide biographical information on the justices.

Legal Information Institute (http://supct.law.cornell.edu/supct/). The law school at Cornell University provides this Web site, which includes collections of Supreme Court decisions and other kinds of information about the Court as well as links to other sites. Connected with the Web site is a free e-mail subscription service that sends copies of the syllabi that summarize the Court's decisions on the same day they are handed down. Those syllabi are linked to the text of the opinions in each case.

On the Docket (http://docket.medill.northwestern.edu/). This site is maintained by the Medill School of Journalism at Northwestern University. It provides summaries and links to information sources for each case that is scheduled for oral argument during the current term.

The Oyez Project (www.oyez.org/oyez/frontpage). Jerry Goldman of Northwestern University has created this site, which has several types of information on the Supreme Court. The most important feature is an extensive collection of audiotapes of oral arguments in the Court. The site also provides a "virtual tour" of the Supreme Court building.

Office of the Solicitor General (www.usdoj.gov/osg/). This Web site provides several types of information on the solicitor general's office and on the Court. The site includes a file of briefs filed by the solicitor general's office in the Supreme Court. The site also provides considerable information on the solicitor general's office itself, including an extensive bibliography.

The Constitution of the United States of America: Analysis and Interpretation (www.gpoaccess.gov/constitution/browse.html). For many years the Congressional Research Service of the Library of Congress has compiled a highly detailed summary of the Supreme Court's interpretations of each provision of the Constitution, along with citations of the relevant cases. Also included are lists of all federal, state, and local statutes that the Court has declared unconstitutional and all Supreme Court decisions overruled by subsequent decisions. Editions of this compilation and supplements to those editions since 1992 are available at this site.

Case Index

Case titles normally are followed by case citations. These begin with the volume of the reporter in which the case appears, for example, 374 in the first case listed below. This is followed by the abbreviated name of the reporter; "U.S." is the United States Reports, the official reporter of Supreme Court decisions. The last part of the citation is the page on which the case begins (203 in the first case below). There is some delay before cases are published in the United States Reports; recent Supreme Court decisions therefore are cited to unofficial reporters. In this text, the Lawyers' Edition (L. Ed. 2d) is the unofficial reporter used for that purpose. Lower court decisions have their own reporters, including the Federal Reports (F.3d) for the federal courts of appeals and various regional reporters for decisions of state supreme courts. For lower courts, the year of the decision is preceded by a designation of the specific court—the circuit for the federal courts of appeals, the district for the federal district courts, and the state for state supreme courts. This index also includes several citations to some other reporters for lower-court decisions that are not officially published.

Index